# Living WITH Grief

## WHO WE ARE

## HOW WE GRIEVE

Edited by Kenneth J. Doka
and Joyce D. Davidson

Foreword by Jack D. Gordon, President
Hospice Foundation of America

# Living with Grief: Who We Are, How We Grieve

*Edited by Kenneth J. Doka*
*and Joyce D. Davidson*

HOSPICE FOUNDATION
OF AMERICA

Ordering information:

Bookstores and individuals order additional copies from
Brunner/Mazel
325 Chestnut Street, Suite 800
Philadelphia, PA 19106

To order by phone, call toll-free: 1-800-821-8312
or send orders on a 24-hour telefax: 1-215-785-5515
Orders can be placed via e-mail: bkorders@tandfpa.com

For bulk quantity orders, call Hospice Foundation of America
at 1-800-854-3402

or write:
Hospice Foundation of America
2001 S St. NW #300
Washington, DC 20009
www.hospicefoundation.org
hfa@hospicefoundation.org

Typesetting and Design by Page Productions, Cheverly MD

Hospice Foundation of America staff assistance: Lisa McGahey Veglahn, Michon Lartigue, Chris Procunier, and Jon Radulovic

Library of Congress Cataloging-In-Print data available upon request

ISBN: 0-87630-898-1

*To All Who Have Contributed
to the Struggle for
Human Dignity
and
the Celebration of Diversity*

Cover photo by Bruce Gemmill, Campbell Associates

The cover photo is a detail taken from the *Adams Memorial*, a sculpture by Augustus Saint-Gaudens, commissioned by Henry Adams, located in the historic Rock Creek Cemetery in Washington, DC.

The memorial was best described in a letter written by John Hay to Henry Adams in March of 1891, the year in which the sculpture was installed.

> *The work is indescribably noble and imposing. It is…full of poetry and suggestion. Infinite wisdom; a past without beginning and a future without end; a repose, after limitless experience; a peace, to which nothing matters—all embodied in this austere and beautiful face and form.*

Many have been greatly moved by the grace and universality of the memorial. Theodore Roosevelt, Samuel Clemens, and Eleanor Roosevelt are among those who frequently visited the monument and considered it a special place of contemplation and a source of strength. The serenity and majesty of the figure make it a meaningful and appropriate image for *Living With Grief: Who We Are, How We Grieve*.

# Contents

# Foreword

*Jack D. Gordon*
*President, Hospice Foundation of America*

I often hear the comment that hospice care is essentially a mainstream, middle-class movement. I agree that more attention must be given to broadening the use of hospice among all segments of society. Making a sincere effort to do this, however, requires an examination of the factors which have created these perceived barriers to hospice care. Are we talking about differences in age, gender, ethnic background, religious beliefs, social or economic class, educational background, or any others that come to mind? And how do the overwhelming concerns that accompany dying and bereavement add to these issues?

We do know that any of these differences or combinations thereof undoubtedly affect both the use of hospice and the people working in hospice programs. That's why we chose to examine these topics in our 1998 National Bereavement Teleconference and collect these essays in this book. Although some of these questions have been written about before, we know of no place where all of these concerns about the way that "who we are" affects our attitudes toward dying and death are examined, by so many disparate voices, in one volume.

I've always thought that hospice people are the last significant group of idealists in the healthcare system; their commitment to helping anyone in need of their services is certainly a hallmark of the movement. So I feel certain that the hospice family, and indeed all whose lives are touched by grief either professionally or personally, will gain new insights from this book. And I sincerely hope that the lessons learned from this book will lead to the provision of hospice care to an ever-widening number of people, as well as exercise a humane influence on the entire healthcare system (which certainly needs it).

After all, the idea behind this book embodies the hospice philosophy of care. Hospice care takes all facets of the person into account—the physical, the emotional, the spiritual. Hospice care recognizes the importance of family and friends—those whose lives are deeply interconnected with the dying person—as the essential unit of care. And the care is administered by a group of caring professionals and volunteers, all of whom bring their own individual strengths to provide truly holistic support at the end of life. By examining and embracing the differences that define us all, I feel certain that we can make progress in broadening the use of hospice care, expanding the role of hospice in the healthcare system, and learning something about ourselves in the process.

# Acknowledgments

Each year as I reread previous acknowledgments, they almost seem to be a journal of all the changes one experiences in the ongoing rhythms of life. As I write this year, the theme seems to be one of continuity—I continue to acknowledge and to thank many of the same people for their ongoing support and presence.

As always, I want to thank Cokie Roberts for her continued support of and participation in the annual Hospice Foundation of America teleconference. I also want to thank Jack Gordon, the Foundation president, for the vision that makes this teleconference an annual reality. It would be amiss not to acknowledge the pioneering role of Hugh Westbrook and Carole Shields in the hospice field and in creating the Foundation. And of course I need to acknowledge the Hospice Foundation staff—David Abrams, Sophie Viteri Berman, Lisa McGahey Veglahn, Sheila Day, Michon Lartigue, Chris Procunier, Jon Radulovic, Gennett Shields, and Johana Silva—for making that vision a reality. Chris deserves special mention for his service as copy editor.

It would not be possible to produce the book without the ongoing support of the Hospice Foundation. Nor would it be possible without the active support of my coeditor, Joyce Davidson. And needless to say, I continue to thank the authors of these chapters, who annually respond to impossible deadlines with quality pieces. This year's group of authors responded with the same efficiency and performance. What is so interesting, and so fitting for a book on diversity, is how each of them spoke in his or her own voice and yet produced a book so harmonious in tone. I also need to thank my colleagues in the International Work Group on Death, Dying and Bereavement, as well as the Association for Death Education and Counseling. Many members have contributed chapters. And the stimulation of others is evident throughout this volume.

The College of New Rochelle continues to offer, too, a rich and stimulating environment. For that I thank our President Steve Sweeney, Academic Vice President Joan Bailey, Dean Laura Ellis, and my Division Chair, Jerri Frantzve. I cannot help but acknowledge the two secretaries, Rosemary Stroebel and Vera Mezzaucella, who continue to offer their own cheerful competence.

I want to acknowledge as well my family and friends, especially Kathy. In the post-parenting phase of life, I am delighted by the continued visits of my son, Michael, and his girlfriend, Angela. My godson Keith and his friends, Matt and Mike, also occasionally enliven the house with their music and noise. (Sometimes it is hard to tell the difference.)

Finally I need to acknowledge and to recognize all those who over the years have shared their journeys through illness and grief. They have taught me much about dying, death, and grief, and even more importantly about life, love, and the human spirit.

Kenneth J. Doka

I join Ken in acknowledging the staff at the Hospice Foundation for their hard work and support in producing both the teleconference and this book. And to Ken, thank you for giving me the opportunity once again to collaborate on this project and for providing me with such a firm foundation on this most gratifying journey.

On a more personal note, I want to thank my husband, Rex, my enthusiastic supporter, and my children, Adam and Anne, my greatest teachers. I understand now why writers and editors express such gratitude to their families—they are called upon to make so many adjustments and sacrifices, and for the ones my family made I am most grateful.

Finally, I must thank Pat Murphy for opening her very large heart to me and for giving me so many "golden opportunities," making it possible for me to bear witness to the "amazing grace" of the dying and bereaved. We stand on sacred ground.

Joyce D. Davidson

# Who We Are, How We Grieve

*Kenneth J. Doka*

## Introduction

A little boy, told that his beloved grandfather has died, stamps his foot in anger, crying, "Who is going to take me fishing now?" Later, he is outside playing.

When her eight-year-old daughter died of leukemia, Maura cried continuously. Joining a support group, she expressed her concern over her husband, Tom: "He's never cried." Tom, instead, busied himself managing a series of investments in a scholarship fund under his daughter's name.

When her mother died after a long and painful illness, Lydia took comfort in the fact that "she was now with God." Her sister, Miriam, faced a crisis of faith. She could not understand why God would allow her mother, so kind and caring, to suffer so much.

When John attended the funeral of his business partner, Tim, he was uncomfortable with the wide range of emotions expressed there, from wailing and arguing to loud laughter. His family funerals had been more subdued. He had made a sizable contribution to a charity in memory of Tim, and was surprised that Tim's widow seemed a bit offended that he did not send flowers.

In the early days of the study of grief, researchers and theorists attempted to find predictable stages or phases that individuals experienced as they grieved or coped with loss (e.g., Kübler-Ross, 1969; Parkes, 1972). Recently there has been a move away from such approaches, which tend to homogenize the processing of grief. In other words, they seem to imply that all individuals, irrespective of their many differences, will grieve in a similar way.

In fact, there are many differences among individuals. Each of these affects the ways individuals experience and adapt to loss. Among the most critical variables identified are:

- the nature of the loss;

- the relationship and attachment to the loss;

- the circumstances surrounding the loss;

- the extent of, and response to, prior loss;

- the psychology and personality of the bereaved;

- personal variables such as health, lifestyle, and stress management; and

- a variety of social variables including age, gender, developmental level, social class, cultural and religious beliefs and practices, family, and external and internal support (e.g., Worden, 1991; Rando, 1984).

Recent research has been inconsistent in assessing the actual degree to which these factors do affect bereavement outcomes (e.g., Stroebe and Stroebe, 1993; Sanders, 1993). There are a number of reasons why these variables are so difficult to assess. Two bear special mention. First, many factors can simultaneously complicate and facilitate the grieving process. For example, believing that a loss is God's will can both assist one in finding meaning in the loss and create anger toward a God who would allow such an act, perhaps generating guilt, isolation from spiritual support, and spiritual pain. Similarly, social support can be both helpful by assisting others with daily tasks or listening, or unhelpful by placing unrealistic expectations upon the bereaved. Second, all of these factors interact with one another, making it difficult to analyze individual effects.

While there are many variables that influence the grieving process, this volume emphasizes the way in which key aspects of identity (who we are) affect the ways we grieve. Though mindful of other variables, it explores how culture, spirituality, age and developmental level, class, and gender affect the grieving process. It is hoped that this book will remind caregivers of the need to consider such variables in working with clients and designing interventive and supportive programs. Only by acknowledging such diversity can caregivers effectively assist the bereaved. In addition, we hope that this book will offer reassurance and insight to survivors of loss, reminding them of the many reasons their grief is unique.

Subsequent sections will elaborate further on the nature of social and developmental variables, but it seems worthwhile to make a few general statements here. Age, gender, culture, spirituality, and class are major sources of social diversity. They are the variables that make us different. They are the variables that identify us.

And, they affect the way we grieve.

For example, we have long recognized that age and developmental level are critical variables in responses to loss. Children and adolescents are in the process of developing. As they age, their ability to understand complex concepts such as "death" increases. Obviously, a young child who has not fully mastered such a concept, who does not comprehend some of the attributes of death, such as nonfunctionality, will respond to such a loss in a different way than children who are more developmentally advanced. But development is not only cognitive. Children develop in other ways as well. Crenshaw (1991) reminds us that most children have a "short feeling span," allowing them to sustain strong emotions for only short periods of time. He recommends, then, that in working with children one deal with shorter, closely spaced time periods.

Children grow spiritually as well. Coles (1990) calls them "spiritual pioneers," pressing on and exploring issues of meaning, even though the territory is new and not fully understood. Children also develop socially. When they are younger they view loss from the prism of self. For example, the six-year-old boy who asked who would now take him fishing after his grandfather's death, five years later comforted his mother at the death of her sister. "I will miss Aunt Margaret," he shared, "but you will miss her more since she is your sister." Now at another developmental level, he could understand the web of relationships.

From the very beginning, we have acknowledged that different interventive strategies and approaches should be used, then, with children. We have come to understand that children and adolescents grieve, but in different ways from adults.

For many years, we perhaps were not as ready to acknowledge the need to take into account other variables such as gender, spirituality, culture, and class in designing and modifying interventions. For example, Rando (1993) chides therapists who seek to have males grieve as their female counterparts. It is "unwise," she reminds us, and "unfruitful." In recent years, too, more attention has been given to cultural and spiritual variables. And there has been increasing acknowledgment of the need for culturally sensitive approaches.

This need is critical. Culture is defined as a way of life. While culture often is identified with ethnicity, it is a far broader concept which encompasses spirituality and class. Stretching the concept, we can even acknowledge that gender and age are a way of life: There is a culture of *females* or *males,* as well as a culture (or perhaps co-culture or subculture) of *adolescents* and *aged.*

All of these variables help define our worldview, our beliefs and assumptions about how the world works (Sue and Sue, 1990). This worldview guides us in our decisions and responses to the world. It is shaped by our experiences, and therefore influenced by our age, ethnicity, gender, spirituality, and social class. Most critically, it offers meanings by which we view death and understand loss and grief.

These meanings may differ among individuals. They may differ, too, among caregivers. The danger is in assuming that one's worldview is the sole one of value, judging others' perspectives or worldviews by how closely they adhere to our perspectives, forgetting that a basic goal of caregiving is to assist clients in understanding the ways their own worldview can provide strength, comfort, and meaning rather than attempting to impose another worldview on them.

Ethnocentrism is an easy trap to fall into. There is a wonderful article entitled "Body Ritual Among The Nacirema" (Miner, 1956), which purports to be an anthropological study of some unusual rituals of an obscure North American tribe. As we read it, we're somewhat shocked and amused by their strange customs. Then as it unfolds, we begin to get a vague feeling of familiarity. Finally we recognize the joke. "Nacirema" is "American" spelled backwards.

The article is instructive because it allows us to look at our own culture through a more distant perspective. And it sensitizes us to the ways in which we may misunderstand other perspectives. It is hoped that this book can offer a similar gift—that it may challenge us to explore further the individual ways people define loss and death, as well as express, experience, and adapt to grief.

In many ways this is a time in the study of grief when perspectives and understandings are under review. We have begun to recognize the wide variety of contexts and losses that can engender grief (e.g., Doka, 1989). We are acknowledging the ways that individuals maintain connections to their loss (e.g., Klass, Silverman, and Nickman, 1996). We are applying newer modes and approaches to our work, testing different assumptions (e.g., Rando, 1993; Stroebe and Schut, 1995). We are affirming the role of cognitive and behavioral strategies in responding and adapting to loss (Neimeyer, 1997; Martin and Doka, 1996). And we are recognizing that individuals not only cope with significant losses, they are profoundly changed by them (Sanders, 1989, 1992; Prend, 1997). All of these newer understandings help us understand grief for what it is: not a process that makes all individuals the same, but rather one that is as complex and multi-faceted as the individuals who experience it.

---

*Kenneth J. Doka, PhD, is Professor of Gerontology at the College of New Rochelle. Dr. Doka is the associate editor of* Omega, *and editor of* Journeys, Hospice Foundation of America's *newsletter for the bereaved.*

# PART I

# Spirituality, Loss, and Grief

In the introductory section, we emphasized that one of the critical issues in grief is finding or reconstructing meaning after the loss, for losses often challenge our faith or philosophical systems (Doka, 1993). The ways we previously looked at the world may be difficult to sustain in the face of the loss experienced. Bereaved individuals may need to search their own belief system for the answers to questions inevitably raised by death. Sometimes, of course, these answers may be readily available. In other cases, they may need to struggle or wrestle with their spirituality. And the beliefs that emerge, that allow an answer, may differ from the beliefs they held at the beginning of the struggle.

So the search for meaning is inherently a spiritual task. Spirituality is elusive and difficult to define. The International Work Group on Death, Dying and Bereavement reminds us that "spirituality is concerned with the transcendental, inspirational and existential way to live one's life…" (1990, p.75). Miller (1994) describes the dilemma in defining spirituality:

> "Spirituality" relates to our souls.
>
> It involves that deep inner essence of who we are.
>
> It is an openness to the possibility that the soul within each of us is somehow related to the Soul of all that is.
>
> Spirituality is what happens to us that is so memorable we cannot forget it, and yet we find it difficult to talk about because words fail to describe it.

Miller also differentiates spirituality from religion, reminding us that, while religion draws from spirituality, for most of us it remains only a part of our spirituality.

Spirituality is the act of looking for meaning in the very deepest sense, and looking for it in the way that is most authentically ours.

Now "religion," on the other hand, works in a different way.

While spirituality is necessarily very personal, religion is more communal.

In fact, if you take the word back to its origins, "religion" means "that which binds together," "that which ties things into a package."

Religion has to do with collecting and consolidating and unifying.

Religion says, "Here are special words that are meant to be passed on. Take them to heart."

Religion says, "Here is a set of beliefs that forms a coherent whole. Take it as your own."

Religion says, "Here are people for you to revere and historical events for you to recall. Remember them."

Religion says, "Here's a way for you to act when you come together as a group, and here's a way for you to behave when you're apart."

Now religion is a natural outgrowth of spirituality.

All major religions began as intensely meaningful spiritual experiences, first within a single individual or among a small group of people, and then among a larger group, which became larger still, because something had happened, something was real, and it attracted people.

Such a definition is critical in that it reinforces the concept that religiousness and spirituality are distinct. The latter is far broader, for it refers to all the ways we invest life with meaning, including theistic beliefs, philosophies, and ideologies. Spirituality is universal. While individuals may or may not have religious beliefs (i.e., adhere to an organized set of doctrines), spirituality is inherent.

The four chapters in this section emphasize that one of the key distinctions among grievers is that they differ in the religious and spiritual perspectives from which they seek answers, search for meaning, and to which they turn for ritual, comfort, and support. These perspectives both transcend, and in many ways help define, different cultural systems. Thus, understanding a person's response to grief, and assessing the ways his or her spirituality both facilitates and complicates the adjustment to loss, remain critical tasks.

Yet this must move beyond simple definitions of religious and denominational affiliation. Each of the chapters affirms that there are many strains of belief within the major religious traditions (Eastern religions, Judaism, Christianity, and Islam) surveyed here. Broadly understanding the ways these traditions speak to issues of loss, death, dying, and grief, is simply a starting point. It helps us begin to ask the right questions.

Each of these chapters, reflecting its author's style and perhaps his or her own spiritual journey, is very different. Three are written by adherents. One is authored by two scholars steeped in that tradition: Klass and Goss broadly survey several Eastern religions, centering on one religion, Buddhism, particularly as it is practiced in one country, Japan. They then offer an interesting digression on the mixed religious traditions of the Chinese as practiced in American immigrant culture. That latter discussion affirms that, for many, spirituality draws from many eclectic sources. It reminds us as well of the inevitable changes that occur as immigrants become acquainted with American culture.

McConnell's chapter on Christianity speaks of a poignant dilemma: the need to affirm hope in the afterlife while simultaneously acknowledging the loss. He also reminds us of another critical point, recognized as well in chapters by Grollman and Raad: Christianity is the source of the dominant religious customs in North America. Comparatively few North Americans may be able to define Yom Kippur or Ramadan, yet most, regardless of religious affiliation, understand Easter and Christmas. This reminds us of the special sensitivities that healthcare and bereavement personnel must exercise in dealing with members of non-dominant traditions. Sensitivity to rituals and beliefs will be much appreciated. Grollman's discussion of religious services that are intended to be interfaith but are, in fact, interdenominational (i.e. within Christianity), underscores this point. An important point reinforced throughout the varied discussions of culture is that when one is a cultural minority, whether based on race, spirituality, sexual orientation, or whatever, personal identification is the salient issue. Christians in North America, for example, do not see their identity challenged as much as religious minorities do. Grollman's very title humorously raises that issue. In a very empathic and, as he's wont, most practical way, he offers sage advice and wise understanding.

Raad's chapter is very different. In a highly personal account of her response to her husband's illness and death, she provides testimony of the ways in which her faith, Islam, offered comfort, strength, and support. Her chapter reminds healthcare providers of the fact that not every culture values the same things. There was an inherent conflict between the physician's understanding of the patient's right to know and Raad's desire to protect.

Together these chapters affirm three basic points: Bereaved individuals may find comfort in their beliefs, in rituals, and in their faith community. The caregiver's role is to empower them to utilize these resources.

First, beliefs, of course, remain the heart of the matter, for they speak to the existential issue of *Why?* Why did he have to suffer? Why did she have to die? Why am I in such pain? What will happen to the person? What will happen to me?

Sometimes these belief systems will provide comforting answers. But sometimes they will not. Perhaps the faith is too fragile, or too rigid, to overcome the adversity. For example, one client's belief was that good deeds would be rewarded. When her husband was shot and mugged stopping to assist what he believed was a disabled car, her faith was shattered. In other cases, the belief system itself may be a source of spiritual pain. For example, religious beliefs that see suicide as an unforgivable sin offer scant comfort to survivors. In such cases, caregivers may benefit from two strategies. First, it is necessary to understand, as stated earlier, that faith and traditions alone do not constitute a person's spirituality. Caregivers must explore the "faith themes" that underlie one's beliefs. A person's perspective of God as gracious will have far different implications than a perspective of a punishing God. Once these themes are understood, persons may find it helpful to consider other ideas that are illustrated within their own religious traditions and services.

In one case, a Christian who believed that his son, who had committed suicide, was damned, was greatly helped when directed to Hebrews 11:32. That verse reminded him that Samson, who too committed suicide, was listed among the faithful. Often this reframing is best done by someone who shares that tradition.

Second, rituals are powerful therapeutic tools. It is beyond the scope of this section to describe fully that role (cf. Rando, 1989). Nonetheless, these chapters illustrate many roles they can play for the bereaved. Rituals remind us of the ways our faith speaks to loss. They can structure grief, providing points throughout the time of grief at which the loss is acknowledged, be it the *yahrzeit*, or annual observance of the death in Judaism, or the anniversary mass of Catholicism. And rituals provide opportunities to mark transitions or ongoing connections, to affirm the person, or to find reconciliation.

Third, each of the chapters reaffirms the role of the faith community. That ministry of ongoing presence is, too, a special gift.

A fourth point emerges from these chapters as well: While each of these faith traditions speaks to death differently, each *does* speak to it. For as Raad reminds us, life and death are the two questions every faith must address.

# ONE

# Asian Ways of Grief

*Dennis Klass and Robert E. Goss*

There is no "Eastern" way of grieving or of coming to terms with death, just as there is no "Western" way. Americans and Europeans are familiar with the cultural differences in grieving between the emotionally controlled English and the emotionally expressive Sicilians, though both are Christian. Yet, Tibetans and Japanese are often lumped into the East, when, in fact, Lhasa and Tokyo are twice as far from each other as London and Palermo.

Partly because the land route taken by Marco Polo was so difficult, Europeans expanded their sphere of influence to Asia by sea. It seemed to them that Asia was a world apart rather than a land mass contiguous with Europe. Europeans projected both their hopes and fears onto the Asians. One of the results was *orientalism*, a tendency to cast all Asian cultures into a single entity and to think that the Eastern way could have all the truth that seemed to be lacking in European religious traditions after the Enlightenment. The East is a big place. It extends from the southern tip of India and eastern side of ancient Mesopotamia to the northwest tip of Siberia. The East includes several large religious traditions, each of which has a great deal of diversity within it.

As Americans have begun to come to terms with death and dying after nearly a century of being a death-denying culture, some people have found that their own religious and cultural symbols are no longer adequate to their experience of suffering and dying. The East of the Western imagination has offered an attractive alternative, mostly because it was the East in imagination, not in reality.

Steven Levine's loose amalgam of Hinduism and Buddhism has been popular with Americans working with the grieving and dying. For Levine (1982), "impermanence holds within it the key to life itself. The confrontation with death tunes us deeply to the life we imagine we will lose with the extinction of the body.... We imagine we will die only because we believe we were born" (p.3). Levine jumps from the human experience of grief right to the Second Noble Truth of Buddhism, that the cause of suffering is desire, with none of the intervening steps understood by the various Buddhist cultures. Clinging to life, he says, is clinging to suffering. The goal of resolution in his theory of grief is the survivor's sense of being at one with the universe, that no boundaries exist—unity consciousness. The abyss that once separated *I* and *other* melts away and they become one, beyond the form, beyond the ideas and models of who each might have been. The forms are seen as illusory and only the love is felt.

No Asian religion asks its adherents to resolve grief in this way. Rather, the various cultures provide a wide variety of rituals and social customs into which grief is channeled. As in Western cultures, religions and societies provide ways by which individuals and families can come to terms with the disruption death brings to human life.

There are many different Asian traditions. As a way of showing how ritual works, one religion, Buddhism, in one culture, Japan, will be examined in some detail, followed by a hybrid religious tradition, Chinese American immigrant culture. Because of the wide variation in Asian traditions, it is impossible to predict the particular culture or tradition of bereaved families with whom one comes into contact, so in conclusion several questions are posed that caregivers can ask as a way of orienting themselves to the particular ritual and custom that a given family may follow.

## One Asian Tradition—Japanese Ancestor Ritual

The Japanese ritual way of responding to death is usually referred to as 'ancestor worship' in English. The translation is not accurate because ancestor worship is not worship in any Western sense, but is a series of rituals performed by survivors lasting between 33 and 50 years after someone has died. The rituals for the first 49 days accomplish what in the West is called *grief work*. The rituals install both the living and the dead into their new status and provide a vehicle for the living to express their sorrow and for the community to provide social support. For the next three to five decades, however, they provide means by which the living can manage their ongoing attachment to the dead. Thus, for the Japanese, both early grief and the continuing bonds with the dead are part of the cultural and religious response to significant deaths (Klass, Silverman, and Nickman, 1996).

The ancestors are those who can be reborn, though rebirth is not a personal matter; that is, there is not a particular set of past lives which can be identified for an individual. The goal of the various Buddhist meditation practices is to escape rebirth. But ordinary people become a Buddha only when they die. Where are these spirits of the dead?

> The world beyond cannot be described in any but equivocal phrases. Spatially it is both here and there, temporally both then and now. The departed and ancestors always are close by; they can be contacted immediately at the household shelf, the graveyard, or elsewhere. Yet when they return "there" after the midsummer reunion they are seen off as for a great journey. They are perpetually present, yet they come to and go from periodic household foregatherings. (Plath, 1964, p.308)

Some Japanese spirits are in a Pure Land, some in a kind of hell, but most spirits are still on earth, available for interaction. They may be in the mountains, but usually they are thought of as being at the grave or on the altar where they are venerated. So the spirit may be contacted by addressing the stone or tablet, and may be called back in the *Bon festival*, the summer festival when the dead return to visit the living for three days.

## EARLY RITUALS: TRANSFORMATION, RESTRUCTURING, AND RECONCILIATION

The death of a person sets in motion a series of rites and ceremonies that culminate in the observance of a final memorial service, most commonly on the 33rd or 50th anniversary of the death (Smith, 1974). Between a person's last breath and the final prayers said on their behalf, the spirit is ritually and symbolically purified and elevated. It passes gradually from the stage of immediate association with the corpse, which is thought to be both dangerous and polluting, to the moment when it loses its individual identity and enters the realm of the generalized ancestral spirits, essentially purified. The names by which the dead are called show this progression (Smith, 1974):

> *shirei* (or *shir'yo*) — spirits of the newly dead
> *nī-hotoke* — new Buddhas
> *hotoke* — Buddhas
> *senzo* — ancestors
> *kami* — gods

The initial transformation from the newly dead to a new Buddha is usually accomplished in the first set of rituals, which takes 49 days. During that time, the dead are installed in their new status and there is a restructuring of the relationship between the survivor and the dead person.

### Installing the dead in their new status

During the 49 days there is very little time when people are left alone. There is lots of activity: the service the night of the death, the service during the cremation, followed by continual services and activities. At the end of 49 days the dead person has safely become a *hotoke*. The initial funeral rites are to help the dead to their new place. The 49-day period may be extended if the death is not settled. If, for example, the person died as a result of a crime or in an airplane accident, the person can't truly rest and become a *hotoke* until the investigation is complete. In those cases people say, "My 49 days are not over."

A central part of the ritual is to inform the person that he/she is dead. As one Japanese person described it, the person is told, "You are dead, you have to go away now. We regret that you have to go away, but you can't stay here any more." If the deceased continues hovering around because they have some unfinished business, such as an unfulfilled wish to get married and have children, the survivors will have to kindly tell the dead person, "Well, you can't do that now, it's time for you to go away. You need to go to the other side of that river." And if the dead person continues to hover around, then a priest might be called in, who will tell them, "You have to go away now."

Each person who attends the funeral says, "Now you are experiencing how the end of life is." It is a formalized expression, used only on this occasion. In effect, it is an announcement of the survivors' status. Thus, the issues of denial which are often a problem in American discussions of death are handled directly and in a ritualized way. The dead are told, "You are dead now. You must go away. I am sorry." And the living are told, "You are now experiencing what the end of life is." The ritual begins with reality orientation.

The cremation (in Japanese no euphemism is used; they say "burned") and placing of bones in the grave also provide a strong dose of reality. The cremation is to be completed within a day or two after death. After cremation, within the first week after death, the family gathers, and the bones are brought out on a tray. Two people, each with a set of chopsticks, pick up the bones and put them into a pot. The pot is then put in the family tomb. The bones of all family members are in the same pot, so the symbolism of the recently deceased joining the other dead of the family is strong.

### Reconstruction and reconciliation

The issue of regret, which is central to the dependence that structures interpersonal relationships in Japanese culture (Doi, 1973), is critical in the restructuring of the relationship between the dead and the survivors during this 49 days. In Japan, when a guest leaves, instead of saying, "Thank you for coming," the host apologizes, "I'm sorry. I should have done more for you." In other words, the core feeling is "I am not good enough in my relationship with you; I am never enough." The sadness of grief may not be for the loss that death brings, but rather regret at unsatisfied obligations and regret that the mourner does not have the power to satisfy those obligations. Thus the survivor, in saying good-bye to the dead, as in every good-bye, is saying, "I'm sorry. I should have done more for you." The survivor ends up with a feeling of sadness, which is not just sadness at being left, but the sadness of self-blame that the relationship which was full of ambivalence did not get resolved, so the survivor remains in the deceased's debt.

There are many folk beliefs involving the newly dead as harmful, wandering spirits. Indeed, *shirei* ('newly dead') can be translated as 'ghost,' in the sense of spook. Until the dead are safely *hotoke*, they may cause harm to the living, though most Japanese are reluctant to say what the harm might be or why a person to whom they were so close would now harm them. Part of the reason for the ritual is to make sure the dead do not remain wandering spirits. Dead spirits wander when no ritual is performed for them. One of the acts of compassion a person can do is to take in a spirit, that is, to perform rituals for spirits who have no one to care for them. At many Buddhist temples there are places where the stones of families with no survivors are kept. In front of the stones is a place where rituals can be performed.

There are many kinds of harmful spirits that can disrupt the lives of the living. Some of these are *gaki*, 'hungry ghosts,' those grotesque beings at the outer edge of the diamond mandala; others are the newly dead who die without people to perform the proper rituals for them; others have met a violent or unusual death. The Buddhist rituals are partly to purify these spirits so they become *hotoke* and partly to cast spells which will protect individuals and community from harm.

During the 49 days there is some sort of a reconciliation that takes place. It is very common for the dead to return in a dream and say, "It's OK, you did your best." In effect, the dead forgive the living, or tell them the relationship is now even. The survivor feels at some point during that 49 days that, "It's OK, the deceased is happy and has forgiven me." It is at the point when the survivor lets go of the ambivalence in the relationship that the deceased is free to go on and become a *hotoke*.

## RITUAL TO MANAGE CONTINUING BONDS

We can illustrate the continuing ritual and personal interaction with the dead by looking first at some very human interactions which take place before the *butsudan*, the household altar that contains the memorial tablets for the dead, and then by looking at some of the rituals of *O bon*, the summer festival when the dead return to visit the living for three days.

### Interactions at the Buddha Altar

Yamamoto and his colleagues note that the altar, with its tablets, is a transitional object (1969; Winnicott, 1953). The phrase was first used to describe things like a child's security blanket. Volkan (1981) noted that such transitional objects are common in grief. He called them "linking objects." They evoke the presence of the dead. But the concept of linking objects does not convey the lively, personal relationship between the living and the dead. Yamamoto et al. (1969) give us a sense of the personal quality of ancestor worship:

> If you would for a moment give up your Judeo-Christian beliefs and attitudes about one's destiny after death and pretend to be a Japanese, you might be able to feel how you are in direct daily communication with your ancestors. The family altar would be your "hotline." As such, you could immediately ring the bell, light incense, and talk over the current crisis with one whom you have loved and cherished. When you were happy, you could smile and share your good feelings with him. When you were sad your tears would be in his presence. With all those who share the grief he can be cherished, fed, berated, and idealized, and the relationship would be continuous from the live object to the revered ancestor. (p. 1663)

Many of the interactions in front of the Buddha altar are continuations of the bond which existed in life. Offerings on the altar are often food or flowers that the deceased liked (Plath, 1964). Smith (1974) tells of a widow at an anniversary ritual who had a chocolate cake, her husband's favorite, with a decorative inscription saying "Happy Anniversary." The first slice was placed at his tablet on the altar and the rest served to guests. A young man about to take college entrance exams may go to the altar where his mother's tablet is and ask for her to look after him as he takes the exam. If he passes, he may say, "Thanks to you, everything went well. Thank you." If he fails, he will apologize and promise to try harder next time. Smith notes that these interactions are entirely within the developmental phase-appropriate son-mother relationship, for if the mother were living, getting him to pass the exams would consume most of her energy and would be the central focus of their relationship at that time.

The dead still care for the living, not by granting favors like Catholic saints, but in the sense that the dead share the joys of any positive achievement of a family member, and indeed may be given credit for the success. In a TV drama about a recently widowed woman and her 20-year-old daughter, the daughter waits for a letter telling her she has been hired for a job she really wants. When the letter arrives, she opens it, clasps the letter to her breast, beams tearfully to her mother, and hurries into the living room. There she kneels before the altar, opens its doors, holds up the letter to her father's photograph and tablet, and bows low. The camera pans to the mother's tear-streaked face (Smith, 1974, p.142).

Some of the distinct ways in which Japanese relate to the dead are more differences in child-rearing technique or typical family relationships than differences in the relationship of the survivor to the dead. Plath (1964) quotes a sociology book written in the early 1960s which assumes it is a common experience for a child after misbehaving to be dragged by dad or mom to the front of the household shelf and asked, "Do you think you can give any excuse to the ancestors for doing that?" The shelf is associated with the household and with society, so that rebelling before it is like rebelling against the whole world, and that is why a lecture in front of the shelf has such potency (p.312).

A Japanese psychologist reports that when children have been bad, instead of being sent to their room, as may be done in America, they may be sent into the room with the Buddha altar and told to sit and reflect on their behavior in the presence of their ancestors. This use of the ancestors in child rearing does not seem restricted to the Japanese. A colleague raised in the Bronx, when told about children being shamed in front of the shrine, put his hands in the air, imitated his grandmother's accent, and said, "It is good your grandfather died that he shouldn't live to see this day."

## Bon Festival

*O Bon*, the major summer festival in Japan, celebrates the temporary return of the dead to visit the living. The analogous festival in the United States is Halloween, which illustrates how differently Americans manage the bonds with their dead. At *bon* the rituals all have as their purpose the welcoming of spirits of the dead into the village. Spirits of people who have died since the last *bon* have a special place in the ceremony. The newly dead are welcomed back in some places with expressions such as, "You must be very sad," indicating that the family understands that it is as hard for the dead to leave the world of the living as it is hard for the survivors who are left behind.

"The periodic merging of the two worlds (living and dead) strengthens the sense of continuity of the house and reassures the dead of the living's continuing concern for their well-being. Neither death nor time can destroy the unity of the members of the house" (Smith, 1974, p.104). Smith quotes a survey on people's thoughts at *bon*: A 63-year-old woman said, "Maybe they come and maybe they don't. I feel that they are here." A 67-year-old man said, "I live in their presence and make a welcoming fire early and a sending-off fire late at *bon*, so that the ancestors will stay longer." A Japanese physician said that he feels the presence of his ancestors, especially at *bon* and at New Year. Of their presence he said, "I don't feel so lonely."

As with other parts of ancestor worship, it is difficult to define the meaning of *bon* in the modern world. To the extent that the rituals are not public, the *bon* ceremony has become privatized. It would seem, then, that the ceremony takes on a more psychological character, because the remaining reasons for the rituals reside in the personal relationship with the dead. In the countryside, the traditions are kept by almost everyone. In many urban areas, the public parts of *bon* are hardly celebrated now, or have become simply summer activities. Yet virtually everybody who lives in urban areas, especially Tokyo, thinks of themselves as being from somewhere else. At *bon* there are huge traffic jams as people go back to their ancestral home towns.

In smaller towns these days the celebration is a more informal family gathering. Some family members have come from the big city, and some have come from the realm of the dead. Neither are ever really far away. Different varieties of squash are brought into the house, and chopsticks are stuck into them so that they can be put together as a decorative sign that the ancestors can come. Then the ancestors come to the Buddha altar and are made welcome. Candles are lit and food is offered.

Even though the public festival has largely fallen into disuse, the traditional ceremonies represent a way of understanding what now seems more internal and psychological. There is a great deal of local variation, but the following is a typical, though not a normative, description (the following relies heavily on Gilday, 1993; and Smith, 1974).

The festival takes place over three days in late summer. After sunset on the first day, lanterns at the family grave sites are lit and incense burned to invite the spirits home. The color of these lanterns varies depending on whether a family has lost a member during the preceding year: if so, white; otherwise, red or blue/green. There is one lantern for each deceased member still remembered by someone in the household. Fires are lit at the doorway of the house to guide the spirits. In some areas the entire village forms a torch-lit procession, singing and dancing through the village to those homes that have lost a member in the previous year.

On the second day of *bon*, people visit the grave again and may go to temple. Buddhist priests make rounds to each family in their parish and offer brief prayers at each house. But the day is a family affair, and the priest may not even be invited in.

On the third day, the spirits depart. There is a large gathering and a dance in which the spirits are entertained before their departure, after which the spirits return "over there." In some places the gathering just disbands, and it seems that the dead can find their own way back. In other places lanterns are lit by individual families to send the spirits off. Formal farewells are made with expressions such as, "Come back next year." In some areas, a candlelight procession moves toward the river, where one by one representatives of each household place small boats bearing the candles into the current. As far as the eye can see the flickering flotilla plies on. When the candle goes out, it is said the spirit has been released to the other world.

## An Immigrant Community—Chinese Americans

Chinese religions blend Confucianism and Taoism, as well as some indigenous shamanistic traditions. For Confucians, human beings are social creatures, and the supreme good is a society based on filial relationships of parents and children and the promulgation of ethical principles. Taoism, on the other hand, is a naturalistic philosophy that links humans to nature in an attempt to get in touch with the Tao. The Tao manifests itself in all becoming and change. Taoism evolved from a philosophy into a popular religion that stressed the balance of yin (feminine energies) and yang (masculine energies) and the five elements (earth, water, wood, fire, and metal) to achieve immortality. For a great many Chinese, Confucian and Taoist strands of religious culture are not mutually exclusive. At certain periods of Chinese history and in certain regions, Buddhism was factored into this non-exclusive practice. Buddhism introduced the notion of rebirth into China. Today some Chinese temples in Hawaii and California blend Taoism and Buddhism.

Chinese culture has always stressed the importance of familial obligation to bury the dead and honor the ancestors with religious rites. Traditionally, the most important obligation in life is to perform burial rites appropriately. Funeral rites for males and heads of the household are more elaborate than for females and other family members. While funerals in Taiwan are held in a Buddhist temple and the family house, Chinese Americans hold funerals at funeral homes or mortuaries.

Close friends of the family come immediately to the home upon the death of a family member, even before visiting hours have been set at the funeral home. Women are more demonstrative in their grieving. Usually a box of tissues and a plate of wrapped candy are set out. Mourners take a tissue to pat their eyes as a family member recounts the story of the person's death. Mourners pick up a wrapped candy as they leave and are supposed to eat it and discard the wrappers before they reach their homes. The candy wards off bad luck for the mourners who have come into the proximity of death. On the day of the funeral, children jump over a can of burning paper spirit money at the entrance of the home.

Funeral rites may be performed by a Buddhist and/or Taoist priest. Family mourners usually wear white clothes rather than black or dark colors to express their grief. The exception to wearing white clothes is for the death of an old person, where bright-colored clothes are worn to celebrate the longevity of the deceased's life. This tradition has begun to break down, and some Chinese Americans now follow mainstream American tradition by wearing black or dark clothes to funerals. Incense, ritual paper money, and other symbolic items are burned to ensure the welfare of the deceased's soul in the next life. Women wail loudly while the men remain silent. Up to 60 days after the funeral, the men of the family do not shave and women do not wash their hair (Horn, 1971).

After the funeral rites, a procession begins with the loud beating of drums, music, wailing, and firecrackers. Paper money is thrown to ward off hungry ghosts who can cause harm, misfortune, or illness. The procession ends at the grave site, where the family throws a handful of dirt on the coffin in the grave. Confucian tradition predominates over Buddhist influences in the disposition of the deceased's body. Most Chinese Americans practice burial rather than cremation. The procession from the grave symbolizes the movement back to life without the deceased. These rites symbolize the separation of the deceased from the living. Some Chinese Americans exhume the body 25 or 30 years later, clean the bones, and ship them for burial to mainland China.

After the coffin is lowered into the grave, all attendees are invited to a banquet held at the family home or a restaurant. The more expensive the feast, the more successful the deceased was. If the deceased lived a long life, guests take a bowl of rice and chopsticks home with them from the post-funeral meal. After some funeral feasts, the guests are sent home with a piece of wrapped candy and a quarter so that they may buy some more sweets.

Post-funeral ceremonies resume three days later when the family burns paper money and leaves food at the grave site. Rituals usually continue on the 21st, 35th, and 49th days. Then families make offerings of food and drink on the 1st and 15th days of the Chinese lunar month, family occasions, and anniversaries of the death date. These can be at the grave site or within the household. The offerings to the deceased serve to reinforce a bond between the living and the dead ancestors. Confucius understood filial piety to continue in relationships between the living and the dead: "That parents, when alive, should be served according to propriety, and that, when dead, they should be buried according to propriety and that they should be sacrificed to according to propriety" (Lee, 1995, p.181). Many Chinese Americans complement traditional ways of resolving grief with some newer cultural innovations and rites. They accept the reality of death but use the funeral rituals and post-funeral offerings as means of resolving their grief by maintaining a continued bond with deceased family members. The offerings to the dead serve as a mode of communication with the dead and remind the living of the presence of the dead among the living family.

## Conclusion—Asking Questions

In America there are both immigrant Asian communities and Westerners who have converted to Asian traditions. Hospice and bereavement workers will encounter many Asian traditions and cannot assume that what is true of one tradition is true of another. Before acting, sensitively ask a series of questions to help understand how the community involved responds to dying and grief. As outsiders, it is okay to ask; indeed, most Asians will understand asking how to behave appropriately as a sign of respect.

Here are some questions to ask:

*What happens to the body at various times in the funeral process?*

- How long is it kept in the house?
- What are the household rituals?
- What happens when it leaves the house?

- What rituals are involved?
- What is correct behavior?
- How is the body finally disposed?
- What happens to the remains?
- What rituals continue around the remains?
- What are the community events after the body disposal?
- Who is invited?

*What are the cultural expectations of mourners and those who would help?*

- What should people wear and what colors are important?
- What expressions of emotions are expected and acceptable?
- When and with whom is it appropriate to express emotions?
- Who is expected to show emotion and who is not, i.e., are there gender differences?
- How are outsiders to express their solidarity with family members?

*What are the mourning periods?*

- What periodic rituals exist and how long will they go on?
- When does the mourning period end?
- What is an outsider's appropriate response to the periodic rituals?

*How does the community continue to include the deceased in its ongoing life?*

- What obligations do the living continue to owe the deceased?
- What obligations do the deceased owe the living?

---

*Dennis Klass, PhD, is a professor and Department Chair at Webster University. He is on the editorial boards of* Death Studies *and* Omega.

*Robert E. Goss, ThD, teaches Comparative Religion at Webster University. Goss is managing editor of the journal* Religion & Education, *and has written several books.*

# TWO

# What You Always Wanted to Know About Your Jewish Clients' Perspectives Concerning Death and Dying—But were Afraid to Ask

*Earl A. Grollman*

*"Comfort ye—comfort ye my people" Isaiah 40:1*

### *"What is the Jewish view of…?"*

Jews come in different sizes and shapes and have varying and sometimes conflicting views. I know this sounds simplistic. Yet so often I am asked, for example, "What is the Jewish perspective of an afterlife?" Jokingly, I respond, "The only similarity that one Jew has in common with a second Jew is the agreement on what a third Jew should give to charity."

Seriously though, there are labels like *Orthodox, Conservative, Reform*, and *Reconstructionist*. However, within these distinct movements there is great flexibility. Chassidic Judaism, a religious movement which originated in the 18th century, may be worlds apart from modern neo-Orthodoxy. In fact, in Israel today there are some right-wing Jews who do not accept the reality of the State of Israel. They are first awaiting the coming of the Messiah.

Generally, theology may not play as major a role in Judaism as in Roman Catholicism or Protestantism. Polls show that while three quarters of African Americans, 57 percent of White Catholics, and 47 percent of White Protestants declare religion important in their lives, scarcely a third of Jews do (Boston Globe, 1997).

Despite this fact, a strong majority have a compelling ethnic tie to their faith. Alan M. Dershowitz, in his recent book, *The Vanishing Jew: In Search of Jewish Identity for the Next Century* (1997), pleads for a "new more positive Jewish identity based on a 3,500-year-old tradition of education, scholarship, learning, creativity, justice, and compassion" (p.174). Secular Jews usually emphasize prophetic Judaism with a stress on social action, the State of Israel, and Holocaust memoralization. More traditional Jews maintain the theological components of God, Torah (the Bible and subsequent sacred literature), and the primacy of synagogue affiliation and active participation.

How often have we thanatologists declared that grief is as individual as snowflakes and fingerprints? So, too, are Jews singularly different. In short, forget stereotypes.

### How can non-Jews understand and help their Jewish clients in the quest for spirituality?

So glad you mentioned *spirituality*. Spiritual concerns of dying people and their families are often overlooked in healthcare literature. In a holistic approach to death, the client is viewed not only as a physical entity, but also as a whole person with bio-psychological and spiritual needs as well. The concept of spirituality is broader than Jews' identity with formal religion. It is the search for meaning, especially during the crisis of dying and death.

Assist them in their spiritual journey. The approach should be gentle, compassionate, and non-proselytizing. Do not argue if your spiritual or religious traditions and beliefs differ from theirs. If they inquire about your precepts, of course, respond. Do not volunteer and do not push; you are not there to legislate your particular faith.

What is important is what is meaningful to *them*, not to *you*. Is there a reading from the Psalms where they may find a measure of comfort? Or perhaps the *Siddur*, the prayerbook? They might find consolation from musical settings in Hebrew, English, or Yiddish.

With a calm presence, you could seek both their spiritual needs assessment and care plan with some of the following questions: "Is there a rabbi with whom you might like to speak?" "Have you a synagogue affiliation?" "Are there some symbols and items that you would like near you, like the Star of David, Prayerbook, Bible?" "Would you like to tell me of your perceptions of God?" (just or punitive, all-loving or unconcerned, all-powerful or impotent?) "How has the illness or death affected you spiritually?" "Are there other spiritual life/death issues that you might want to discuss?" And above all, remember the Yiddish aphorism that "God gave us two ears and one mouth so we can listen more than we speak." The fact that you listen and care is itself supportive and spiritual.

### When death occurs, should I visit the family before the funeral?

The Jewish burial usually takes place within a few days of the death. The bereaved are engrossed in a myriad of details. It is often a time of confusion and disorientation. It's also the time for arranging the funeral and making other decisions. If there is a visitation before the funeral, it is mostly confined to family members. Always in order, though, is a telephone call to the survivors relaying your personal condolences. Your presence will be most appreciated *after* the funeral.

### How about sending flowers?

In ancient days, fragrant flowers and spices were used to offset the odor of decaying bodies. Today, with refrigeration, flowers are generally not part of the Jewish funeral. The method of tribute considered more lasting and meaningful is a contribution to a hospital, hospice, synagogue, or medical research foundation. Check the obituary: "In lieu of flowers, please make contributions to...." If in doubt, contact the funeral director to determine whether specific wishes were cited by the mourners.

### Is cremation permissible in Judaism?

Since a natural decomposition of the body is required, cremation is contrary to traditional Jewish law. However, the practice is permitted in Reform and Reconstructionist Judaism, as long as a funeral is held with the body present. Even though in ancient times bodies were buried in mausoleums, caves, and tombs, earth burial is the most accepted form of interment.

### Can I see the dead body? What about organ donations?

Public viewing of the body and cosmetization of the body is against Jewish law (there is no equivalent to the Christian wake). The rabbis urge that we remember the dead as they were in life. However, the family may desire to view the body privately before the funeral begins since the casket is permanently sealed before the service. Embalming is prohibited in traditional Judaism except when government regulations require it or when the body is to be transported a long distance for burial. There are branches of Judaism which encourage organ donation when the overriding principle of *pikkuach nefesh*, the saving of the lives of the living, is paramount so that death serves life.

### How is the body dressed?

The loved one may be buried in ordinary clothes. Adult males usually wear a *talit* (a prayer shawl) and a *yarmelka* (a head covering). Others are buried in *tachrichim* (plain shrouds) to emphasize equality in death, for there are no pockets in shrouds. Says the *Ethics of the Fathers* (16:9): "In the hour of departure from this world, neither gold nor precious stones nor pearls accompany the dead, only Torah (learning) and good deeds."

### Where is the funeral held?

Years ago, most Jewish funerals were held in the home, except for great scholars, whose services were conducted in the synagogue. Today, most funerals are conducted at a funeral home, synagogue, cemetery chapel, or grave side. Funerals are held during the day and not on the Sabbath (Saturday) or major Jewish holidays.

### To go to the funeral or not?

"Rabbi, one of my dear friends just died. She was Jewish. I'm a member of St. Joseph Church. Is it permissible for a Christian to attend a Jewish funeral? Will I feel out of place? How do I act? Help!"

I have received literally hundreds of these calls from confused, anxiety-ridden friends. I truly understand their consternation.

Because Jewish people comprise less than two percent of the American population, many people know virtually nothing of Jewish customs, rituals, and ceremonies. They may never have attended a Jewish worship service.

Should you go? The simple answer is, "Of course!" Being there demonstrates that although someone has died, friends like you still remain. Being there is the most eloquent statement that you care.

All may attend Jewish services and are always welcome. Today, many people describe themselves as African American or Irish American. The first word merely designates one's ethnic or racial origin. The second word, *American*, affirms that in diversity, there is unity. The first word in the phrase *Jewish friend* indicates religious preference. The second word, *friend*, is all-important and, according to Webster, means "one attached to another by affection or esteem." You are a friend in sorrow, memory, and love. A public funeral affords an entire community the opportunity to offer support and share sorrow. How often have I heard: "I can't tell you how pleased I was that the hospice worker (or therapist) actually came to the service."

The Jewish funeral is a ceremony where no one may be invited, but all are encouraged to attend. For good reason, too. Dr. Regina Flesch, in a study supported by the National Institute of Mental Health, (1977), emphasizes that the caller must overcome the mistaken belief that mourners prefer to be alone. Pain suffered in solitude is more difficult to bear than anguish that is shared. As John Donne wrote: "No man is an island. Every man's death diminishes us." That's true whatever one's religious beliefs may be.

### What happens at the funeral?

Usually, an ordained rabbi will conduct the funeral service, though any informed Jew may perform it. Members of the family and friends of different faiths sometimes participate in the sharing of memories. Prayers are recited in English and Hebrew.

At the funeral, the rabbi recites those prayers which are both expressive of the spirit of Judaism and the memory of the deceased. The most commonly used scripture, Psalm 23, expresses the faith of the members of the flock in the justice of the Divine Shepherd. From the Psalm, "O Lord, what is humankind?" we hear that although "our days are a passing shadow" there is immortality for those who have "treasured their days with a heart of wisdom." During the recitation of the prayer *El Molah Rachamim*, the name of the loved one is mentioned. The eulogy of the dead (*Hesped*) is included in the service to recognize not only that a death has occurred but that a life has been lived.

Jewish worshippers do not kneel at services. All that is required is to stand or be seated at appropriate moments of the liturgy. As a sign of respect, hats or yarmelkas may be distributed. Wearing one is not a contradiction of Christian principle. I recall the late Cardinal Cushing coming to my temple and insisting that he wear his own yarmelka, which he obtained in Israel.

The casket is mostly present at the service. Jewish law, *halacha*, requires that the casket be made completely of wood, without metal nails or handles. Metal retards the natural process alluded to in Genesis 3:10: "For dust you are and to dust you shall return." As in Christianity, Jewish ritual also takes many, many variations.

### Why are black ribbons sometimes worn by mourners?

At the service, the family members perform *keria*, meaning 'tear.' This practice derives from Genesis; when Jacob believed that his son, Joseph, was killed, the father "rent his garments" (37:34). Today many mourners indicate their anguish by cutting a black ribbon, usually at the funeral chapel or at the cemetery prior to interment. The ceremony is performed standing up to teach the bereaved to "meet all sorrow standing upright." Instead of a ribbon, traditional Jews may tear a coat or dress. The torn garment or black ribbon is usually worn after the funeral for seven days and for some, thirty days.

### Is it acceptable to go to the cemetery?

In Judaism accompanying the dead to the grave, *halavayat hamet*, is considered the highest form of loving kindness, *hessed shel emet*. The funeral does not end in the chapel, but after the dead person has been accompanied to the final burial place. Witnessing the burial, *k'vurah*, emphasizes the importance of leave-taking and affords basic emotional tools for dealing with unfinished feelings. An expression of consolation recited by friends as the mourners leave the grave is the Hebrew: "*Ha-makom yinachem et-chem b'toch sh'ar a-vay-lay tzion virushalaymim*," 'May God comfort you along with all the mourners of Zion and Jerusalem.'

### What happens after the interment?

*Shiva* (meaning 'seven') consists of the seven days of mourning when most family members remain at home and refrain from their ordinary pursuits and occupations. Children may go back to school for some of the period if both parents and child together make this decision.

In returning to the *beit aveil*, the mourners' home, some may wash their hands, which according to one sage symbolically indicates that our hands are clean of death; we did everything to help this person live or to ease his/her pain.

Immediately upon returning from the cemetery, a light, or *shiva candle*, is kindled and remains burning for the entire seven days. Before his death, the great sage, Judah Ha-Nasi, the 3rd century editor of the Talmud, instructed that a light should be kept aflame in his home for "Light is the symbol of the divine. The Lord is my light and my salvation."

The practice of covering mirrors is not based explicitly upon Jewish law. Some authorities regard this practice as superstitious and discourage its use. Others interpret the rite symbolically. The reason: "We ought not to gaze upon our reflection in the mirror of the house of mourning. In so doing, we appear to be reflecting upon ourselves."

During the week, the community reaches out to both adult and child. Friends demonstrate their concern and love. The first food, *seudat havra'ah*, is traditionally prepared by others. The meal usually includes bread or rolls, the staff of life, and hard boiled eggs, symbolizing the cycle of life and death.

During *shiva*, religious services may be observed in the mourners' home. The bereaved recite the *Kaddish* prayer "May God's name be magnified and exalted...", a pledge of rededication to the God of Life. They belong to the largest company in the world—the company of those who have known anguish and death. The great, universal sense of sorrow helps to unite human hearts and dissolve all other feelings into those of common sympathy and understanding.

*Sh-loshim* (meaning 'thirty') is the 30-day period after death. During *sh-loshim* mourners gradually return to their normal living, but avoid joyful social events. For most mourners, *sh-loshim* concludes the period of bereavement, but for those whose parents have died, mourning concludes 12 months from the day of the death.

The anniversary of the death, *yahrzeit*, is observed annually on the date of death, commencing on the preceding day and concluding on the anniversary day at sunset. *Kaddish* is recited in the synagogue and a *yahrzeit* candle is kindled.

The service of commemoration of the tombstone or plaque is called *the unveiling*. The time of the unveiling may be any time after *sh-loshim* and usually before the first year of mourning is over. Unveilings are not held on the Sabbath or Festivals. Any member of the family or a close friend may intone the appropriate prayers.

### What does one say when visiting the family?

The obituary usually contains the place and time when the mourners will be together. When you enter, custom has it that one should remain silent and permit the bereaved to speak first. Take your cues from the mourners. You might share some remembrances of your client. If you also write a personal letter, it will be cherished forever. Encourage the family to relate their reminiscences and feelings. Their emotions may be non-verbal. If they cry, tell them that this is a normal way to express emotion. Most importantly, just your presence will afford them comfort and reassurance.

### Is there a Jewish view of life after death?

There are Jewish views of life after death, with a variety of beliefs in the more than 3000-year-old history. The great scholar George F. Moore declared: "Any attempt to systematize the Jewish notions of the hereafter imposes upon them an order and consistency which does not exist in them" (1954).

As mentioned, Judaism has no dogmatic creed. During the many centuries, many ideas have been presented. All Jews accept the fact that death is real and memories never die. Some believe in the immortality of the soul and the reunion of body and soul, *tehiyath hamathem*, 'bodily resurrection.'

Many beliefs have been offered, yet none is declared authoritative and final. Tradition teaches but at the same time seems to say that there is so much we do not know and still more we have to learn. Only God can completely discern the mysteries of life and death.

The emphasis in Judaism is upon life and living. "Better is one hour of repentance and good deeds in this world than the whole life of the world-to-come" (*Ethics of the Fathers*, 4:17).

## Are Jews permitted to participate in non-sectarian worship?

Nearly always when a congregant hears that I will be lecturing in another community, the inevitable question is, "What synagogue?" Even though I am a rabbi, my audiences are predominantly, and often exclusively, non-Jewish. (Grief is grief, whatever one's theology.)

I speak in about fifty Christian seminaries a year. Some of the students who have never seen a rabbi are disappointed that I don't fit their stereotypical pictures, replete with flowing beard and a "beanie" (a small black hat called a yarmelka).

As a Jew, I feel at home in any house of worship. Judaism is not a missionary faith and forbids the perspective that only Jews know the way to the spiritual life. The sages of old taught: "The pious and the righteous of all nations have a share in the world to be."

Of course, we know that all faiths are not identical because we approach the God of love from different theological and cultural traditions.

Brotherhood does not mean *otherhood*. Ecumenism does not demand the dilution of dissimiltude, but rather the creation of a climate of understanding in which each can thrive and develop the best that each possesses for the ultimate benefit of all faiths. When religions are easily interchangeable, their value on the exchange market of movements that are life-shapers and influence-makers is zero.

I delight in speaking in churches and experiencing the singular majesty of each historical tradition. How disappointed I was when a pastor recently told me that he was inserting into the service the Jewish hymn, *Yigdal*, to "make me feel more comfortable." Faith should not be watered down from its separatist qualities nor neutralized of its distinctive features. Uniformity is never our goal, rather unity through diversity.

This is best illustrated in my recently being invited to participate in a non-sectarian memorial service for an annual meeting of hospices. The name of Jesus Christ was repeatedly invoked in this so-called non-sectarian worship. Of course, we all know that Christ is from the Greek, *Christos*, literally 'anointed' or 'Messiah.' Though Jesus was born a Jew, he is not considered a messiah in Judaism.

Obviously this Christological reference is apart from Judaism and non-sectarian service. According to Webster's dictionary, non-sectarian means "not having a sectarian character, not affiliated with or restricted to a particular religious group."

Memorial services are significant community rituals especially for those of us who are devoted to helping the dying and healing the survivors. In a pluralistic society, there could well be the desire for traditional theological modes. Do not schedule an interfaith service and invoke the name of Jesus. Let there be truth in advertising.

### In summary, are there Hebrew terms that may be helpful?

*Alav Hashalom* (pronounced Ah-la-hv Ha-shaw-lome) 'Peace be upon him.' Used after the name of the departed.

*Alehaw Hashalom* (All-leh-haw Ha-shaw-lome) 'Peace be upon her.' Used after the name of the departed.

*Avelim* (Ah-veh-leem) 'Mourners' Laws of mourning apply in case of death of one of seven relatives: father, mother, husband, wife, son or daughter, brother or sister.

*El Moleh Rachamin* (Ale-moh-lay Ra-cha-meen) 'God full of compassion' Memorial prayer recited at funerals.

*Hesped* (Hes-peed) Eulogy delivered by rabbi for the dead, usually includes an account of life accomplishments of the departed.

*Keria* (Ka-ree-ah) Custom of mourner tearing a section of his garment or a black ribbon as symbol of grief.

*Matzevah* (Mah-tzave-vah) Tombstone that is erected toward the end of the first year of interment.

*Minyan.* Minimum number of ten Jews above the age of thirteen required for public services. According to Jewish law, a minyan is required for community recital of the Kaddish.

*Seudat Havra-ah* (S-oo-dat Chav-vey-rah) Meal of consolation.

*Sh-loshim* (Sh-lo-sheem) 'Thirty' Mourning begins on the first day of the funeral and ends on morning of the thirtieth day.

*Shiva* (Shee-vah) Refers to the first seven days of mourning after burial.

*Nefesh* (Neh-fesh), *Neshamah* (N'sha'ma) and *Ruach* (Rue-ach) 'Soul' Derived from roots meaning 'breath' and 'wind.' Soul is the source without which there can be no life.

*Tachrichim* (Ta-ch-re-cheem) Robe in which some dead are buried. Made of white linen cloth.

*Tehiyyath Hamathem* (Th-chee-yaht Ha-may-teem) 'Resurrection of the dead' Belief by some that at the end of time the bodies of the dead will rise from the grave.

*Yahrzeit* (Yohr-tzite) Yiddish term for the anniversary of death.

*Yizkor* (Yz-core) Prayer "May God remember the soul of my revered…" on major holidays, Day of Atonement, Feast of *Yom Kippur*, Tabernacles (*Succoth*), Passover, and Feast of Weeks (*Shavuot*).

---

*Rabbi Earl A. Grollman, DHL, DD, is a pioneer in the field of crisis intervention and has written 25 books. He often appears on radio and television and is a frequent lecturer in the US and abroad.*

# THREE

# Christians in Grief

*Stephen D. McConnell*

*"Listen, mother," said Father Zossima. "Once in olden times a holy saint saw in the Temple a mother like you weeping for her little one, her only one, whom God had taken. 'Knowest thou not,' said the saint to her, 'how bold these little ones are before the throne of God? Verily, there are none bolder than they in the kingdom of heaven. 'Thou didst give us life, oh Lord,' they say, 'and scarcely had we looked upon it when Thou didst take it back again.' And so boldly they ask and ask again that God gives them at once the rank of angels....' That's what the saint said to the weeping mother of old. He was a great saint and he could not have spoken falsely."*

Fyodor Doestoevsky, *The Brothers Karamazov*

As it is with every orientation of life, the Christian faith offers both great comforts and great challenges to the person in grief. In the lines above, Doestoevsky indicates what some of those comforts and challenges might be. Among them are questions concerning who God is and God's participation in the death of a loved one, the life beyond, and the role of the church in the grief process.

Christianity is such an entrenched aspect of Western culture that it pervades secular writing, music, and art, as well as rituals and customs. Consider, for example, how many people who are not practicing Christians celebrate Christmas and Easter, or how many of our cultural ceremonies, rituals, weddings, and funerals have their basis in Christian doctrine. The majority of non-Christians in our culture have some familiarity with these customs.

This chapter, however, deals not so much with the cultural aspects of Christianity as with the actual beliefs of the faith community and how those beliefs may complicate or facilitate grief and loss. There is tremendous variation to be found among practicing Christians. So what chance is there to approach even a general review of how "Christians" grieve? Certainly there is no formula by which Christians express the pain that comes from profound loss. But this discussion explores the impact of a range of beliefs and offers suggestions for effectively caring for the believer walking through the "valley of the shadow of death."

A Christian is a believer. Of course people are all believers in some way or another, but to minister to a Christian in grief is to take into account the impact the individual's beliefs will have upon the way he or she grieves. As in the Doestoevsky passage, there are some shared and understood beliefs that allow the saint to minister to the weeping mother.

The first of these is, of course, the afterlife, or in more specific Christian terms, heaven, the ultimate hope of the suffering or grieving Christian—the belief that one's loved one has not merely departed but has, in fact, arrived elsewhere, a better place, the ultimate destination. Heaven remains for most people a subjective concept, and there are nearly as many different images of the afterlife as there are Christians, many of which vary greatly from the literal Biblical image. However, I have not yet found anyone who paints heaven as anything less than pure joy and fulfilled dreams. For the Christian, heaven is the light at the end of the tunnel of grief: "I can go on, because I know he is in a better place, and because I know I will see him again someday."

This rather simplistic view of heaven is often a quick panacea offered by the caregiver who doesn't really want to deal with the pain of the grieving person and would prefer to hurry them along to a more comfortable state. "Well, I'm sure you're comforted to know that Harold is in a better place. Oh, would you look at the time! I have to go." Such an approach misses the mark, rather like the floral shop that mixed up two orders. One basket of flowers went to a bank that had just relocated and the card said, "Deepest sympathy on your most recent loss," while the other basket went to a funeral home, with a card reading, "Congratulations on your new location." Christians in grief are apt to find themselves between those two expressions: the deep pain of losing a loved one and the joy of believing that he or she is in a wonderful place beyond the reach of earthly suffering.

Unfortunately, a grieving Christian can begin to feel guilty or selfish that he or she is not actually experiencing the joy that comes from knowing the deceased is experiencing the wonder of heaven. Often the pain of separation trumps the imagined joy of the deceased loved one—especially in the early hands. An anguished father whose child had recently died expressed it this way: "I just miss him so much. I know he's there, but he's not here." It is important for the caregiver, regardless of his or her own beliefs, to affirm that anguish.

Bereaved people often sense the spiritual presence of the deceased and, for the most part, find comfort from such experiences. Some, though not all, followers of the Christian faith believe that these experiences (i.e., the ability of deceased loved ones to visit and communicate with mortals) are not consistent with the Christian understanding of the life beyond. Who is to judge? The caregiver is wise to affirm the grieving person in these encounters. As researcher and writer Louis LaGrand (1997) writes, "The challenge is to set aside our personal beliefs about the hard-to-explain and be open to the possibilities that can present themselves when the extraordinary experience occurs in the life of the mourner" (p.5). The therapeutic value of such experiences can be very real. But it is important for both the caregiver and the bereaved individual to recognize that they may well meet with differing opinions within the Christian community as to the validity of such experiences. Being confronted with conflicting views may complicate the grieving process, and a discussion ahead of time on how to process and respond to those contradictory views can be most helpful.

All too often within the Christian community bereaved individuals are not given permission to feel and express the deep pain that may remain in spite of the assurance of eternal life for their loved one. Sadly, there are even those who are likely to cast doubt upon the faith of a griever who continues to traverse the valley of the shadow of death longer than expected or who wonders aloud why God would allow such a death to occur.

Sometimes the church becomes a challenging place for people to continue their grieving, either because fellow believers wish to rush them beyond the pain of loss to the joy of heaven, or because it is simply difficult for the acutely grieving person to participate in the celebrations of the faith community. Typically, the church does well in the crisis moments of death and immediate grief, but is often not prepared to walk with the bereaved down the long path. Casseroles and cards that were quick to come the week after death cease to appear within a month or two, when, of course, moments of grief and isolation still occur. The caregiver would do well to familiarize the local church with the ongoing needs of the bereaved. Grief workshops and seminars that sensitize the faith community to these issues not only empower those who want to reach out to grieving people but also provide them with tools that can be used when they themselves join the ranks of the bereaved.

Many widows and widowers who participated actively with their spouse in the church find it hard to return because of all the memories that abide there. Or perhaps their place in the pew remains empty as a silent protest against a God who appears to have acted quite cruelly or unfairly.

Which leads to the ever-present issue of God's participation in suffering. To be a Christian is to believe in the beneficence of a God who gives us life and calls it good. It is also to believe that God continues to play an active role in our lives. And yet when death comes too soon, too suddenly, or too cruelly it is often that same believer who is left to wonder why God would allow such a thing to happen. Grief can become even more confusing and painful when one hears words of "assurance" from well-meaning friends within the faith community who say, "It must have been God's will." The Christian is left with not only the fresh pain of loss, but also the question, "Why would a good God do this?" It is, of course, the age-old question that remains, for the most part, shrouded in mystery, one that theologians and philosophers have pondered throughout history.

So the question for the grieving Christian remains, "Am I allowed to be angry at the God who has allowed my loved one to die?" The answer, of course, is yes. But it is important for the caregiver to understand the complexity of such anger. It is an anger that shakes its fists at a God whose purposes are good yet unknown. It is an anger that will never get a completely satisfying answer to the question of how involved God was in this death. A Christian is loathe to believe that death is a meaningless thing and is eager to believe that God will somehow work it into something meaningful. Yet a long time can pass before there is even a hint of that meaning and purpose. A lengthy, sometimes arduous, journey can be counted upon, and the compassionate, non-judgmental companionship of others within the Christian community can be pivotal in determining the direction the journey will take.

All in all, a good God who promises to be faithful can often be an easy target for the grieving person. As caregivers, those in the Christian community should not feel as much the obligation to defend God (God can take it) as to make sure that the griever does not pull punches in the expression of that anger. Affirming the full range of intense emotions that often threaten to overwhelm the griever can be a particularly valuable role for the caregiver.

There is no better treatment of this issue than in *A Grief Observed*, penned by C.S. Lewis (1961). Lewis, who is perhaps the most popular Christian theologian of the 20th century, writes about his own profound grief over the death of his wife:

> Meanwhile, where is God? This is one of the most disquieting symptoms. When you are happy, so happy that you have no sense of needing Him, so happy that you are tempted to feel His claims upon you as an interruption, if you remember yourself and turn to Him with gratitude and praise, you will be—or so it feels—welcomed with open arms. But go to Him when your need is desperate, when all other help is in vain, and what do you find? A door slammed in your face, and a sound of bolting and double bolting on the inside. After that, silence. You may as well turn away. The longer you wait, the more emphatic the silence will become. There are no lights in the windows. It might be an empty house. Was it

ever inhabited? It seemed so once. And that seeming was as strong as this. What can this mean? Why is He so present a commander in our time of prosperity and so very absent a help in time of trouble? (p.17)

Lewis so vividly puts into words the feelings that a fervent Christian is apt to feel in the deep moments of grief: feelings not only of anger, but of bewilderment over God's silence. A lust for some sort of answer, a hunger for some sense of assurance. A desperate plea for God to somehow fill the void left behind by the departed loved one. To encourage Christians to express that anger and bewilderment is to keep them in conversation with the God in whom they have so assuredly believed, and encourages them to keep asking the questions until the time when faith allows the questions to go unanswered. Peace comes in believing that God will disclose His reasons in His time.

A discussion of Christian beliefs regarding death and response to it is incomplete without touching on the issue of salvation and judgment. Many Christians believe that heaven is not necessarily a guaranteed destination. Thus grief can be complicated by a bereaved person's doubts about the salvation of the deceased and the possibility that, due to God's judgment, he or she is, in fact, not in heaven but in hell. And some Christian traditions understand other dimensions of the afterlife, including purgatory and limbo, which encourage the joint participation of the griever and deceased in the journey to full communion with God.

The temptation on the part of the caregiver might be to minimize these possibilities or dismiss them all together. Caution: To do so is to invalidate what may be core tenets for the believer and thus to call into question what has been a foundation of his or her life. This is a reality that the grieving person has to work through. Always, the Christian holds out the hope that God's grace will abound and persevere for the sake of the deceased, but the lingering doubt of whether or not a person really is in heaven can intensify or prolong the grieving process. What is key here is that once again we are back to the mystery that lies between God and humankind, and the caregiver would be wise to encourage the grieving believer not to presume God's acts or intentions.

The unique symbols that Christians carry into grief are the images of Jesus Christ crucified and Jesus Christ resurrected. These images are the heart of Christian faith and can serve as the heart of a Christian's response to death. It is the crucified Christ that helps to remind Christians that they are not alone in their suffering but that God, in Jesus Christ, has suffered with us, experiencing the pain of seeming betrayal by the Father in heaven and the abandonment of earthly friends. Comfort comes in knowing that there is a God who understands, and has felt, our pain. Coupled with this image of the cross is the empty tomb: the sign of Christ's resurrection, the belief that death is now conquered and that life does not end with our last earthly breath. This is the message that the Christian celebrates time and again and yet might find difficult to celebrate in moments of deep grief.

A man whose wife of many years died just a few days before Easter appeared in church on Easter Sunday. People were glad to see him, but were surprised that he had returned so soon after burying his beloved. When it was time for congregational singing he found he couldn't sing. When it was time for the prayer he found he couldn't pray. The sermon fell upon the widower's deaf ears and numb heart. Later, when asked to reflect upon the experience of his return to church and worship, he said, "On that Easter morning I found it very hard to believe and feel the resurrection, but I also found it very comforting to know and to see that there were people feeling and believing it for me even when I couldn't."

And therein lie both the comforts and the challenges of a Christian in grief: The hope and assurance of what is promised to us in the beyond, and the doubt and pain that can come to us in our present loss. The psalmist speaks of these comforts and challenges in that wonderful poem (Psalm 23) often heard at the time of death, and for good reason:

The Lord is my shepherd, I shall not want.
He maketh me to lie down in green pastures,
He leadeth me beside the still waters, he restoreth
my soul.
He leadeth me in the paths of righteousness for his name's
sake.
Yea, though I walk through the valley of the shadow
of death,
I will fear no evil; for thou art with me;
thy rod and thy staff, they comfort me.
Thou preparest a table before me in the presence
of mine enemies;
thou anointest my head with oil, my cup runneth over.
For surely goodness and mercy will follow me all the days
of my life;
and I will dwell in the house of the Lord forever.

And so these are the places between which the Christian in grief is apt to be found: walking through "the valley of death," and yet believing that "goodness and mercy will follow me all the days of my life and I will dwell in the house of the Lord forever." The caregiver will do well to simply walk alongside, wherever the path leads and for as long as the journey takes.

---

*Reverend Stephen D. McConnell is the pastor of the Liberty Corner Presbyterian Church. He is a graduate of Westminster College and Princeton Theological Seminary.*

# FOUR

# Grief: A Muslim Perspective

*Shukria Alimi Raad*

My husband, Mohammad Azim Raad, died on January 15, 1989, from pancreatic cancer that had been discovered during an operation in April of 1988. Those eight months will always be with me, and the story is not an easy one for me to tell. I knew that I would have him with me for a very short time. While his illness was not prolonged, the grief that I have learned to live with is.

I am a Muslim woman. For those readers not familiar with my faith and beliefs, Islam means "surrender to the will and purpose of God." We worship Him alone and ask Him alone for help. This surrender to Allah frees us from the shackles of superstition, and from fear and frustration. I believe that my faith is the reason I survived and learned to live with grief and pain.

No matter how different we look, what kind of religion we practice, or which direction our faith takes us, we all have two things in common in this world: life and death. We are all born the same way and will die one day. We have no control over death. The Qur'an tells us:

> And behold! Ye come
> To Us Bare and Alone
> As We Created You
> For the First Time:

Ye Have Left Behind You
All (the favours) which
We bestowed on you:
We see not with you.
(S.VI 93)

I was born in Afghanistan and lived there until I was 37 years old. I was a broadcast journalist and my husband was a prominent attorney and well-known poet. Our lives were very comfortable, but we left the country with our son, Aziz, and daughter, Haida, after the Soviet invasion in 1980, when our lives, like millions of other Afghans', were turned upside down.

Our escape from Afghanistan is another story. For a long period of time I was alone in India, my husband was inside Afghanistan, and our children were alone in Pakistan. Those were very harsh days for us. We weren't sure that we would ever see each other again. When at last we were reunited, we were among the most fortunate of Afghan families because we reached the United States unharmed.

We left everything behind. Can you imagine how unbearable our lives had become that we agreed to leave our homeland? We buried all of our memories there and agreed to live in a country where nobody knew us, ready to speak a totally different language and leave behind our history, literature, and tradition. We could not bring anything out of Afghanistan but our faith and love. As a Muslim, I believe that

The man of Faith holds fast to his faith
Because he knows it is true.
The man of the world, rejecting Faith, clings
hard to worldly interests, but let him not Force
his interests on men sincere and true, by favor,
force or fraud.
(S.CIX)

We really and truly believed in holding fast to our faith, the faith which guided us all our lives to believe in and trust God the Creator of the universe. All of our hardships, being uprooted, becoming very poor, uncertainty about our future, were tolerable and can hardly be remembered now. The only grief that we will never forget, though we have learned to live with it, is the loss of Azim, who died just when everything was beginning to go smoothly in our new life in the United States. At the time, the children were studying hard, and Azim and I both had jobs we liked. We wondered why death had come to us now. Was God testing us?

> In gulps will he sip it,
> But never will he be near
> Swallowing it down his throat
> Death will come to him.
> (S.XIV 17)

Muslims believe it is the biggest test of our lives to lose someone very dear to us and still have faith and trust in God.

I am not a scholar of Islam and therefore cannot write with authority about all the various Islamic sects. There is one Holy Book, the Qur'an, in which all Muslims believe. The major Islamic sects are the Sunnis, who comprise four fifths of all Muslims, and the Shi'ites, who live primarily in Iran and parts of Iraq. Other sects include Ahmadias and Sufi Muslims. These groups may pray or fast in different ways, but when it comes to questions of life and death, we all believe the Qur'an when it says:

> Every soul shall have a taste of death:
> And only on the Day of Judgment shall
> you be paid your full recompense.
> (S.III 85)

Parents talk about death, teachers teach about it, and poets write about it. It is part of our culture and faith. Children are taught from an early age that the purpose of life on earth is to prepare oneself for the next life. I remember my mother talking about death when I was barely seven years old. My father died when I was only one year old. I was told that death is very close to us, closer than we think. I hated this closeness because I was reminded day after day how cruelly death parted people. Death is mentioned in the Qur'an many times in order to prepare us for our life after death. I often wonder if it is mentioned so often in other religions.

We Muslims strongly believe that death is not the end but a beginning to our new lives. In spite of all these preparations for the life to come, Azim's death was not only a tremendous shock but has left behind grief like a wound that will never heal.

Funeral and burial practices differ somewhat among the wide variety of cultures in which Islam is practiced, but there are general patterns based on the advice given by the Prophet. When death is very near, someone is called to read verses of the Qur'an at the bedside. At the moment of death, the eyes are closed and the jaw bound up (Smith, 1991).

An important part of the process is the washing (or ablution) of the body, which is often done by a professional washer at home or at a hospital. All items used in the ablution must be newly purchased, and the water must be disposed of carefully. During the washing ceremony, verses from the Qur'an are usually recited. Often, cotton plugs are placed in the body's orifices and the body is wrapped in a shroud (Smith, 1991).

Muslims are advised to mourn communally for just three days. We are told not to hurt ourselves physically. Even though women are advised to refrain from screaming, scratching their faces, or hitting themselves, there are traditions in Islamic countries which still practice such behavior. In Afghanistan women who are in mourning wear black and keep their heads covered for at least 40 days. No makeup and no colorful dress is worn during the mourning period. In contrast, Indian Muslim women wear white during this period, and sometimes for the rest of their lives. Cultural practices may vary but the grief is the same.

## The Shock

My grief started with a shock when I was told that Azim had a very short time to live. I would ask myself: How can I possibly survive? When I came to the United States I left behind my mother, my sister, and my friends. I adored and worshipped Azim; he was everything to me. I never loved anyone so dearly in my life, not even my mother or my children. Even now, nine years later, as I write about him the tears roll down my face, and I can still see his kind face through my tears. It is still difficult for me to use the past tense when I speak of him.

Azim was sick, but he did not tell us. Day by day he was changing. He lost weight, did not eat much, and visited his doctors regularly. One night he could not hide it any longer, so he told me that he wanted to go to the hospital.

One doctor after another gave us different opinions. They and the nurses used medical jargon that none of us understood. But there was one word that we understood all too well: cancer.

After each test, we were told that the result was negative and was not cancer. Even the endoscopy didn't show any signs of cancer. We were told that the only way to know what was wrong with any certainty was to agree to an operation.

It was two weeks before Azim was fit for the operation, and I spent most of that time beside his hospital bed. I observed clergy and counselors comforting the families of those with serious illnesses, but I was never told about Azim's illness. Even the night before the operation the surgeon told me he was hopeful that Azim did not have cancer.

The next morning my children and I went to the hospital filled with hope and prayers. Azim was smiling. The surgeon told me the operation would take three to four hours. I was miserable as I sat in the waiting room for what seemed like an eternity. When the doctor came out I looked at my watch: I had been waiting less than an hour.

The surgeon motioned me to meet him in the hall. My whole life depended on what he was going to say. I only remember his saying, "Your husband has cancer and has only about two weeks to live." I don't remember what happened next. It got dark and I fainted. I heard my daughter crying. There was no one from the hospital or from the chapel to comfort the children or me. I have never felt so lonely in my life. Later, someone from the hospital came to have me sign papers and to ask my permission for a bypass.

I signed the papers and pleaded with the surgeon and nurses not to tell my husband the bad news. When Azim opened his eyes and asked about the operation, I told him that everything would be just fine. I stayed with him that night and just sat on the floor of the little room. As he slept I prayed and asked God to give me strength to deal with this terrible shock and to help me keep Azim happy for the short time he had with us.

The doctors forced me to tell him about his illness. Azim was very brave. He was worried about us because he did not have life insurance, but we were worried only about him. My concern was to keep him happy during his last few days, and since he did have very good health insurance I made sure that he had the best. I wanted him to have the best oncologist, the best chemotherapist, and the best hospital.

It is most important in our culture for families to be together. When Azim was in the hospital, the children did not go to school and we were with him constantly. Since the hospital had visiting time rules and regulations, I often hid in the restroom and when the coast was clear I went to Azim's room. I had obtained a private room for him, but the room did not have a cot for me to rest on, only an armchair. Day and night I sat on this chair. When I got very tired I would sleep on the floor.

Azim and I talked and cried during the long nights in the hospital room. It made him uncomfortable to see me on the chair or on the floor, but for me this was not a problem as long as I was with him. However, I was afraid to ask for anything that would let anyone know that I was spending nights in the hospital room.

Although Azim lived longer than expected, after a while the cancer took over and the doctors talked to me about hospice. This was the first time that I had heard of it.

Hospice was something that we all needed. The children wanted to be with Azim. He was happy to go home and we were even happier to spend more time with him. We left the hospital around Christmas. The hospice nurse brought everything that was needed to our house. She taught me how to change the IV and how to find the veins. Azim was almost skin and bones, and finding his veins was not an easy job.

I look back now and think about how we all adapt when the need arises. I have always been terrified of needles. There was a time when I could not even watch my children getting a shot. Once when my daughter was very small and got a shot at a clinic, I fainted. Then the day came when I knew that Azim's life depended on it and there I was, struggling to find a vein so that I could pierce it with the needle for his IV.

Azim did not take morphine or any other pain killer. He wanted his mind to be clear, and most of all he wanted to remember the few days that we had left with each other. He was very weak at the end, but I still remember him talking to all of us as much as he could. With the help of meditation, rather than medication, it seemed that he did control the pain. The doctor was amazed at Azim's pain tolerance. Whenever I told him that Azim did not have much pain, the doctor reminded me that he did, but that he had even stronger willpower.

The familiar environment made Azim more comfortable. Now, in the privacy of our own home, he started talking about death. He explained to us how he felt about his past and how he remembered those days. I will never forget when he told me that if he were to do everything over again, he would marry the same woman and would want the same children and family.

By this time, we had all surrendered to God's will. My son and I were taking turns staying up at night. My daughter was in very bad shape. She was especially close to her father and spent the nights in her room praying. She was the one who drove him for his radiation and chemotherapy for three months, and she knew how much her father suffered.

When she drove him to the clinic, Azim would wait by the front door until she parked the car. One day she sadly told me, "I saw Dad sitting on the curb today while I was parking the car. He is so weak now." My husband knew that she was the fragile one and he had many talks with her. He talked to her about death and how we should all accept it. She tells me now that while riding in the car, her father would look out the window and admire everything around him. He told her to do things that she enjoys because life is so short. Azim did so himself.

His friends visited him every day now. Some stayed overnight, and one of his friends even came from Germany and stayed for a couple of weeks. We all ignored the changes in his appearance and simply enjoyed the pleasure of having him with us. Gradually I noticed that his veins were shrinking and I could no longer get the needle in. I became panicky and called the hospice nurse, who came and explained to me that it was the end, and we couldn't do anything to postpone it any further.

The horrible time was here: Azim was leaving us. He also knew that it was the end, or rather the beginning of another life for him. We were so busy during those months that we hadn't even thought about a site for his grave or the funeral service. One night he had asked me to look for the phone number of the Muslim Community Center. He said, "Please call them now because I need some place to be buried." I dialed the number and started crying. I asked the woman who answered the phone for some information about a grave for my husband. She started to cry as well. I will never forget her kind and pleasant voice and her sincere compassion. She said, "Sister, do not panic. You are not alone, we are all here for you."

Afterwards, I thought about how God helps us during the hardest days in our lives. The woman and her husband were involved in helping people in the Muslim Community Center. When I told them that my husband wanted us to purchase a grave site in the middle of the night, they agreed to help us and they gave me their home address. They also gave us the addresses of funeral homes. My nephew and I went and obtained four sites in the cemetery. Azim told me that night how relieved he was.

The following night he started talking to himself. He said, "How green and peaceful this place looks." My son and I asked him what or where was so green and peaceful. Azim did not answer.

One thing that did become clear to me at the end was that Azim was in pain. After his death Haida told me that he had asked her to pray that the end would come soon because he could no longer tolerate the pain. I was with him day and night but did not see the pain, because he hid it from me. Often he was silent and sometimes even trembling; when I asked what was wrong, he would say that he was praying. During the first days in the hospital, I had heard other cancer patients screaming from pain, and I was so worried about Azim. I know now that his pain had started a long time before but he had always managed to hide it from me.

## The Last Day

It is still very hard for me to write about this day. On January 15, 1989, the doctor and two hospice nurses were with us. The doctor told me that Azim may have a seizure and that that would be the end. He left his telephone number with the nurses. As he said good-bye to his patient and left the room his eyes were moist. He told me that Azim was very different from his other patients, who asked for the strongest pain medication. He said, "Mr. Raad not only admits that he has pain but he gives us a smile, too."

That same day, at about one o'clock in the afternoon, Azim asked all of us to sit beside his bed. He started praying. Whenever he missed a verse, I repeated it for him. Two of his friends were reciting the Qur'an. He asked me where my nephew, who lived with us, was. I said that he would be back soon. When my nephew walked in, Azim just looked at each one of us. One of the nurses touched his feet and told me that this was it. She told me in English to tell him that the children and I were going to be fine and that he could now surrender and go. I suddenly remembered the *suras* of the Qur'an, "Yield up your souls," and "Return unto Him."

Azim died peacefully. When the nurse closed his eyes, I said: "No, he is going to have a seizure, the doctor said so." She smiled and said, "Doctors cannot predict everything." I cried, we all cried, even Azim's doctor came later and cried, too. Tears are rolling even now as I write these lines.

Afterwards, I did not go to any sort of bereavement support group. In Islamic communities, friends and relatives never leave the mourner alone. They take turns bringing food and staying overnight. Women mostly share their grief and join in the mourner's weeping. I remember that when I lived in Afghanistan I had been critical of these gatherings. But now, when I was mourning, and my friends and relatives surrounded me, I realized how much this tradition meant. Every Thursday night, people brought dinner to our home and talked with me until late into the night. This went on for 40 days. On the 40th day, almost all of our friends and relatives came over, recited the Qur'an, and dedicated it to the dead person's soul. This was a sort of group therapy for me.

We all need help or a shoulder to cry on—Christians, Muslims, Jews, Buddhists, all of us. I really needed somebody to approach me and to offer a little sympathy when I was in the hospital with Azim. I am certain now that the hospital staff was not sure how to deal with another religion, culture, and tradition, and so did not reach out to us as they did to others.

I am one of the millions of people who greatly admired Mother Teresa. Azim and I lived in India for five years. During that time we helped many Afghans who had come to India for surgery or other medical reasons and who did not speak the language or needed a place to stay. This was one of the reasons that hundreds of Afghans came from all over the United States and Canada, even as far away as Europe, for Azim's funeral.

We all need a hug, a shoulder to cry on, or a simple handshake when we face the biggest tragedy of our lives, losing someone we love. We cannot prevent death, but as Mother Teresa said, "We can help people to die with dignity." And within an atmosphere of human caring and compassion, no matter our culture or religion.

---

*Shukria Alimi Raad was a journalist in Afghanistan until she and her family came to the US in 1980. She has been a broadcaster with the Voice of America since 1982.*

# PART II

# Ethnicity and Culture

This volume has emphasized that culture is more than ethnicity, yet ethnicity cannot be ignored in understanding culture and grief. In fact, ethnicity remains one of the major ways that culture is defined. Glazer and Moynihan's classic story, *Beyond the Melting Pot*, shattered the myth of assimilation. Instead, it showed that cultural differences persisted for generations, even when ethnic groups migrated to the United States. A hybrid culture was formed, one where earlier cultural themes were retained.

This is clearly the case with death and grief. Kalish and Reynolds' 1981 study found that experiences, attitudes, practices, and beliefs about dying, death, and bereavement varied among ethnic groups. For example, for many racial minorities in the US, infant mortality is higher, and life expectancy is lower, than the national average. Moreover, the ways that individuals find meaning in loss, the support they look for and receive within and outside the family, as well as the beliefs that guide decisions about death all vary among different ethnicities (Kalish, 1981; Irish, Lundquist, and Nelsen, 1993).

These differences are rooted in history. For example, slavery and racial segregation both influenced and, in some ways, enhanced the role of African American funerals. Many customs survived from Africa (Barrett, 1995; Perry, 1993). In a segregated society, providing funeral services was one of few professional roles open to African Americans, offering community prominence as well as relative prosperity. In slavery, the funeral persisted as one of the few opportunities to build a sense of community (Perry, 1993).

The chapters in this section explore the effects of culture and ethnicity on our experiences of grief. Since culture hides from those who know it best, Cable begins by describing the ways that the common experiences of American culture frame our responses to loss. He notes that dramatic changes in mortality have tended to associate death and aging. In addition, the bureaucratization of death, de-ritualization, cultural diversity, and geographic mobility have all limited social support in grief.

Cable's contribution seems twofold. First, he reminds us that cultural practices can both facilitate and complicate grieving. While Cable's discussion emphasizes the latter, we can point to factors such as the rise of the self-help movement that have done much to ease the isolation of the bereaved. A second contribution is more incidental. Implicit in this chapter is a call to create a common ritual. Perhaps it might be as simple as a black or purple ribbon that would denote the mourner as someone needing social support.

Chapters by Barrett and Showalter offer two perspectives on ethnic/racial cultures: Barrett on African Americans; Showalter on Native American culture. Individually and together these chapters offer a number of sensitive observations. First, they remind us of the extensive variations within particular ethnic groups. Barrett's inferential model notes that variations in culture, social class, and spirituality remain lines of division within the Black experience. Native Americans come from tribal groupings that varied in many ways at the time of European contact, including economic, political, linguistic, social, and spiritual differences.

Second, one must remember that these groups' experiences of death may be different as well. Both may have different value systems as well as sensitivities that healthcare workers and counselors should acknowledge. For example, in working among Alaskan Native people, it is critical to allow relationship building and story telling. A "down to business" approach can be alienating. Even the general values of counseling—self-expressiveness, affective openness, and individual actualization—may not be shared across all groups (Sue and Sue, 1990).

Third, as stated before, each group has practices that may complicate or facilitate the grief process. For example, the Native Americans in Alaska share a strong sense of ritual and community that facilitate grieving. But the harsh environment, the extent of sudden loss, and high rates of alcoholism are complicating factors (Doka, 1997). Both Barrett and Showalter provide similar illustrations, which remind counselors and caregivers of the need to build upon cultural strengths, including cultivating local resources such as clergy, traditional healers, or whoever can, and traditionally does, provide bereavement support. Ignoring such assets or focusing upon complicating factors can increase mistrust and perceptions of insensitivity.

Finally, both authors remind us of the difference between stereotypes and useful generalization. A major difference is simply that the latter provides a basis for exploration. It allows for questions rather than answers.

DeSpelder's chapter provides a natural conclusion to this section as she offers sage advice on ways to develop cultural competence. She admonishes us not to search for a magic solution, but rather a non-judgmental openness and an ability to listen that foster increased understanding.

Naturally, this section leaves unexplored many other ethnic groups. Rather than being definitive, these chapters are intended to be illustrative of the ways ethnicity affects the grieving process. Readers may find it useful to supplement this with other sources, such as Irish, Lundquist, and Nelsen (1993); Parkes, Laungani, and Young (1997); or Walsh and McGoldrick (1991).

# FIVE

# Grief in the American Culture

*Dana G. Cable*

Contemporary American culture glorifies youth, beauty, and health. In so doing, it tends to deny the reality of death and thus, the human experience of grief. On the whole, American culture provides little in the way of support to those who are grieving. We are expected to hide our feelings and emotions, to grieve alone and in silence. We are encouraged to replace our loss as soon as possible.

The American experience of grief has changed dramatically. This century has seen science conquer numerous diseases and add nearly 30 years to life expectancy. We have come to expect, therefore, that one will die in old age and that this is acceptable. We see no need to learn to cope with grief, since those who die will be old. Yet statistics show that people of all ages die and we must do our grief work. Even if death only came to the old, we would still need to grieve.

Geographic mobility has had an impact on the experience of grief. A century ago people were born, lived, and died in the same community. The community knew you and your family. They watched you grow up, marry, and raise your children. Your life unfolded in front of them. A death impacted everyone because it meant that a part of the community had died. But today our families are scattered far and wide. When we learn of a death in a neighbor's family, it may well be someone we never met or knew only slightly. We are not significantly affected by the loss. Our support, therefore, is often minimal. Rando (1993) has suggested that this lack of social support can inhibit the readjustment of the mourner. Support must involve consolation and empathy, but it also needs to include practical help and information. Rarely do we offer this type of support following a death.

In addition, in recent years, the American experience of grief has become de-ritualized. For much of this century and before, when a death occurred, we had some fairly standard sets of responses which were seen as assisting the grief process. For example, wearing black as the color of mourning was customary. Black arm bands on clothing and black wreaths on the front door of the home were outward signs of the grief inside. All those around the mourner could recognize the grief and provide support. And this outward recognition continued for a long period of time, which made it easier for the griever to obtain ongoing support from others.

Early in this century families were more a part of the death experience and, therefore, the grief experience. Most deaths occurred at home with the family present. The survivors participated in the care of the dying and, following death, helped prepare the body. Later, they would often return the body to the home for viewing and visitation. Friends would come and provide comfort for the bereaved. They would speak of the dead and their memories of the person. They would stay to support the family.

Also in generations past, grief was experienced early in life. Most families saw at least one, if not more, of their children die. All learned early that death and grief were natural experiences shared with others. There were many who had experienced similar losses and could be of support to the newly bereaved. Most importantly, the bereaved were not alone, but rather part of the larger community of grievers.

Today, however, death is seen and dealt with in a more taboo and negative way (Aries, 1974). Death is unacceptable in today's society. Many deaths, particularly deaths as a result of suicide, AIDS, alcohol abuse, and the like, are seen as the fault of the dead. His or her lifestyle, choices, etc., are viewed as having brought on the death. Consequently, society provides less understanding and support for the survivors.

Perhaps even more significant for this discussion is the fact that today mourning is regarded by some as morbid, even pathological (Corr, 1997). We want the bereaved to express their grief in private, and we make all kinds of efforts to encourage them to do so. Such statements as, *You are doing so well, You have to be brave for the children*, and *Big boys don't cry*, effectively discourage outward signs of mourning. We even go so far as to suggest that the loss is easily replaceable, as in the statement, *You're young, you can have another baby*.

Children particularly are shielded from the experience of grief. In our society they are often excluded from the rituals of saying good-bye. Even if they experience the death of a pet goldfish, we immediately replace it so they will not be sad. Thus the child grows into an adult who has never learned what the process of grieving is really like.

We even avoid the language of death in order to make the pain less intense. We rarely speak of someone dying. Rather, they *pass away*, are *promoted to glory*, *kick the bucket*, or *expire*. All of these euphemisms serve to reduce the sense of loss and avoid the emotional response of mourning. In all respects, we discourage the direct expression of grief. Grief has come to represent a failure to adjust.

Much of this response is a function of our own discomfort with death and our lack of knowledge of what to say to grievers. We do not like to see people sad, and we attempt to cheer them up. Therefore, we communicate the subtle message that if someone wants our company and support, they should "be happy." If they start to speak of the dead, we try to change the subject. If that doesn't work, we begin to avoid them. It doesn't take long for them to get the message: "Don't show your grief to me." In turn, they withdraw, or learn how to cover up their real feelings when they are with us.

We live in the days of fast food, high-speed modems, supersonic transports, and cellular telephones. Everything and everyone must operate at top efficiency. Mourning is seen as serving no useful purpose and simply getting in the way of our progress (Kastenbaum, 1998). Most employers allow the bereaved three days off work following a death. The not-so-subtle message is that we should be ready to get "back to normal." The very fact that grief is not seen as normal speaks volumes about our society. We are encouraged, directly and indirectly, to hold back our emotions and show how strong we are. To do otherwise is seen by many as pathological.

None of this is to suggest that people should not return to work and other routine activities of life. Often these routines serve to fill time and allow the bereaved some escape from their thoughts and emotions. But that does not mean that grief has ended. Grievers need ongoing support. Unfortunately we try to provide the griever with a timetable that is not always appropriate for them. We imply that they should return to work within a week or so. We want to see the widow dating again, but not too soon. Our timetable fails to take into account the unique, individual nature of every relationship, loss, and grief experience.

Much of our avoidance is rooted in our own fears associated with death and grief. We don't really know what to say to a griever. Our question, "How are you?" is asked in an attempt to evoke social conversation. We are not prepared to respond when the answer is, "I'm not doing well." Many of us would not ask how someone was doing if we thought they would give us an honest answer.

We also maintain a morbid curiosity about some deaths. If the death was a suicide or murder, we want the griever to tell us everything. This is not an attempt to help them in their grief, but simply voyeurism.

Even our attempts to provide comfort and support are often failures. We make statements such as *I know how you feel*, *They certainly lived a long life*, and *You were lucky to have them as long as you did*, which are meant to help, but rather show the speaker's lack of understanding. None of us can truly know how someone else feels in their grief. If we have experienced a very similar loss, we can have some understanding. But every death, every relationship, and every person's grief is unique.

Occasionally an event occurs which does bring about an outward and shared mourning experience among many people at the same time. In 1997 many tried to come to grips with a sense of loss over the deaths of Princess Diana and Mother Teresa. Many Americans sat in front of their televisions and watched the whole world mourn. Many people who would not feel comfortable showing their grief over a very personal death felt they had permission to grieve with the rest of the world. At embassies and shrines around the world people came and left floral tributes, notes, candles, and other symbols of their shared grief. And these outward displays of grief have been acceptable.

The feeling of loss over these deaths is, I believe, genuine. Yet perhaps it also expresses the pent-up grief that many of us have over personal deaths. These public deaths and rituals have given us an opportunity to openly express our feelings and perhaps, in our own way, deal with other personal grief.

Yet, if we see someone we know grieving a personal loss in this way, we react very differently. Rather than validating their grief, we try to encourage *containment*. We avoid grievers who so outwardly show their emotions. We see this response as excessive and inappropriate. We try to get them to mute their grief. All too often the griever complies. He or she recognizes the discomfort of others. Accordingly, in public, the bereaved will try not to show the feelings and emotions that are inside. They learn to grieve in private over their own personal losses.

Among the changes that have taken place in our death system, perhaps none has had as dramatic an impact on the grief experience as our tendency to avoid confrontation with the dead body. Grief counselors know that viewing the body can facilitate adjustment to the death, whether immediately after death, or during the funeral rituals that follow (Raphael, 1983). This confrontation with death often marks the beginning of the grief process. It forces people to face the reality of death and begin to let go of any denial. Yet today, individuals often elect to have closed caskets or immediate disposition for cremation, thus denying that opportunity. It is not uncommon to find that these grievers later have considerable difficulty with their grief. As a society, we must reevaluate the significance of death rituals for the grief process and encourage the return to meaningful rituals, which facilitate grief for the survivors.

In today's industrialized America, we value control and predictability. Emotions go against these values. We even discourage children from expressing anger and sadness. Yet these are two of the most basic elements in grief (Scheff, 1975). Children learn that regardless of their inner feelings, they should control their outward show of emotion. When President Kennedy died, Americans admired the stoicism of Jacqueline Kennedy and her children. Yet this denial of emotions only serves to avoid and delay the actual grief.

Guilt is another emotion that is often part of the grief process. Grievers avoid expressing the guilt for fear that no one will understand. The natural response is to try to remove the guilt by saying something such as *There wasn't anything you could do*, or *You did your best*. We need to recognize that guilt is a part of the grief process. Grievers need to be allowed to resolve their own feelings with our support. They need to be reminded of the things they have done that were right.

American culture, correctly or incorrectly, is generally seen as being primarily Christian in its religion and White in terms of race (Irish, Lundquist, and Nelsen, 1993). Therefore, the emphasis in our understanding and support of the bereaved has centered around this image. Our literature on bereavement and our training of professionals have assumed that this is the universal image of the grieving American.

But this image is false. America is a blended society of many diverse racial, ethnic, and religious groups. To a large extent these groups have maintained their own identity and customs surrounding death and grief. We are not the melting pot we once described. Rather, today people hold on to their customs and traditions. This is as true of death and mourning as it is of other areas of life.

Recent decades have seen many immigrants arrive in the United States from such places as Cuba, Southeast Asia, and Africa. These immigrants have brought their cultures with them. They have enriched our society with their customs. Yet we fail to understand these customs.

How would we react to the drums and firecrackers of a Chinese American funeral (Tanner, 1995)? Or the picnic on the grave three days later? Can we understand those cultures where emotional expression includes extensive wailing and throwing oneself on the casket? Or what about those where no emotion is shown? We have a very difficult time understanding those grief responses which are not part of our own behavior.

Kastenbaum (1998) discusses the mourning patterns of the Hmong people. Many Hmong came to the United States from Laos in the 1970s. Their funeral and mourning practices are very complex and involve many people. But our cultural approach to death intrudes on many of these practices. For example, our medical system may require an autopsy. The Hmong believe that this is horrible and means the person will be born mutilated in the next life (Bliatout, 1993). It is important for the Hmong to attend to the deceased. Yet in our culture washing and dressing of the body is done by professionals.

There are also significant differences in the patterns of grief we see even among religions that are more familiar to us. One could explore the basic Protestant denominations and discover great variations in the patterns of grief. In some denominations a funeral is meant to be a celebration of life. In others it is a chance to find redemption and to prepare for one's own death and afterlife. In still others it is a mournful time.

One important way to examine the usefulness of the American culture in assisting grief is to explore how our grief system assists us in moving through the tasks of grieving. Worden (1991) suggests four tasks of mourning. The griever needs to accomplish these tasks in order for mourning to be completed.

The first task is to accept the reality of the loss. In almost any death there is a sense of disbelief. Often, the rituals of death and the confrontation with the body assist one in accomplishing this particular task. In the American culture today, survivors often decide on closed caskets and/or memorial services. This avoidance of the body, for whatever reason, makes the acceptance of the reality of death more difficult. Particularly in the case of sudden death, where one had no forewarning, seeing the body is important.

The language of death may also be a factor in accomplishing this task. With the inclination in our culture to use euphemisms and non-threatening words, denial often persists. In counseling sessions it is usually very important to get the mourner to use the word *died*. Such words bring the reality home.

The second task is to work through to the pain of grief. If this pain is not worked through and experienced, it may well lead to the development of significant and complicated symptoms. Once again, the values of American society may hinder the completion of this task. Because of our discomfort with grief and feelings, we discourage the direct expression of grief. Our message is that showing grief is not appropriate or healthy. For a time, this denial of emotion may make the griever feel more comfortable. But ultimately the pain must be experienced. If not, depression or other psychiatric issues may emerge.

Worden's third task is to adjust to an environment in which the deceased is missing. For the bereaved this means they must be willing to take on new roles that were filled by the deceased and they must develop a new sense of self-worth. Our culture does seem to assist grievers with this task to some extent. We do encourage grievers to move on and assume some of those other roles. Perhaps we actually push them too fast. We need to encourage the griever, and reinforce the positive changes they make, without making them feel they are moving too slowly.

The last of the tasks suggested by Worden is that of emotionally relocating the deceased and moving on with life. This represents the ability to find an appropriate place for the deceased in one's memory and emotional life, but at the same time to recognize that one must go on without the person as part of their physical world.

In our culture, the tendency is to urge grievers to forget, rather than relocate. We are seemingly more comfortable if we do not have to encounter pictures or words about the deceased. We want people to "get over their grief." We fail to encourage appropriate memorialization.

Another significant issue in our culture's response to grief has to do with the social recognition of a loss (Rando, 1988). Our culture evaluates relationships and their loss and may not validate or acknowledge the loss. For example, a miscarriage, stillbirth, or neonatal death is often treated by others as though the mourners have not even experienced a loss. There is no recognition of the degree of attachment that may have formed, and hence little in the way of long-term support.

The death of a pet is another example. Those who come to a local support group for pet loss speak of being confronted by the fact that society as a whole does not look at them as experiencing valid grief. After all, *It was only a dog.* These grievers are forced to deal with their grief alone and without the comfort of supportive friends.

A third situation arises when the death occurs in a relationship that is not socially sanctioned. The death of a partner in a gay relationship or in an extra-marital affair is an example of this type of loss. Many in our society do not accept these relationships and thus do not provide support when the relationship ends from a death.

Fourth, our support for grief may be influenced by the way in which a person dies. With a suicide, we may see it as a choice the person made and therefore provide little support to the bereaved. We respond similarly when the death is a result of alcohol or drug abuse. We forget that the griever has still experienced the loss. Indeed, in deaths from causes such as these, perhaps more support is needed rather than less.

American culture does have a significant impact on the experience of grief. Our cultural system has changed over time in many ways. These changes, some of which have been very valuable, have in turn brought about changes in our response to grief. Unfortunately, many of those changes have meant a de-emphasis on the grief process and on society's support for grievers. More and more, grievers have found themselves alone with their emotions, in a society that does not provide guidance and help.

But one can maintain hope that the support of the past will return. The rapid development of hospice in our society has taken death out of the closet, and with it grief has also emerged. We are once again recognizing the importance of the grief process and the need for support of the griever. Many hospices have grief support programs that are far larger than the patient population of the hospice, available not only to survivors of patients in the hospice but to grievers in the community at large.

Perhaps too, the public nature of grief over the deaths of Princess Diana and Mother Teresa will also cause a reevaluation of our response to grief. Our need to remember is great. Once again, we may see the community share that need and the grief as well.

––––––––––––––––––––––––––––––––

*Dana G. Cable, PhD, is Professor of Psychology at Hood College. Dr. Cable is on the editorial board of the* American Journal of Hospice and Palliative Care, *and a frequent presenter of programs on grief for professionals throughout the US.*

# SIX

# Looking Through Different Eyes: Beyond Cultural Diversity

*Sherry E. Showalter*

Following are some reflections surrounding Native American belief, thoughts, and spirituality, and their effect on interactions with modern medical care—in particular, hospice care. Incorporating knowledge of Native American cultures and groups into practice is vital in all specialties. Of course, it is important to note that there are no "generic" tribes, cultures or beliefs. Each tribe, clan, and descendant of Native American heritage will have their own culture, language, tradition. However, it is safe to say that all embrace some similar fundamental thoughts on life, death, hope, and healing. The diversity among Native cultures is far too great to allow for a comprehensive treatment, but as many as possible have been included here.

It is only when we as professional providers glean the particulars of a person's heritage and culture that we can genuinely accept our patients and their families *where they live*. Then we are able to offer added support and knowledge, as well as enhance the quality of care within their enduring supportive surroundings.

We have much to learn from those we are privileged to serve. Native people were "doing" hospice hundreds of years before the modern day movement. Caring holistically for members of the community, while including the family and other kinship groups, is a way of life for the Native American. Today, the range of alternatives in services, delivery systems, conceptualization of illness, impact of spirituality, and treatment modalities is staggering. But we need to begin to understand ways in which other cultures cope with serious illness, view the dying process, and express their personal grief and bereavement.

## The Challenge

I would like to challenge you to *look through different eyes*. As hospice professionals, healthcare professionals, and mental health professionals, we are forever challenged to provide quality care in a holistic manner. Awareness of cultural diversity is significant at all levels of care. Ethnocentric approaches to hospice philosophy are ineffectual in meeting the needs of our culturally diverse patients, families, and communities. When working to enhance services, it is important to integrate a *working wisdom* of our patients and their families. By looking through different eyes we are able to find universal threads that consistently connect and intertwine in the fabric of our lives.

As professionals we may be used to the concept of cultural diversity with regard to racial and ethnic differences. However, changing populations give rise to the increased cultural diversity that challenges healthcare professionals, who find it necessary to refine their knowledge and skills. Hospice care, along with other healthcare delivery systems, must be strengthened to work with culturally diverse peoples.

Native Americans are a part of many communities—in major cities, in fancy homes, subsidized housing, condos, Reservations, cabins in the mountains, and at the beaches. You may not think they look so different from yourself; you may feel the desire to ask, "Are you part Indian or full-blood?" and with that question you will have insulted and offended. It is often difficult to recognize them as different: no war paint, no headdresses, often just ordinary-looking people. History has taught people that it is best to fit in. Native Americans have assimilated modern ways, times, and illnesses. Professional helpers need to listen hard in order to hear the stories of relations and ancestors who have remained an intact and integral part of many Native Americans. More often than not you will need to look through different eyes to see today's Native American clearly.

Native people will utilize services that are identified and respected by their communities and/or meaning systems. Impressions of illness, health, dying, hospice are all a part of the cultural belief system of a group. Before hospice became a philosophy of modern healthcare, Native American extended families cared for patients, while communities rallied with the necessary provisions to care for the patient, those who loved the patient, family, and friends. Tribal Elders used their wisdom to restore balance before and after a death, while the community mourned for the patient, the family, and the community itself. There is much to learn from Native American cultures, as there is to learn from other cultures that differ from the mainstream.

The ways in which Native Americans demonstrated care and expressed their accompanying emotions may be an unfamiliar notion to modern day hospice professionals. Hospice care would be much richer and more effective were we to incorporate the past into the present delivery of holistic care. This is the challenge of looking through different eyes.

Each member of the hospice team brings his or her own cultural and philosophical views, education, religion, spirituality, and life experiences to the professional setting. It is important to understand that the work—the journey—will involve three cultural systems: the particular culture of each team member, the culture of the patient/family, and the culture of the setting. Holistic care can be further enhanced by providing culturally relevant, responsive, non-judgmental services. Hospice care must be culturally sensitive, as should all healthcare and bereavement services. Within hospice, professionals advocate for patients and their families, recognizing cultural diversity and integrating cultural knowledge. Providing services in a culturally appropriate manner enables hospice professionals to be more authentic in the application of hospice philosophy. Educational programs are needed to address the beliefs, values, and ideas of cultures different from that of the hospice team member.

By looking through different eyes hospice professionals are likely to find many similarities among groups. There are many universal aspects to life, family, trust, love, hope, understanding, funeral customs, grieving techniques, and caring. Cultural diversity has been referred to as the differences between people that are based on shared teachings, treasured beliefs, norms, customs, language, and meanings symbolized in daily living. These differences contribute to the conceptions of health, hospice care, treatment, spirituality, death, and bereavement for individuals and communities.

As professionals we will be forever challenged to look beyond ethnocentrism and the world as we have experienced it. This attitude can place barriers between hospice professionals and patients/families of diverse cultural groups (e.g., Cherokee, Lakota, Pueblo, Tewa, Choctaw).

Another example of looking through different eyes includes the ability to recognize differences across cultural groups. For example, White Americans tend to seek counselors or psychiatrists; Southeast Asian Americans will often consult herbalists; African Americans look to ministers and priests; Haitians often turn to priests of voodoo; while Native Americans seek and trust medicine men/women, the Creator, and the interconnectedness of life. As professionals we would do well to learn about the many cultures in our service areas; focus on the family structure, the perceptions, language, and communication styles of patients and their families; and be aware of their perspectives of illness and end-of-life issues. In doing so, we strive to find healing ways to blend our skills within each unique system in order to enhance the supports and beliefs that exist within a cultural setting.

Knowledge, understanding, sensitivity, and respect for differences can and does enhance care. It can be an empowering experience to tell a patient, "I do not know much about your culture and beliefs, but I am interested in learning from you what I may need to know so that I may care for you in the best way possible." By attending to the humanness that connects all people, we can enhance our services and provide holistic care for our patients and those who love them. It is crucial to recognize that we live in a multicultural society. We may experience people belonging to other clans, cultures, tribes, and communities that are thousands of years old. We are not always the experts; the real experts are our patients and those who know them. At our best, we can hope to complement their care while working with their families and communities. The challenges are formidable. There may be contrasting values that must be acknowledged and appreciated.

*"I may be forced to adopt a new way of life, but my heart and spirit spring from the red earth."*

Painted Wolf

## Those Differences

I would like to tell you about "Indian Time." Many Native Americans view time as flowing, always being with us. Time is relative, things will get done as they need be. Legend has it that we developed the fine art of procrastination! This view of time is radically different from that of mainstream society, in which careful scheduling of activities is important (hospice visits, doctor's appointments, counseling sessions). Non-Indians may mistakenly construe an Indian's dissimilar attitude toward time as "irresponsible," which may equate with being "non-compliant." This difference alone can create very real obstacles to holistic care.

With ongoing education, training, and sensitivity, hospice professionals can surmount barriers and develop trusting relationships with patients and their families while providing supportive care. With wisdom comes knowledge; by looking through different eyes we may be able to step inside other cultures, and as much as possible to feel culture as our patients and families feel it. It is significant to understand that there are no generic cultures or tribes. We must develop an awareness of diversity among bands, tribes, cultures, clans, languages, spirituality—both historically and in today's world. Recognizing the diversity of cultural subgroups—whether traditional, assimilated, bi-cultural, or uncertain—will assist us in our personal and professional awareness of the uniqueness of the individual apart from culturally defined differences. In doing so, we have not only enhanced our practice but we have also enhanced our personal lives. Increasing awareness allows us to respond to actual rather than assumed needs of those we are privileged to serve and honored to walk beside.

## It is Time to Tell You Stories

It may just be that stories touch an uncivilized part of our professional selves, often allowing us to look through different eyes from a sacred place in our hearts. I have heard it said: A non-Indian man asked an old Cherokee woman, "How long do you think it will take your loved one to eat those plates of food you set out every evening?" The old woman glanced at him, smiled, and quietly replied, "Ah, I think it will take maybe the same time as it will for your aunt's soul to smell those flowers you take to the grave on Sundays."

Dr. Terry Tafoya, a Taos-Pueblo, often tells the story of a coastal Indian woman who was admitted to the locked psychiatric unit of a hospital. Her examining psychiatrist had noted that she had suicidal ideation, based on her cutting her hair and describing "knives around the doorway." While in lock-up, the woman had a session with Dr. Tafoya. In talking with this woman, Dr. Tafoya discovered that the woman was an active member of the Shaker Indian Church, a Northwest coastal religion that is a syncretic blend of traditional beliefs and Christianity. The woman's uncle had died and her extended family, members of a fundamentalist sect, did not want to participate in what were considered the appropriate mourning ceremonies of the Shakers (the uncle was of the Shaker faith). The woman cut her hair, following an accustomed practice intended to show the loss of a loved one. The cutting of one's hair is practiced in many Native American tribes. And if you have ever been on an Indian Reservation, you may have noticed that much of the federally-built Reservation housing leaves much to be desired. The construction is scant and locks seem to fail to work after a while, so it is common practice to place butter knives around the door frames to serve as a wedge lock in order to keep undesirables (nocturnal drunks and mean-spirited people) out of your home. The woman was trying to tell her psychiatrist this when she spoke of the "knives around the doorway." By learning to look through different eyes we open doors of communication along with the windows of opportunity to understand, hear, and complement care.

Within the last 30 years cancer has become the third leading cause of death for Native Americans. Most common are cancers of the lung, colon and rectum, breast, prostate, cervix, stomach, pancreas, and gallbladder. Upon diagnosis, many Native Americans seek out medicine men or women, utilize the sweat lodge for purification rituals, and seek to restore balance within the heart, mind, body and soul. Conventional hospice care is often not viewed as being willing to work within this belief system. Education regarding holistic care is imperative. Many older Native American people prefer traditional medicine to that practiced by Western populations. Elders are respected and family members who are ill are often cared for in the home. They are extremely private in their pain and loss, reluctant to confide in those from the outside.

Native Americans are diagnosed as suffering from depression at a rate four to six times the national average. Alcohol is often used to self-medicate depression, Post-traumatic Stress Disorder, and unresolved bereavement and loss. Grief and loss are not new issues for those of Native American heritage. Hundreds of years of cumulative grief have taken their toll. Many have developed a quiet acceptance of the pain of loss both historically and today. Further research on Native American depression indicates a difference in threshold time for diagnosis. By cultural standards, Native individuals may be classified as depressed prior to the standard two weeks' duration suggested by the DSM-IV. Although I have no documentation, I have been told and am inclined to believe that Native peoples have a tremendous pain tolerance and often require a tremendous amount of drug intervention to control pain. The problem is that Native people do not freely discuss their discomfort, their pain, or their needs for intervention.

For many Native Americans there is an old joke about the word "yes" always being the better answer than "no." It seems that many non-Indians tend to stop asking questions if one answers "yes," but will ask more and more questions if they hear "no." Consider the story of the visiting nurse who sat in the home of an old Navaho woman who sells pottery, and has it all around her home. The nurse asked, "Did you make this?" The woman, with her head bowed, says simply, "Yes." There is really nothing left to say, is there? But had the old woman said "No," the next question might have been, "Do you know who made it? How they made it? Were they your relatives?" and so on. By answering the first question "yes," the conversation is really over, and the old woman was able to prevent a long string of questions that may have been personal and uncomfortable. Asking yes/no questions of a Native American may in fact encourage a "yes" answer, so it might be wise to ask open-ended questions. Rather than asking, "Did you sleep well last night?" you may want to try, "How did you sleep?"

## The Medicine Wheel

Many Native Americans look at life as a circle. They may recognize the medicine wheel as a sacred symbol, one that speaks to relationships and the interconnectedness of all things. The fundamental philosophy of reciprocity, giving and taking mutually, is very important in establishing understanding. This way of thinking often seems eccentric to the helping professionals. Most, if not all, clinically trained professionals have been taught and conditioned to be very cognizant of personal/professional boundaries, disclosing as little of their own personal information and background as possible. The practice may work well for some professionals and some cultures, but is inadequate when working with Native American people. The separation of patient/family and the professional will not facilitate understanding nor establish trust with the Native American. These professional boundaries may actually interfere with holistic care when working with Native Americans, who are usually less interested in knowing what the other "does" and much more concerned with what the other "is." This is especially true upon the first few meetings. Questions such as "Where are you from?" and "Are you connected with the world around you?" are a natural attempt to determine any existing relationship.

## Points to Ponder

When working with Native Americans there may be noticeable differences from other groups.

You may find that Native Americans have and/or demonstrate the following characteristics:

- slow, softer speech
- little or no eye contact
- fewer "encouraging signs" (nodding head, saying "Uh huh.")
- delayed response to auditory message
- non-verbal communication
- group needs most important
- harmony/balance with nature
- control of self, not others
- privacy and noninterference with others
- physical punishment rare
- broken English accepted language
- let it happen
- greatest sins: lying and disrespect (especially of Elders), abuse of family, greed, selfishness
- respect for aged; they are useful members in the community
- today is a good day to die
- participants in life and in death and ritual
- life is viewed as circular

I would like to end with a few concrete thoughts for those working with Native Americans. I have heard it said from Elders that a "dead end" is a wonderful place to turn around! It was also said:

— "Sentiment was against the Indian, that they could not be civilized...Could not be educated...were somewhat like human beings...but not quite in line of human rights...." (Wassaja)

— "It may be that some little part of the sacred tree still lives." (Black Elk)

— "These beads are a road between us. Take hold at one end, I will at the other, and hold fast." (Como)

— Food is a symbol of friendship. To refuse to share or accept food may be considered rude.

— Small talk leads to big talk.

— Direct eye contact is considered impolite among many Native Americans, so looking away while talking is not a sign of unfriendliness or disinterest. Many will avert their eyes out of respect.

— Many Native Americans are inexperienced with healthcare systems, home care philosophy, and bereavement services, and may feel ill-prepared to understand and/or speak up for themselves.

— A Native American handshake is often not really a handshake, but a soft touching. Don't be upset if you receive a "limp" greeting... it is a cultural difference, not a personal reflection.

— Pointing may be done mostly with one's lips or chin!

— People will tell you just as much as they want you to know. Be cautious when probing for information with questions of a personal nature.

— Legend says babies who still have a soft spot on their skulls are very vulnerable to evil influences. Because of this legend, approach infants with care, or not at all (unless you ask the parents), even when providing care.

— There is often a great solidarity within a family and extended kinships.

— One of the most difficult things for a Native American to cope with is sarcastic humor. There are elements of a "hit and run" with this type of humor; it is without honor. A joke in which someone is hurt is not humorous in Native American life.

— Children are given great attention by many relatives, including families of choice and extended kinships. Native Americans will often lower their voices when correcting a child. Child rearing is self-exploratory rather than restrictive and often viewed by non-Natives as permissive.

— Personal belongings may adorn a home—perhaps feathers, jewelry, artifacts. These belongings should not be handled without the owner's permission.

— People may come and go from the home while you are present; there may be much activity and not so much talk.

— The Cherokee have a saying, "Listen or your tongue will make you deaf."

— When you can speak from your heart, you will find appreciation of your words. Explain technical words in ways that can be understood by a non-medical person.

— Humor is valued and incorporated into day-to-day living.

— Native Americans will often use sage, sweet grass, and cedar as a ritual for healing, for strength. To non-Natives this smell may be mistaken for an illegal substance! Pretty funny, huh?

— Asking a Native American if they are "part" or "full-blooded" is insulting and often perceived as rude. Would you ask a non-Native if they were part Black, White, Jewish, heterosexual?

— Storytelling is a remarkable instrument in understanding, in healing and treating dis-ease.

— Native Americans are not strangers to issues of pain and loss.

— Native Americans often believe that life after death is a continuation of the life already experienced. "There is no death, just a change of worlds."

I would like to leave you with a gift...a gift to use in your growth, your life, and your healing. This gift is from an Elder Tewa Indian man from San Juan Pueblo, speaking to Vera Laski on life and death in *Seeking Life* (1959). The words of this Elder may sum up the words of this manuscript and provide a wonderful opportunity of looking through different eyes.

What I am trying to say is hard, to tell is hard and hard to under-stand...unless, unless...you have been yourself at the edge of the Deep Canyon and have come back unharmed. Maybe it all depends on something within yourself...whether you are trying to see the Watersnake or the sacred Cornflower, whether you go out to meet death or to seek life. It is like this: as long as you stay within the realm of the great Cloud Beings, you may indeed walk at the very edge of the Deep Canyon and not be harmed. You will be protect-ed by the rainbow and by the Great Ones. You will have no reason to worry and no reason to be sad. You may fight the witches and if you can meet them with a heart which does not tremble, the fight will make you stronger. It will help you to attain your goals in life; it will give you strength to help others, to be loved and liked, and to seek life.

May you walk in beauty along your journey while learning to *look through different eyes* at the beauty which is all around you. *Wado* ("Thank You")

---

*Sherry E. Showalter, MSW, LCSW, is Bereavement Care Coordinator at VNA Community Hospice. She has developed a Comprehensive Bereavement Program blending traditional social work methods with beliefs from her Cherokee heritage.*

# SEVEN

# Sociocultural Considerations for Working with Blacks Experiencing Loss and Grief

*Ronald Keith Barrett*

The focus on cross-cultural studies in the death and dying literature (Irish, Lundquist, and Nelsen, 1993; Parry and Ryan, 1995) reveals subtle and significant differences in the ways distinct groups respond to death, dying, and funeral rites. The unique characterizations of African American funeral rites and customs are well documented in the evolving cross-cultural literature in the field of thanatology (Barrett, 1993, 1994, 1995; Perry, 1993; Sullivan, 1995). This knowledge base can be a valuable resource for clinical practitioners working with Blacks who experience loss and grief.

Sensitivity to subtle but significant cultural traditions and idiosyncrasies can be helpful in affirming and supporting the client's grief recovery. Many of these considerations are difficult for Blacks to talk about, justify, or explain to others (Barrett, 1994). While recent research on Blacks has documented the sociocultural origins of many contemporary practices and customs, even Blacks who are loyal to these traditions may not be fully aware of the origin of long-standing cultural traditions, customs, and practices. Consequently, this important and evolving literature can enhance the awareness and cultural sensitivity of those who work with Blacks in grief recovery.

The primary goal of this chapter is to examine the unique cultural attitudes and beliefs of Blacks regarding death, dying, and funeral practices, including distinctions among subgroupings of Blacks. While many Blacks share common sociocultural influences, this chapter attempts to call attention to the need for more careful study of critical distinctions among Blacks. In that regard, I offer an inferential model for breaking down some of the complexity of working with Blacks experiencing death and grief. A second goal is to call attention to the differences in the rate of death and dying among Blacks in the United States as compared to Whites, and to examine the causes of premature death among Blacks. A third goal is to explore the ways that the unique experiences of Blacks contribute to a sense of mistrust that might affect caregiving and counseling processes. Finally, this chapter attempts to offer practical and useful considerations for caregivers who work with Blacks experiencing loss and grief.

## Self-Reference and Sociocultural Influences

While many people may relate to and regard all Blacks as the same, Blacks themselves make important distinctions among cultural subgroups. In the 1990s we have become sensitive to the practice of referring to all persons of African descent as Blacks. This in an inclusive term that includes all subgroups of persons of African descent, including African Americans. Blacks have similar physical characteristics common to persons of sub-Saharan African descent. While there is great heterogeneity in the physical traits that characterize Blacks (e.g., skin color, facial features, hair color and texture), some common characteristics are visible.

It is very important to note that while it is reasonable to refer to all persons of African descent as Black, there are many subcultural groups with unique sociocultural variations and distinctions. For example, while most persons of African descent may share a strikingly similar physical appearance, African Americans are distinct from other subgroups of Blacks (e.g., persons from Jamaica, Guyana, Trinidad, Barbados) in that they define themselves as being socialized primarily through values inculcated in the United States.

To acknowledge an individual's unique cultural heritage and identity is, first and foremost, an important way of affirming his or her identity. In some cases one might offend and alienate a Black individual by making assumptions based on incorrect identification of his or her cultural or subcultural background. The usage of terms varies extensively, even within a given group. Caregivers are always advised, then, to listen for cues or to directly ask clients the terms they use to define themselves.

It is important to note as well the unique approaches to death, dying, and funerals within the various subcultural groupings of Blacks. For example, while most Blacks might prefer ground burials, Jamaicans traditionally assist with the burying of their loved ones and insist on closing the grave. In addition, Blacks in the Caribbean prefer immediate funeralization and burial of their dead with minimal delays. Because there is a conspicuous absence of detailed documentation of the unique cultural traditions, practices, and customs of many of the subcultural groupings of Blacks, there is an obvious need for more systematic study and research. Cultural sensitivity to the unique characteristics of subgroups among Blacks is a significant first step is acknowledging the role of cultural identity in influencing a Black individual's attitudes towards death and dying (Barrett, 1995, 1997b).

## Race, Ethnicity, and Health: A Collective Identity and Common Fate

The Black experience of death and dying in the United States is fundamentally different from the White experience. While recognizing and acknowledging discrete subgroups among Blacks is an important consideration regarding death and dying, the relationship of race and ethnicity to the quality of health among all Blacks is noteworthy. The overwhelming evidence suggests that most Blacks share a common fate of less robust health and wellness than Whites and others who are more advantaged. This negatively impacts their quality of life and contributes to premature death. Race and ethnicity, along with social class, are significantly correlated with health, wellness, and premature death. Barbara Dixon (1994), in her book *Good Health for African Americans*, reports that Blacks experience premature death at a much higher rate than Whites (see Table 1.0).

In addition to race and ethnicity, a number of other factors influence the quality of life and health of Blacks. While Blacks are estimated to represent 12 percent of the US population, approximately 33 percent of Blacks fall below the poverty level. As a result of poverty, Blacks tend to have less education than Whites and have less access to health insurance (Holsendolph, 1997), transportation, child care, time off work, and, consequently, less access to health care (Washington, 1997).

A 1989 survey conducted at the Harvard School of Public Health found that, even when taking into account lower income, health status, age, and gender, Blacks tend to have a significantly lower number of medical visits than Whites.

The scarcity of doctors within the Black community also contributes to the declining quality of life, wellness, and premature death. Washington (1997) reports that nationally there are 150 doctors per 100,000 people. Yet the rate in New York's Bedford-Stuyvesant, for example, is below 75 per 100,000, while across town, affluent Manhattanites have access to 1,136 doctors per 100,000 people. The relationship of race and ethnicity to health suggests a pronounced trend of racism and classism. It is important to note that fundamental differences between Blacks and Whites in the quality of life, wellness, and premature death contribute to significant additional losses (e.g., loss of health and wellness, role functions, and related financial hardships) that Blacks grieve (Barrett, 1997a).

## Race, Ethnicity and Cultural Mistrust

While many factors contribute to differences in both the quality of life and premature death among Blacks in the United States, the role of *cultural mistrust* has often been overlooked. In an important early study of trust dispositions among Blacks and Whites, Terrell and Barrett (1979) found that Blacks, the poor, and women were more likely to mistrust. The authors explained these empirical findings by referring to the psychology of oppressed groups whose social history does not support a belief system characterized as trusting. Consequently, politically disadvantaged groups who have experienced long-standing discrimination and prejudice tend to mistrust those identified with their oppressors (Terrell and Terrell, 1983). The concept of cultural mistrust is one reason that Blacks tend to under-utilize health services and are more likely to drop out of institution-alized healthcare than Whites (Barrett, 1997b; Washington, 1997). This higher attrition rate is observed in institutional providers of both physical and mental healthcare (Sue and Sue, 1990).

The fear of medicine, or *iatrophobia*, as well as a general cultural mistrust of institutionalized healthcare, contributes to the tendency of many Blacks to avoid doctors and to seek care only at the last minute. In addition, the 1989 Harvard School of Public Health survey found that, considering income, health status, age, and gender, Blacks have a significantly lower number of annual medical visits than Whites. Not incidentally, Blacks also expressed greater dissatisfaction with the way they were treated than Whites (Washington, 1997).

Black individuals who are mistrusting often experience alien-ation from White care providers and are therefore re-victimized by insensitivity to their lack of trust (Barrett, 1986). The tendency to judge the mistrusting individual's alienation from many social estab-lishments is another way in which caregivers may blame the victims. Blacks, as a group, are often mindful of a historical pattern of mis-treatment, betrayal, and victimization by White institutions. Many African Americans share a perception that White physicians are slow to treat and quick to experiment on Blacks in institutional settings. A 1991 *American Journal of Public Health* study reported that Blacks tend to avoid AIDS clinical trials because of the painful legacy of the Tuskegee Syphilis Study, in which treatment was withheld from approximately 400 Black sharecroppers between 1932 and 1972. In addition, Black consumers of healthcare often report that they feel they receive less assiduous treatment than Whites, that they are patronized in the doctor's office, that doctors don't communicate effectively with them, and that they are more likely to leave the doc-tor's office unsure of what their medical problem is or the options for treatment (Washington, 1997).

# Understanding Blacks, Death, and Dying:
# The Barrett (1995) Inferential Model

While there are certain universal aspects to the ways humans respond to grief and loss, a growing body of research suggests there are unique ethnic and cultural differences in attitudes, beliefs, and funeral customs (Kalish and Reynolds, 1981; Irish, Lundquist, and Nelsen, 1993; Parry and Ryan, 1995). Significant variations within discrete ethnic and cultural groups have also been observed, suggesting that race, ethnicity, and culture may not be definitive conceptual tools for understanding the distinctive features within any given racial, ethnic, or cultural grouping (Barrett, 1995). The significant heterogeneity among Blacks suggests that racial, ethnic, and cultural grouping is not enough to provide insight into the attitudes toward death, dying, and funeralization among Blacks.

## RACE, ETHNICITY, AND CULTURAL IDENTIFICATION

The tremendous heterogeneity among Blacks requires that one take into account more than race or ethnicity to understand and appropriately respond to loss within the Black experience. First and foremost, a clear sense of the cultural and subcultural identification of the Black individual is important. It is important to note how strongly the individual identifies with his or her respective cultural heritage. Blacks of all subgroupings who identify themselves as being Africentric will reflect values, beliefs, and attitudes derived from African traditions. Barrett (1993) documents the sociocultural origins of attitudes, beliefs, and funeral practices of African Americans, suggesting a strong link with and influence of West African origin. Research findings by Nichols (1989) also support the thesis that West African culture influences African American funeral practices. This notion is supported by the fact that West Africa was the demographic point of the deportation and transport of slaves during the diaspora and migration to the North American continent. Striking similarities in attitudes, beliefs, and funeralization practices support this thesis (Barrett, 1993).

While distinct identities and traditions may exist among Blacks, evolving research on death and dying among Blacks suggests it may be reasonable to assume that most Blacks share a number of characteristic attitudes towards death, dying, and funeral rites. For example, most Blacks can be characterized as being inclined to

- be "death accepting," that is, viewing death as part of the natural rhythm of life,

- oppose active euthanasia,

- regard death, dying, and the dead with great reverence and respect,

- regard funerals as primary rituals, that is, they invest greatly in the execution of the ritual and closely follow tradition and protocol,

- believe that one's attendance at and participation in funerals represents an important social obligation,

- prefer ground burial for final disposition,

- believe in life after death and the notion that individuals transition to the spirit world,

- acknowledge the existence of dead ancestors within their community, though in the spirit world, and

- engage in a number of rituals and traditions to honor the dead, e.g., naming of infants after the dead, passing babies over the caskets of loved ones, pouring libations on the ground for the dead, and acknowledging the presence of the dead at family gatherings.

Most American Blacks of African descent, particularly from the coast of West Africa, share common African sociocultural traditions blended with Western customs and practices (Barrett, 1993, 1995). Consequently, most Blacks tend to view death as a part of the continuum of life as opposed to the end of life, and also believe in the existence of the afterlife—that upon death one transitions from the physical world to the spirit world. Consistent with this view is the belief that there is an indistinguishable separation between the physical world and the spirit world.

Most Blacks view life and death with reverence, and the funeralization of the dead is given great care and attention. In other words, funerals are regarded as primary rituals (Barrett, 1993) with great social significance (Barrett, 1995). Blacks as a demographic group are inclined to invest considerably more discretionary income on funerals than do Whites (Barrett, 1995). In addition, Blacks tend to value one's attendance at and participation in the final rites of a loved one as a significant gesture of support and condolence. Close relations are expected and obliged to be present and participate; not to honor this social obligation can be perceived as being disrespectful.

## SOCIOECONOMIC STATUS AND SOCIAL CLASS

Socioeconomic status is an important additional influence on attitudes, beliefs, and funeral practices. Blacks of lower socioeconomic status tend to be keepers of tradition and are more conservative in their attitudes, beliefs, and funeral practices (Barrett, 1997b). As Blacks move up in socioeconomic status they have increased exposure to alternative lifestyles and increased opportunities for educational influences. With the enjoyment of wealth and upward socioeconomic status Blacks literally move away from their traditional communities and are exposed to other values systems that influence their attitudes, beliefs, and practices.

For example, lower-class Blacks are more likely to have funeral services characterized as "emotional, traditional homegoing services." On the other hand, middle-class and affluent Blacks are more inclined to have funeral services similar to those of the White middle class, which tend to be significantly less emotional, more stoic, and more formal. Black funerals in general also tend to have a longer planning stage, with a funeral occurring on average of one week after the death. Traditionally, this delay served a pragmatic purpose: it allowed family members to travel from afar and also gave more time for survivors to gather financial resources for the funeral arrangements.

The traditional Black funeral is a social event and does not start until all significant persons have gathered. The more esteemed the deceased loved one, the greater the investment in time, resources and participation in the service. In the Black experience, presence at a funeral is a significant gesture of respect and esteem. Traditional Black funeral services are also longer than White funerals, sometimes lasting for hours, and usually include more spontaneity and musical participation. The traditional funeral could be a full-day affair, including the service, the committal, and the family gathering and repast afterwards.

As Blacks have experienced more mainstream acculturation and have achieved greater socioeconomic status, observation of some of these traditional practices has declined. Consequently, the upper-class Black funeral service may now more closely resemble a White funeral: shorter, less emotional, and more formal, with no wake or social gathering afterwards.

## SPIRITUALITY AND RELIGION

A Black individual's spirituality or religious orientation can have a significant influence on his or her attitudes, beliefs, and funeral practices. The religious orientation of Blacks varies from liberal to conservative on matters related to death, dying, and funeralization (e.g., baptism, anointing, post-mortem examinations, tissue donations, organ transplants, blood transfusions, euthanasia, and final disposition). Barrett (1995) postulates that the conservative or liberal religious orientation of a Black individual may have a more influential role on his or her disposition toward death, dying, and funeral practices than race alone. For example, in a medical emergency, Blacks who are Jehovah's Witnesses, Christian Scientists, or Rastafarians understandably might make choices consistent with their religion and be against blood transfusions. Similarly, Blacks who follow Christian Science, Afro-Caribbean Blacks, or Rastafarians might be against post-mortem examinations. Thus, religion may be a stronger determining factor than race alone. While it is reasonable to assume that one's formative socialization in early childhood may be most influential, more empirical research is needed on the relative influence of one's formative vs. present religious orientation on his or her attitudes, beliefs, and practices regarding dying, death, and funeral rites.

## BLACKS AND EXPRESSIONS OF CONDOLENCES

While funerals in the Western cultural tradition signify the ending of a life, in the Black experience funerals additionally represent the great worth of the deceased within the community. The funeral is a critical moment in the life cycle and is handled with great reverence and attention to detail. Traditionally, in anticipation of their death, Blacks invest heavily in funeral societies and burial policies to assure the execution of a decent and proper funeral. For the average Black, who may have been denied much in life, including any significant measure of human dignity, a grand funeral may represent a final triumph and one last attempt to be regarded as somebody. The contemporary value of funerals as a primary ritual is an extension of the traditional African view of funerals as representational rituals reflecting the value of the individual to the community.

The death of an individual in the Black experience is a defining moment, and there is an implicit social obligation to gather to express support and condolence. Unsolicited expressions of condolence and support are expected and valued greatly. The greater and more personal one's investment in expressing condolence, the greater the associated value and regard for the survivors (Barrett, 1995). For example, upon hearing of a death within the community, characteristically Blacks will immediately gather without solicitation at the home or place of death to provide support and express condolence. While modes of death notification have evolved with technological advancements, Blacks still, for the most part, prefer the more personal word of mouth.

One of the most honorable expressions of condolence is the personal sacrifice of being present during the time of loss (e.g., going to the home upon notification of a death, attending the wake, the funeral, and the burial service and repast afterwards). It is the social norm among Blacks to make offerings of money, resources, or food to survivors at the time of loss. While immediate family members are expected to be present, participate, and make contributions as needed, others who provide personal assistance are held in high regard by survivors. The more personal the sacrifice, the higher the regard for the offering. For example, while the donation of uncooked or store-bought food is appreciated, it is considered less personal and regarded less highly than the sacrifice of an individual who personally prepares and donates food (Barrett, 1995).

For most Blacks, gestures of condolence are valued expressions of respect to the deceased and the survivors during a time of loss and bereavement. As one elderly Black widow commented, "During your time of sorrow you learn who your true friends are." This statement reflects the traditional expectation that friends and relatives should be present and available to the bereaved during a time of loss and grief.

Because of the cultural reverence for death as a critical moment in the life cycle, the appropriateness of one's response to the death often has significant consequences for familial and social relations. Family ties and relationships are often dramatically redefined according to one's participation and conduct during a time of loss and grief. Those who respond appropriately, according to normative expectations, are gathered closer and regarded highly, and those who fail to respond appropriately are often regarded as losses— additional losses to mourn and grieve.

## THE ROLE OF CLERGY AS CAREGIVERS

During illness, dying, and death, Blacks tend to have high expectations of clergy and often are unforgiving of clergy who do not live up to those expectations. Because Blacks have a very reverent regard for death and believe in the spiritual transition of the deceased, the active participation of their spiritual leaders during serious illness and death is very meaningful to members of the deceased's family and community. Blacks typically have the following expectations of a clergy person during the illness and death of a loved one:

- Upon notification of the serious illness of a member of his or her faith community or congregation, the clergy person will make a personal bedside visit to offer prayers and support to the sick person and the family.

- The clergy person will encourage others within the faith community and congregation to pray for and be supportive of those who are ill and their families.

- Upon learning of the death of a member of the faith community or congregation, the clergy person will immediately make a personal visit to the family to offer condolences and assistance with the final arrangements.

- The clergy person will be present at and support the family during the wake or sit-up that occurs prior to the funeral service.

- The clergy person will officiate at the funeral service, delivering a personalized eulogy and offering support and regard for the surviving family members during the service.

- The clergy person will participate in the committal service for the final disposition.

- The clergy person will make an appearance at the social gathering and repast that traditionally follows the committal service.

The active and responsive participation of the clergy or spiritual leader during this important and sacred time is a defining moment in the survivors' relationship with and subsequent regard for the clergy and the religious institution.

## Conclusion

A number of sociocultural considerations are important for caregivers working with Blacks who experience loss. The following practical recommendations are suggested:

1. Understand the sociocultural influences from both African and Western traditions that combine to influence the attitudes, beliefs, and values of most Blacks regarding dying, death, and funeral practices.

2. Acknowledge and appreciate the uniqueness of the sub-groupings of Blacks, understanding the fundamental differences between them. When in doubt, ask a client how he or she would describe his or her cultural identity. (More research is needed to document the differences among these subgroups.)

3. Be sensitive to the fundamental differences in the quality of life and rate of premature death for Blacks compared to Whites. Recognize that these factors contribute to chronic grief.

4. Understand the impact of collective losses that Blacks often must grieve.

5. Recognize that race alone is not sufficient to understanding the experience of loss among Blacks. Consideration of socioeconomic status and spirituality can be helpful in working effectively with Blacks experiencing loss and grief.

6. Become more sensitive to the consistent role of cultural mistrust regarding health, wellness, and premature death among Blacks. Be aware of how that mistrust may contribute to a Black individual's being guarded, especially when working with culturally different caregivers and institutions. Well-intentioned caregivers may not be welcomed with open arms, especially by those Blacks who have had a history of betrayal or victimization. A considerable amount of trust building may be needed to establish rapport and build a working relationship.

7. Be sensitive to the culturally ascribed value Blacks place on expressions of condolence. Understand that for most Blacks, a loved one's death is a major moment in the life cycle. Expressions of condolence are extremely important to survivors and have considerable value during a time of loss and grief.

8. Understand the high expectations Blacks may have of clergy and spiritual leaders during dying, death, and funeralization. Because most Blacks regard death as a critical spiritual event, their expectations of clergy and other spiritual leaders are higher than their expectations of other caregivers.

Finally, I am often asked by those who are culturally different if they can be an effective caregiver for a Black individual who is experiencing loss and grief. While race, culture, and ethnicity should not be taken lightly, they should not be perceived as insurmountable barriers. Be yourself, be honest, be real, and be open to and teachable about those aspects of the Black experience that may be a bit different from your own. Have faith in our common humanity to connect and support one another in our experiences of loss, grief, and pain in spite of our separateness and apparent differences.

## Table 1.0

### COMPARATIVE MORBIDITY RATES FOR BLACKS AND WHITES IN THE UNITED STATES

According to a study conducted at the National Center for Health Statistics for the year 1988 the rate of death for African Americans from the leading causes of death when compared to Whites was as follows:

| Cause of Death | Comparative Mortality Rates |
| --- | --- |
| Accidents | 24 percent higher than Whites |
| Cancer | 32 percent |
| Heart Disease | 38 percent |
| Psoriasis of the liver | 77 percent |
| Strokes | 82 percent |
| Diabetes | 132 percent |
| Kidney failure | 176 percent |
| AIDS/HIV | 250 percent |
| Homicide | 500 percent |

---

*Ronald Keith Barrett, PhD, is Professor of Psychology at Loyola Marymount University. His research has focused on the effects of violence on children.*

# EIGHT

# Developing Cultural Competency

*Lynne Ann DeSpelder*

The television camera was turned off and the interviewer turned to me, lowered her voice, and asked, "Why are Anglo funerals so serious?" Ah, I thought, a woman curious about cultural diversity. I often hear questions like hers. People seem truly interested in exploring and understanding cultural differences. This article presents an opportunity for you to add to your knowledge and gain skills that can be applied in working with people from diverse backgrounds. Take our television reporter. Notice that she used the word "Anglo." Considering her word choice, her name, and her appearance, I guessed that her background was Hispanic. Her use of the word "serious" also caught my attention. Both of these words give some clues to the reporter's experience.

Our attitudes reflect experiences and practices that are a familiar part of our heritage. We all carry our own cultures in that package of attitudes. Paying attention to how people use language reveals a great deal about personal as well as cultural attitudes toward death. By becoming aware of the metaphors, euphemisms, slang, and other linguistic patterns that people use when talking about death, we can appreciate more fully the range of attitudes and responses elicited by death, dying, and bereavement (DeSpelder and Strickland, 1996).

## Cultural Competency

Think about your own cultural heritage. As a child, I traveled widely with my family. Whenever we encountered an attitude or behavior that was unfamiliar to our Midwestern US upbringing, my father would say: "When in Rome, do as the Romans do." Cultural competency does not require that you behave as another, only that you understand and relate to the attitudes and beliefs and practices that are not your own. To the culturally competent, my father's statement needs editing. The advice would be: "When encountering an individual from Rome, pay attention to Roman attitudes and beliefs. Do not assume that all Romans share the same worldview simply because of their cultural origin."

Developing cultural competency requires the ability to listen and gather information. Recall the reporter's question to me. Listening carefully to her question gives me enough information to make a guess about her cultural background. I am not in favor of framing a response based solely upon a guess, however, so I ask, "What has been your experience with Anglo funerals?" Mind you, I don't think at this point that she is actually talking about a British Anglo-Saxon funeral. More likely, she is asking about her experience with Caucasian funerals as contrasted to rituals of her own family or ethnic group. By matching her language and using the term "Anglo" in my response, I encourage her to be more specific in giving me information.

I listen as she describes two recent deaths, one of a Caucasian colleague and the other of a family member. As she talks about the differences in the funeral rituals, her use of the word "serious" is placed in context. I now have much more information about the cultural differences that spark her curiosity. The contrasts between the two funeral ceremonies were quite perplexing to this young woman. The funeral for her uncle was held in his parish church (Catholic) in an area of Miami populated mostly by Cuban immigrants. In her uncle's case, the funeral itself was preceded by several days and nights of viewing at a funeral home where family members, including small children, visited. Cuban music played in the background, and central to the gathering were jokes, laughter, and stories about the deceased. Laughing and crying together, the family visited with other members of the community who came to pay their respects.

The young reporter then described her experience at the visitation and funeral for her colleague. The Caucasian funeral was a Protestant service held at a mortuary. She arrived at the mortuary to find the deceased's body in a small, empty room. Walking through the door, she noticed a condolence book set out for her to sign. She did so, briefly viewed the body, and left. During the funeral, the family sat behind closed curtains, cut off from the view of the casket and the mourners sitting in the public portion of the funeral chapel.

As you imagine the range of differences between these two gatherings, it makes sense that, to the reporter, one seemed to be more "serious" (solemn and staid) than the other.

## Accommodating Cultural Diversity

The key to accommodating cultural diversity is first to understand your own attitudes, beliefs, and practices toward death, dying, and bereavement. Cultural competency begins at home with an examination of your own experience with death.

The way you answer a question like, "What kind of funeral would you choose for yourself?" reveals beliefs and practices that relate to your culture, your religion or spiritual practice, and your family heritage—in short, the package in which you carry your experiences. The more you know about your own preferences, the easier it is to listen to another without projecting or judging.

When I think about cultural diversity, the word *accommodating* comes to mind; that is, providing for something needed or desired, making room for something without crowding. Such is the case when exploring cultural diversity. Although we are long past the time when unfamiliar cultural practices were routinely labeled "bizarre" or "barbaric," we still sometimes hear words like "morbid" when unfamiliar death customs are mentioned.

(Since morbid comes from the Latin *morbidus*, meaning "diseased," it does strike me as humorous that a death custom should be deemed diseased. Of course, the more popular definition of morbid points to gloomy or unwholesome feelings. In the use of the judgment *morbid*, I think that it tells more about the experience of the person using the word than the death custom itself. Perhaps the speaker has dis-ease at the notion of participating in a particular custom. Certainly, its usage is an indication that the speaker is not at ease with the custom.)

The process of making room for cultural diversity in death, dying, and bereavement requires that you respond to unfamiliar practices with an understanding of differences. In order to become more skilled, here are four areas where further study is important: (1) understanding your own attitudes and beliefs, (2) learning to listen to language, (3) gathering information about particular sources of comfort, and (4) knowing about resources.

## KNOW YOUR OWN ATTITUDES, BELIEFS, AND PRACTICES

Your thoughts are related to your past experiences, your family's practices, your religious or spiritual beliefs, and your heritage. What follows here are types of questions that, when answered, can provide you with an understanding of the contents of your cultural package.

- To what extent do you believe in a life after death?
- How appropriate is it for children to attend funerals?
- How was death talked about in your family?
- What most influenced your attitudes toward death?
- How significant is religion in your death attitudes?
- To what extent do you believe in reincarnation?
- How often do you think about your own death?
- If you could choose, when would you die?
- What do you believe causes most deaths?
- What kind of death would you prefer?
- How do you feel about having an autopsy done on your body?
- To what extent should suicide be prevented?
- If you were diagnosed with a terminal disease, would you want to be told?
- What efforts should be made to keep a seriously ill person alive?
- What circumstances would prompt you to refuse medical treatment for a dying family member?
- Are you willing to be an organ donor?

- If a close friend were dying and wanted to talk, how would you feel?
- How helpful to a survivor's grief is viewing the body?
- How do you want your body disposed of after death?
- What is your experience of participating in rituals to remember the dead?

Thinking about your position on a small sample of issues related to death will give you some indication of your cultural background. The ability to know yourself enhances your ability to listen to another person whose attitudes and beliefs are different. The key to being a good listener is to respond with curiosity when meeting an individual whose answers to these questions are vastly different from your own.

## LISTEN FOR AND MIRROR LANGUAGE PATTERNS

As we saw in the example of the young reporter, using language or choosing words in a skillful way will give you more information about an individual's culture. Take the differences in three different ways of describing that a person is dead. You might say *passed away*, or use the expression *passed on*, or perhaps refer to the dead as *passing*. Small differences in language can indicate much about the speaker's experience. For example, passed away might describe the deceased from the survivor's perspective; that is, gone from the living. Passed on indicates that there is some place to go, possibly revealing a belief in life after death. Passing is used by individuals whose belief system of life and death is represented by a circular model rather than a linear one. For example, in the African American community where individuals may often see birth and death as part of a cycle, the dead commonly are said to be passing (Barrett, 1995).

## GATHER INFORMATION ABOUT DISTINCTIVE RITUALS, PRACTICES, AND BELIEFS

Several books with information relating to cultural diversity in healthcare have recently been published (Galanti, 1997; Lipson, Dibble, and Minarik, 1996). The October 1997 issue of *The Director*, the monthly publication of the National Funeral Directors Association (NFDA), is titled, "Cultural Differences in the US." In the same issue, the President of NFDA announces the advent of a FaxBack system to provide information about a faith or culture.

While generalizations about a particular culture or religion may be useful in understanding practices and beliefs, it is crucial to find out which traditions are meaningful to a particular person. In a section on the death rituals of Koreans, one resource (Lipson, Dibble, and Minarik, 1996) suggests that the "imminence of death should be told to a spokesperson who will relay information to the family. They will unite and prepare themselves and patient for death" (p. 198). Such advice should be used as a guideline along with further information about individual and family preferences taken directly from the situation at hand. In my experience, the best way to collect information is to listen, observe, and ask about unfamiliar practices. The ability to ask questions and thereby understand how an individual identifies and expresses his or her cultural background is essential. For example, important personal preferences of an individual might include the following:

- **Appropriate language to describe an individual's cultural heritage.** Is this someone who identifies with being White or Caucasian, Black or African American, Hispanic or Cuban American?
- **Differences in nonverbal communication patterns.** In general, individuals of Japanese decent will avoid eye contact with their elders and superiors. Some people may welcome touch while other cultural groups avoid such contact.
- **Names of the dead.** If calling a person's name is a way of summoning the person, then refraining from using a name will presumably leave its bearer undisturbed. Hence, one practice related to the dead is name avoidance: The deceased is never again mentioned, or else is referred to only obliquely, never by name. At the other end of the spectrum, rather than being avoided, the name of the deceased person is given special emphasis. It may be given to a newborn child in the dead person's family (DeSpelder and Strickland, 1996).

## INVENTORY INTERNAL AND EXTERNAL RESOURCES

Cultural competency involves determining what strengths an individual draws upon when encountering death, dying, or bereavement. These resources can be categorized as internal or external. Examples of internal resources, sometimes thought to be psychological in nature, are an individual's belief system or model of the world. If I believe myself to be capable of surviving a loss through death, then my internal resources will support my survival. An individual's access to past experiences and the comfort of remembered cultural customs are also internal resources. External resources are those support systems that are available to the individual in a social setting. For example, Daoist practices might dictate to bring special amulets and cloths from home to the place of death to provide closure. The ritual objects then become external resources. A survivor support group run by the local hospice is another kind of external resource. Individuals will pick resources that are compatible with their cultural heritage.

# Stereotyping and the Magic Recipe

There is no formula or recipe for understanding a particular cultural group. First, you must know that, while generalizations about beliefs and practices might be helpful guides, the map is not the territory. The last time your route home was blocked by construction or a frequently traveled road was closed reinforces the truth of that statement. Do not assume that all individuals of a particular religion, race, or cultural group share the same beliefs. Each individual is unique. Norms can be used as a guide. They are not a substitute for individual assessment.

Stereotypes will trip you up every time. When I hear a generalization about a particular cultural group, I think, what about the particular family? So, it might be true that in Japan, at the time of this writing, there are issues related to organ transplants and defining the moment of death that preclude organ donation. With Japanese Americans, one factor related to organ donation might be how many generations have passed since immigration. The *Issei* (immigrant generation) may have different beliefs than the *Nissei* (first

American-born generation) or the *Sansei* (children of the first American-born generation). It is likely that the *Issei* will think of organ donation in the same manner as their counterparts in Japan. The *Nissei* or the *Sansei* may favor organ donation.

Just when you think that there is a pattern related to generations, you find the opposite with Vietnamese immigrants. (This is a generalization about a generalization.) The immigrant generation may be more tolerant than the second generation (Lipson, Dibble, and Minarik, 1996).

# The Barrett Inferential Model

Dr. Ronald K. Barrett's research (1995) on African American death customs points out that, even within cultural groups, there is tremendous diversity. His model identifies three variables that are important for understanding cultural diversity.

## CULTURE

Understanding culture requires knowledge of how an individual defines his or her heritage. This definition may be influenced by the length of time an individual has lived in North America. Other factors include geographic location, rural or urban setting, and family influences. The African American experience is more heterogeneous than homogeneous. Thus, skin color is not the determining factor in matters of death, dying, and bereavement.

## SOCIAL CLASS

Celebrating *el Día de los Muertos*, 'the Day of the Dead,' in Mexico, I noticed that the poorer families seemed to make up the largest percentage of the participants. When I asked about my observation, I was told that the Mexican government had instituted a program in the city of Oaxaca to interest the middle and upper classes in the traditions of their ancestors. As noted in the African American research, the affluent in a culture are more likely to move away from their communities of origin, thus becoming less traditional. The poor are more likely to follow traditional practices.

## SPIRITUALITY

Different religions and religious denominations shape spirituality in different ways. The more traditional the religious experience, the more conservative will be the attitudes, beliefs, and values that ultimately affect behavior. The more conservative believers can be characterized as the "keepers of the tradition." They hold to old ways of relating to death, dying, and funeral rites. Many conservative believers object to blood donations, autopsies, and tissue or organ donations. In the African American experience, Dr. Barrett (1995) lists as most conservative the Baha'i faith with Judaism, Black Muslim, Apostolic, Church of God, Seventh-Day Adventist, and Pentecostal following in ascending order towards the more liberal.

# Summary

Skills for developing cultural competency can be learned. Culture differs among societies as well as within societies that include social groups with distinctive customs and lifestyles. The extent to which traditional cultural patterns are maintained by the different groups that make up North American society varies widely, both between the different ethnic groups and among individuals who share a particular ethnic heritage. Nevertheless, in studies of behaviors related to dying, death, and bereavement, ethnic and other cultural differences can be found in methods of coping with life-threatening illness, the perception of pain, social support for the dying, behavioral manifestations of grief, mourning styles, and funeral customs.

In societies that value pluralism, different groups are able to retain distinctive identities while enjoying equal social standing within the culture as a whole. Encouraging diversity in death attitudes and customs allows the entire society to benefit from a wealth of cultural resources that can assist in coping with dying and death.

In contemporary societies, socially sanctioned rites for dealing with death are in flux. The dynamic of the "melting pot" metaphor in North American society is changing as individuals and groups strive to honor and reinterpret, rather than discard, the distinctive attitudes and death customs of their forebears. This variety and dynamism challenges the assumptions of caregivers, who must carry out their professional missions in environments that require attention to individual and group differences (DeSpelder and Strickland, 1986).

---

*Lynne Ann DeSpelder, MA, is an author, counselor, and full-time faculty member at Cabrillo College. She is a member of the International Work Group on Death, Dying and Bereavement, and lectures and conducts training programs and in-service education.*

# Varied Experience: Gender, Development, Class, and Cultural Influences on Grief

Throughout this book we have broadly defined culture as a "way of life." Sometimes that distinct way of life emerges from a shared belief system or common ethnicity. Yet ways of life can emerge from a variety of contexts including shared occupations, classes, genders, or even common sets of experiences. Not only may such variables define categories or people who share such a way of life, they profoundly affect the ways that we grieve, again offering factors that both complicate and facilitate the grieving process.

Social class is one such factor. Will Rogers was once reported to quip, "The rich are different—they have more money." This piece of humor may express a common American perspective of class: In the end, class differences are relatively unimportant. Yet such a distinction ignores the bare reality of class long emphasized in sociological studies (e.g., Warner, 1959; Hollingshead, 1949). Social class dramatically affects the ways we live our lives, from the likelihood of our being born to how and when we die. It even affects where we are buried (Warner, 1959). Moreover, class influences nearly every aspect of life in between: where we go to school, whom we marry, how many children we have, where we live, as well as our values, spirituality, and lifestyle.

In fact, many variables that we attribute to ethnicity are actually more closely related to social class. It is little wonder that Gordon (1978) has defined "ethclass," or the conjunction of the two critical variables of ethnicity and social class as they define a person within his or her society. So, for example, a middle-class African American will share a common experience with all middle-class persons regardless of ethnicity and with all African Americans, irrespective of class.

Given the pervasive influence of class, it would be naive to expect that it would not affect the grieving process in both manifest and subtle ways. For example, Coles (1977), in his study of privileged children, addresses the unique aspects of a *psychology of entitlement* that wealth entails. In Coles' study, this led to higher self-esteem and self-confidence, as well as greater coping skills. We can infer that these qualities may suffer as one copes with loss.

Similarly, wealth also may provide the sophistication and resources to utilize effectively other sources of support. Yet at the same time, the psychology of entitlement may serve to make certain losses, particularly those that are sudden, traumatic, or developmentally out of sequence, incomprehensible.

In one case, a very wealthy woman struggled with her young husband's cancer. At the beginning of his illness, she was confident that their socio-economic status would facilitate his survival—after all, they could afford the best care. Even as his condition deteriorated she remained confident, since their connections made available experimental protocols. When he died in spite of such resources, she had a difficult time accepting his death.

Murphy's chapter insightfully explores the other end of social class, identifying complementary sets of strengths and limitations found in the midst of poverty.

Gender, too, marks a major division in social life. The socialization and experiences of men and women differ from birth. It is reasonable to assume that such differences may affect the grieving process. Both Sanders' and Martin and Doka's chapters explore those effects. Sanders' review of research offers support to Martin and Doka's theorizing about *masculine grief*. Both suggest that these may be different patterns of grieving—related to gender though not determined by it. And both these chapters repeat a common refrain: These are differences, not deficiencies, as each style offers complementary strengths and weaknesses. Sanders, and to a lesser extent, Martin and Doka, emphasize how differences in socialization can affect the grieving process, suggesting that attention be paid to the developmental process.

Corr provides an overview of this process, reminding us of the ways in which distinct developmental issues in each of the major periods of life (childhood, adolescence, adulthood, and old age) affect the grieving process. He challenges us, in our desire to be sensitive to cultural differences, not to neglect other critical variables, such as developmental needs. Corr does not imply that developmental periods are unrelated to culture. Culture informs these distinct periods of human development with all their biological, social, and historical force, defining these periods in their own unique way. So caregivers and grief counselors need to understand both developmental differences and the ways they are perceived in a given culture. Nonetheless, as Corr so clearly indicates, developmental levels do affect grieving.

This point is reiterated in Lavin's chapter on an often neglected population, the developmentally disabled. Here she notes how cognitive deficiencies, overprotection, disenfranchisement, and limited communication, support, and experience, can complicate grieving. Beyond developmental disabilities, Lavin's chapter suggests sensitivities to a variety of conditions that may complicate adjustment to loss. And she offers a reminder to caregivers to enfranchise all those who may be (because of such differences) disenfranchised in their grief.

*Disenfranchised grief* exists when a loss is not socially sanctioned, openly acknowledged, or publicly shared. The individual grieves, but others may not acknowledge that person's right to grieve. There may be a number of reasons for this. The loss may not be acknowledged, the relationship unrecognized, the griever or manner of grieving discounted, among others (Doka, 1989).

The latter category may include not just the developmentally disabled but also those who are critically ill, confused or disoriented, and young children, all of whom may express their grief in ways other than those deemed appropriate in a given society. Yet, all grieve. The concept of disenfranchised grief can also be extended to masculine grievers or those from different cultures who do not grieve or mourn according to societal norms.

Unexplored in this book, but a factor as well, is regional difference. Garreau (1981), for example, identifies nine distinct cultures within North America, noting that each region has its own distinct population mix, history, values, and norms. These norms will influence grief, shaping funeral customs, expressions of grief, and expectations of support. Similarly, one could identify generational differences, noting that each generation group (e.g., baby boomers, depression-era babies, etc.) also has unique historical experiences that shape identity, values, and norms.

Sometimes a shared group identity and experiences can define a common culture. These chapters consider how categories formed by a shared disability, sexual orientation, or occupation can lead to distinct cultural identification. Zieziula, for example, explores Deaf customs, noting how a shared impairment and language have combined to form a very distinct culture. Wilder considers how sexual orientation may affect the experience of grieving. And, finally, Carroll discusses the unique aspects of loss in military culture.

Together these chapters reiterate a series of points. First, they emphasize the many factors that shape the experience of grief. Certainly other chapters could be added about the ways in which different physical or sensory impairments or challenges can affect the grieving process. And just as surely other categories, such as occupational groups (e.g., police or firefighters) may be said to share a common culture that affects the mourning process as well.

Second, they all speak to the issue of disenfranchised grief. For example, relationships within the gay community do not have the same societal acceptance and sanction as heterosexual relationships. While a widow has broad recognition and support in her grief, a lover, even in a long-term relationship, may not have the same support, especially outside the gay community. Similarly, Carroll describes how the common advice extended to the bereaved may ring hollow for military survivors. Zieziula, too, notes how the hearing community may disenfranchise deaf survivors by assuming that they cannot process complicated information.

All of these pieces then stress the critical role of validation. Sometimes, as Zieziula suggests, this can be done by sensitive and sensitized professionals within and outside the community. Sometimes, as Wilder and Carroll suggest, this can be best provided with a support group or individuals who share the common experience. However it is done, all recognize the critical role of validation in normalizing grief and in reminding survivors, whatever their circumstances or differences, that they do not grieve alone.

# NINE

# Dying and Grieving in the Inner City

*Patricia A. Murphy and David M. Price*

The experiences of death, dying, and grieving are universal. Yet few who read these words have lived through loss in the circumstances of urban poverty.

This chapter is written not by sociologists but by health professionals with long experience in the inner city. For the most part, that experience has been in one inner-city community. Readers can decide the extent to which these observations can be generalized to other poor and under-served populations.

## Children

This is not Mr. Rogers' Neighborhood. While there are unquestionably kind and concerned adults in the environment, it is filled with danger. Doors are triple-locked. Knowing too much about what goes on next door can get you killed, like it did your cousin Kenneth. Rasheeda's mother always made her come in off the stoop as soon as the streetlights came on, but a stray bullet found her in the parlor anyway. Most third graders know someone who has been a victim of street violence. For many, the violence has claimed someone in their families, if not as a victim, then as a perpetrator now in jail.

AIDS has decimated families. Many children live with grandparents or in foster homes because both parents are dead, and many of those children acquired the virus at birth. Some of these are or have been very sick. Some die, others expect to die soon.

AIDS came to the inner city in all the well-known ways, but overwhelmingly by way of intravenous drug abuse. Drugs and drug dealing are everywhere. The dealers have cars and sharp clothes. They provide employment opportunities, even to kids too small to push a lawnmower or babysit. The money is far better than anybody ever earned babysitting. The glamour and the pride of good pay for easy work seduces many children into underestimating the dangers.

More than a few children have multiple primary caretakers while growing up. Death, jail, drug-related disability, and mental illness, sometimes in combination, interrupt the continuity of parenting. Large numbers of children are in foster care; many more are placed indefinitely with aunts and grandmothers "until the mom can get straightened out."

## Young Adults

Older teens and young adults in great numbers come unprepared to adult roles. They have few marketable skills and poor educational backgrounds. If they expected to get a job at age 18, they find that there are none, or at least far fewer than there are people just like them who are looking. Unless they have grown up in one of the too few households with consistent role models and expectations for achievement through hard work, these young people are ill-prepared for either continued schooling or successful competition in today's job market. The manufacturing base that once absorbed large numbers of the young, marginally educated urban poor has long since moved elsewhere, typically to underdeveloped countries.

That so many young adults seem directionless, discouraged, and disaffected is no surprise, given their circumstances and the circumstances of their childhood. Loss has been a constant companion and hope a stranger. Like young people everywhere, they do not think about the distant future or imagine themselves growing old. Unlike their privileged counterparts, they do not expect the near future to be better and many expect to die young.

## Grandmothers

Without grandmothers, the children of the inner city would be in unimaginably worse shape. Because AIDS, violence, and imprisonment have removed so many parents and because emptied-out mental hospitals have freed so many under-treated, but fertile, young adults to "begin their own families," middle-aged women (and, where those women are married, middle-aged men) are raising their second set of children. They are doing so out of duty and love, not preference. In many instances, their intervention is saving the children from chaos and likely disaster. In some cases, it is too late.

Such grandmothers are well acquainted with grief. They have lost their children to gunfire or prison or drugs or mental illness or "the virus." Now they try to protect and nurture children who have themselves known too much loss and may even be fatally wounded in body or spirit by their perilous early lives.

There are many, many such grandmothers in the inner city. Just what will be the long-term consequences of this truncated generational cycle is hard to imagine. In the short run, one cannot help but be relieved that these often quite remarkable middle-aged women are able and willing to catch the children that fall from the tatters of their own children's lives.

## Obstacles to Dying and Grieving

It is perhaps easy to see some of the barriers to successful coping that are associated with life in poor neighborhoods of American cities. For many people, there is a deep sense of fear. Crime, especially drug-related crime, truly is reason to be fearful. One must be on guard. Many children really do feel that they are safer if they carry knives or guns. The incidence of crime is probably under-reported because of fear.

Fear breeds distrust. So does the reality of authority figures who fail to protect—or care. The service system, from schools to clinics to police to child protective agencies, is sometimes corrupt, often fragmented, and always overburdened. Gains in one segment seem to be matched by losses in another. The safety net, never very reliable, has recently developed new holes.

The attitudes of self-reliance, self-worth, and social competence that middle-class parents, teachers, and health professionals attempt to instill in all children are a hard sell among urban poor children in the 1990s. There seems to be a pervasive sense that control lies elsewhere than in oneself, that neither effort nor goodness is rewarded, and that external forces, not individual choices, will prevail. Even those souls whose faith allows them to believe that goodness and peace and spiritual riches will abound are inclined to think that this will come about by God's agency, not by humankind's, and surely not by theirs. Resignation reigns.

Institutions serving the urban poor also tend to be poor. From schools to grocery stores to motor vehicle agencies, the inner-city service sector outlets are understaffed and shabby. Even those whose staff members do not share in the resignation and defeat of their clientele often lack the combination of extra money and community support that seems to make the crucial difference between a school and a good school, between a clinic that is merely open for business and a clinic that is a healing environment.

Consider the experience of Hessie, a 59-year-old, single, licensed practical nurse who had lived all her life in a poor neighborhood of a poor city. Hessie had a 24-year-old son with "mental problems" who shared her household. She developed lung cancer, which spread to the brain and bones.

Hessie was clear that she wanted to be cared for at home, with no aggressive treatment of her already advanced disease, but with vigorous attention to pain and other symptoms. Hospice home care was arranged with Hessie's son, Ben, as the principal caregiver, though Hessie had expressed concern about whether Ben could manage.

One night soon after the home care plan was implemented, Hessie became quite confused, presumably as a result of her brain tumor. She would not allow Ben to care for her and accused him of trying to kill her. In a panic, Ben called 911 and Hessie was taken to a local hospital. When her confusion cleared, Hessie refused to return home, insisting that Ben "can't handle it."

Financial barriers proved daunting as the hospital staff tried to arrange an inpatient hospice placement. Hessie had a private managed care policy through her employer, but it would not cover indefinite inpatient hospice care. A covered "transitional" program was limited to fourteen days. Hessie was too young for Medicare, too "wealthy" for Medicaid, and too poor to pay. The nearest hospice that would provide free inpatient care had a waiting list and was in another state, too far for frequent visits by friends and family.

Accordingly, a network of neighbors and church friends was patched together to support Ben in caring for Hessie at home. Without much confidence in this plan, but with no better alternatives in sight, Hessie returned home.

Only two days later, the stress proved too much for Ben. Hessie had become markedly confused again and Ben, thinking that the confusion was a drug side-effect, stopped her medication. He distrusted the neighbors and church friends, barring them from the house. After three days without gaining entry, Hessie's frustrated friends phoned the hospice nurse who finally convinced Ben to let her in.

The hospice nurse found Hessie in terrible pain and being force-fed by Ben, who was convinced that he could prevent his mother's death if she would only eat well enough. Both Hessie and Ben were relieved when the hospice nurse arranged for immediate rehospitalization.

Hessie arrived at the emergency room in terrible pain. It took hours to get her onto the oncology floor and to get her pain under control. Hessie stayed in the hospital until she died nine days later. The hospice nurse cooperated with Hessie's oncologist in her care. The hospital was reimbursed at the hospice per diem rate.

This account of Hessie's dying leads to several observations. Hospice home care faces major challenges in caring for the urban poor. Problems that are occasional in the suburbs are frequent in inner-city neighborhoods. Hospitals are not equipped to provide excellent palliative care. Yet a higher proportion of urban residents die in hospitals than do people from suburban and rural areas. "Systems of care" remain an elusive goal; fragmentation and discontinuity seem more common, despite the caring and committed efforts of individual professionals. Meanwhile, many of the chronically under-served do not seem to have the information, skills or, most importantly, expectations that are needed to make the system work for them.

## Strengths

There are some features of inner-city life that have potential to provide support in the experience of coping with death and the restorative work of bereavement. Some of these features can be seen in the foregoing account of Hessie's dying. Though they were largely frustrated in carrying through their plan, and though the plan was more or less cobbled together, the "church ladies" were willing and available to help. In many affluent communities, one would be hard pressed to find a cadre of women prepared to go into a home to provide bedside and household care.

Other strengths can be seen in the case of Helen, who was also in the terminal stage of cancer. A 75-year-old single grandmother, she lived in two large rooms with fifteen other people, five or six of them small children.

Though Helen was eager to go home, social workers and nurses in the hospital busied themselves with developing options for alternative care settings. "We are still trying to find a good place for you," they assured her.

"But I have a place," she insisted. "Just let me go home."

"Now, Helen, you don't want to have all those people around when you don't feel well. And the children right on top of you?!"

"Your middle class is showing," Helen said with a smile. "Those are my people. They won't bother me."

Helen went home promptly. She died peacefully a short time later, in the midst of the warmth and bustle of the household.

Such strong family support exists side by side in the inner city with homes where dying cancer patients would be at risk of a caretaker appropriating prescription medication for sale or their own use. While it is commonly emphasized that one should always carefully assess the actual needs and preferences of the dying, Helen's story reminds us of two corollaries especially relevant to inner-city America: Generalizations are useful in their place, but individuals and individual families cover a wide spectrum; and, if professionals make assumptions, rather than careful inquiries, their "middle class" is almost certain to show itself.

Helen's story also suggests another feature of inner-city life that may represent an advantage for some. As mentioned earlier, the environment affords many people more experience of loss and thereby more opportunity to learn how to respond to it and grow through it. There seems to be less denial of the possibility of loss, and less separation from death. The readiness with which Helen chose to die at home, a three-generational, densely packed household, and the apparent easy acceptance of that plan by others in her family may both reflect and reinforce an acceptance of dying that may not be nearly as common in affluent communities.

## Implications for Caregivers

Good care always begins with good listening. Helen pointedly reminded one very seasoned and sophisticated professional that the middle-class orientation, background, and attitudes of most caregivers necessitate awareness that urban poor clients may have both obstacles and strengths that are hard to perceive.

The remedy is to ask what is needed, rather than to assume, and then immediately set about identifying and overcoming obstacles so that those needs get met.

It has been useful for some working in inner-city environments to remember Maslow's theory of need satisfaction. In very simple form, Maslow taught that until human beings' most basic needs are more or less satisfied, they will not attend to or pursue fulfillment of higher-level needs. His hierarchy of needs looks like this:

  I.   Physiological needs (e.g., food, oxygen, sleep)
  II.  Safety needs
  III. Needs to belong and to be loved
  IV.  Esteem needs
  V.   Self-actualization needs

The urban poor, for whom some of the lower-level needs are matters of uncertainty, may not be able to address some of the developmental tasks that we sometimes associate with the last days of life:

life review, putting one's affairs in order, saying one's good-byes. In Hessie's case, almost all the energy expended both by her and by her professional caregivers was quite appropriately focused on providing a safe environment. For Hessie to have sat down with her son or with a hospice volunteer to reminisce over a family scrapbook would have had to come well after more basic needs were satisfied. It is sad that, for Hessie, there was too little time for scrapbooks after fulfillment of these needs. That does not mean that scrapbooks should or could have come first. Maslow's concept seems to apply very well to the care of dying persons generally, especially among those for whom food, shelter, and safety are uncertain.

All people who experience significant loss should have support and practical assistance. Exactly what kinds of support and help are most needed must await *care-full* listening and assessment. It may be helpful, however, to recall that many of the urban poor need assistance with such ordinary tasks as transportation or reading consent forms, as well as guidance through difficult decision-making processes and emotion-laden events.

For those whom the fates have blessed with security, education, status, self-esteem, and the attitudes and expectations that come with privilege, it can be humbling to know people who endure and even triumph despite disadvantage. While it is commonplace for those who work with dying people to speak of how uplifting and inspiring the work can be, there may be special spiritual reward for those who work with dying poor people: incredible dignity in the face of indignity, faith in spite of social wrong and political betrayal, and generosity in the midst of want. It is a blessing to be in the presence of such amazing grace.

---

*Patricia A. Murphy, PhD, RN, CS, FAAN, is Clinical Specialist in Bereavement and Ethics at Newark Beth Israel Medical Center. Dr. Murphy also maintains a private practice and is a speaker on bereavement and end-of-life care.*

*David M. Price, MDiv, PhD, teaches professional ethics at New Jersey Medical School and is the hospital ethicist at St. Barnabas Medical Center. He is a founding member of the ethics committees of several hospitals, nursing homes, and a hospice.*

# TEN

# Gender Differences in Bereavement Expression Across the Life Span

*Catherine M. Sanders*

*I couldn't break down...show my real feelings. Everyone depended on me and I couldn't let them down. But Mary didn't understand, I guess. She took my holding together to mean I didn't care. How could she ever feel that way? Our son didn't have a chance ...his life over at fifteen. If I ever started to bend a little, I would dissolve. And then where would we all be?*

Bereaved father, age 49

It seems impossible that two people could manifest such different responses to the same loss. Yet the truth is that there are often broad differences in the way men and women react, differences that come about from early socialization and linger in varying degrees throughout life. That men and women generally react differently to grief may be a recognized fact for some theorists; however, there still appears to be a considerable difference of opinion among others. Some researchers have noted that widows exhibit more health problems than do widowers, and that mothers tend to grieve more openly than fathers. It is possible that the difference in both these situations lies in the ability of women to express their grief in a more open manner than men. This is not to suggest that men show no grief or feel no grief when they lose a loved one. It just means that there are different expressions of grief shown by each gender. Of course, many factors contribute to these findings, not the least of which are cultural conditioning and learned behavioral reactions across the life span.

While gender differences before adolescence have not been widely noted, there are strong indications that early socialization has an effect on the way children respond to loss. The grieving behavior of a child will often mimic that of the surviving parent of the same sex. For example, after his mother's death, a son will sometimes behave in a stoic manner not unlike his father. While some friends may say in an admiring way, "What a little man!" or, "He is acting so grown up!" these remarks tend to discourage the important emotional development necessary to produce a fully functioning adult. But more importantly, they send the message to the child to suppress natural emotions and behave in a manner that hides true feelings rather than to react in a normal way.

As stated earlier, gender differences begin to appear in the literature as adolescent behavior is discussed. Because of the newly emerging world of the adolescent, as well as the developmental changes taking place, living is emphasized both in concept and in practice. Everything focuses on life, change, and growth. Therefore, bereavement to an adolescent is dealt with unwillingly. The extra burden of stress is added to an already full plate of life changes. Some of these changes include:

1. body changes in height, weight and development of secondary sexual characteristics;

2. major endocrine changes leading to powerful sexual feelings associated with moodiness;

3. revival of Oedipal conflicts from childhood development;

4. cognitive developmental changes allowing a move toward form and operations (use of abstraction, reasoning, development of reflective self);

5. increase in self-consciousness and self-centeredness;

6. development of social self as a result of interaction with the community, new friends, and acquaintances. (Raphael, 1984)

Because depression, misery, and unhappiness are common in adolescent development, it is often difficult to determine which reactions are caused by grief and which are simply a part of normal adolescent behavior. As difficult as it is, the actual experience of grief is an aid to the adolescent's eventual acceptance of the fact of death. Still, death for the young person is a fearful reminder of his own possible demise. It is difficult for the adolescent to seek care directly from others during the time of bereavement, primarily because the request for help might suggest weakness, and it may also draw attention to oneself when the real desire is to simply fade into the background.

There are definite gender differences during adolescence. With girls, the sadness and emptiness of loss, particularly that of a parent, will generate a longing for reassurance: to be held and consoled. This is often manifested outside the family in sexual relationships which offer a sense of wholeness, of closeness with another. While this behavior will not completely assuage the pain and longing, it will sometimes offer a temporary sense of belonging to something or someone now that the parent is no longer present. Promiscuity may result in pregnancy, offering the assurance of having something of her own to love. Yet acting out is likely to add to the guilt she may already carry regarding the death. Of course, there are many avenues by which these problems might be resolved; her family may stabilize or friends may help her resolve her loss.

For the adolescent boy, stress is likely to be acted out in a more risk-taking, aggressive manner. Fights, alcohol and other drugs, or testing authority are only a few of the possibilities. These activities serve not only to release tension but also to dole out punishment for the guilt felt for surviving. Sexual acting out may result from grief, in an attempt to find body comfort and care or even to achieve "adulthood," sexual behavior being equated with being an adult. Unless he is able to deal with his own loss, there are definite possibilities for negative outcomes which would make grieving even more difficult for the adolescent boy.

There are times when adult decisions are thrust upon the eldest son, especially in cases when there is only a single parent, for example, when the mother, who has been the sole caregiver, is the one to die. Timothy, an eldest child who was only 17, saw it as his duty to make the funeral arrangements. Regarding this as an unpleasant job, he tried to shield his sisters and grandparents from the responsibility. Yet when he was criticized by the family for excluding them from the funeral planning, Timothy was embarrassed and reacted in anger, saying things he had not intended to. He tried to explain his position:

> I was very insulted, very embarrassed...I never even raised my voice to my grandmother before. I had no reason to... but this one time, boy, if I hadn't, if I didn't know that I can control myself, my temper...The first thing she does is she jumps up and runs out of the room to where my uncle was, then he comes running in there, wanting to go outside with me because I'm talking to his mother like I am.

A year and half later, the family still avoided each other. Timothy, in his desire to protect everyone, had not taken into account the fact that his grandparents were the bereaved parents of his mother and needed special consideration.

In dealing with a grieving adolescent, it is important for the caregiver to be aware of the many variables—the life changes, the anger, as well as the acting out—which are a call for others to pay attention to their needs. It may be easier for girls to ask for help in getting their needs met; for boys it is much more difficult, primarily because they may see neediness as childish or unmasculine. A sensitive caregiver will be able to spot defensiveness and offer necessary support.

Gender differences in bereavement expression begin to become more pronounced as adults mature and experience loss more often. This is not to say that masculine grief becomes more open and expressive or that feminine grief becomes less so. Due in large part to social conditioning and learned behaviors, feelings and emotions tend to become more clearly differentiated between the sexes, particularly after marriage.

Martin and Doka (1996), studying adult bereavement, found several consistent patterns. They note that masculine grief can be described by the following generalizations:

1. Feelings are limited or toned down.

2. Thinking precedes and often dominates feeling.

3. The focus is on problem-solving rather than expression of feelings.

4. The outward expression of feelings often involves anger and/or guilt.

5. Internal adjustments to the loss are usually expressed through activity.

6. Intense feelings may only be expressed privately; there is a general reluctance to discuss these with others.

7. Intense grief is usually expressed immediately after the loss, often during post-death rituals.

Martin and Doka point out that caregivers tend to overlook much of the masculine reaction to grief and focus instead on feminine grief, ignoring the potential differences. The following case exemplifies the dilemma men are placed in when they must fulfill the expectations of everyone else as well as their own expectations of themselves.

John had survived the cancer deaths of two wives and was still trying to regain his footing after the second loss when he first came to my office. He had been married to Jane only two years when she was diagnosed with metastatic breast cancer. His first wife had died of colon cancer five years before. He felt cheated that he and Jane had not been able to carry out the plans they had made together. He was at the hospital every day until she died; agonizing days that gave him little time to prepare himself.

After the rituals were complete and family members had returned to their homes, John had time to think about the events of his life and ask many questions as he struggled with an acceptance of his losses. But then John had to return to his job, where his boss poured work on him, thinking it was the best way to help him through his grief. For John, this worked out well because he had no need to discuss his feelings with anyone—or so he thought. He would come home from work, try to read and then try to sleep. But he couldn't get past the feelings of guilt and terrible anger he felt from watching Jane die and being able to do nothing to change it. Twice he had been robbed of his marriage and twice he had no control over any of it.

John suffered from isolation, sleeplessness, and guilt. It wasn't long before his work suffered as well, and he was put on temporary probation. His boss suggested that John seek professional help to work through some of the painful issues he had kept to himself. John had to contemplate the implications of his losses before he could deal with the pain of his separations.

In a study that looked at gender differences, Stroebe and Stroebe (1987) found that widowers did indeed suffer from greater health impairment than did the control group of married men. The writers reasoned that this difference was due to the loss of social support that had been provided by their wives. On the other hand, these same researchers found that widowers, in using avoidance strategies in grief work, actually showed a better adjustment than did widows after a two-year period. The researchers felt that the results were due to the men working outside the home, a social environment which discouraged their dwelling on their grief. Yet widowers evidenced more depression than married men, which Stroebe and Stroebe interpreted as resulting, in some degree, from the bereaved men needing to withdraw from others. Their sense of distance with friends left them feeling solitary and lonely.

In looking at health aspects of gender differences, Parkes and Brown (1972) noted that men had fewer physical complaints than did women in either the bereaved group or the non-bereaved controls. As a matter of fact, this control group of women reported almost the same number of symptoms as bereaved men. Apparently, men reported fewer symptoms than women, making it appear that women were more acutely depressed than men.

An interesting turn in these same results showed that widows had higher depression scores after the first year of bereavement, but in a two-to-four-year follow-up the widows suffered from no more depression than married women about the same age. Widowers, on the other hand, indicated significantly more depression than married men. Because men are more likely to rely on their wives for emotional support as well as for social interaction, there is a tendency to pull back, avoid others and go it on their own as did John. Yet it has been shown that men who were active in their church or temple showed less depression than those without a social or spiritual affiliation. Having meaningful activities in which to participate has been shown to facilitate the grieving process.

For the most part, women are conditioned differently from men. Early on, a young girl is encouraged to express her feelings, whether it be crying on the playground or expressing her fears without being called a "fraidy cat." As she continues toward teenage years, she is given typically feminine household tasks. In short, a girl is generally taught to fill the role of homemaker even when she is also encouraged to seek a career of her own. Many of the duties at home stem in part from helping her to eventually nurture a family of her own. So, as such, a mother is socialized to fill a different role from her masculine counterpart. She is expected to be the nurturer, caregiver, hub of the family, to communicate with each member, and help the members communicate with each other.

We have learned much about feminine grief from studies regarding parental bereavement. Because the death of a child is one of the most difficult and painful traumas to bear, and because of the prevalence of marital problems following such a tragedy, much of the focus of interactions between the parents after the death of a child seems to stem from the need to search for and locate helpful intervention strategies.

Recognizing that the bonding of mother and child begins before birth and continues as long as either lives, it is understandable that a strong connection remains. The connection is more than one of blood. Deep emotional ties bind the mother to her children throughout life. When a permanent separation occurs, the bond is broken and leaves the mother feeling empty and isolated. A father is traditionally involved in a job that takes him away from the home the greater part of the day. As mentioned earlier, this time offers a temporary respite from his sorrow.

Unless she is among the minority of women with full-time jobs, the mother is either taking care of the household or caring for her

other children. She is used to carrying the emotional burden of the
family and creating the family circle. When a child dies, the circle is
broken. Grief freezes the mother into a shell, and she cannot function
in her role as she once did. She grieves not only for her child but
also for the loss of the delicate balance in the family system.
Feminine grievers have been shown to have these characteristics
(Sanders, 1995):

1. can express anguish in tears and laments;

2. socialized to be nurturing and empathetic;

3. are not afraid to discuss grief;

4. seek support;

5. have difficulty expressing anger;

6. are prone to guilty feelings;

7. are caregivers to friends and family;

8. are keepers of the family circle.

Sudden death is impossibly painful in its stark reality. Sarah
and Joseph were asleep when the doorbell awakened them at 3:30 in
the morning. Joseph knew exactly when the police arrived. Quickly
getting out of bed, he tried to find his robe in the dark. Sarah was
half out of bed, her face reflecting the terror she already felt—
the cold, gripping terror that one feels when one knows something
is dreadfully wrong. She urgently asked, "William, what's the matter?
Who's here?"

"Not sure—you stay here. I'll go check," William said.

But she didn't wait. Sarah knew something was wrong and she
felt that William might need help. She was right behind him when he
opened the front door. Two police officers identified themselves and
asked if they were Mr. and Mrs. Kramer. The taller officer spoke: "Mr.
Kramer, there's been an accident. Your son has been badly hurt. We'd
like you to come to the hospital with us." That pronouncement
pierced the air like a pistol shot, removing any shadow of a doubt that
something very serious had happened.

Sarah tried to hear what they were saying. She asked aloud to everyone, "Is Billy okay? Has he been hurt?" When no one answered, she saw from their stricken faces that the news must be awful. It was then that she began to scream. For her everything was blank from then on. But William remembered all of it: Sarah's hysteria, her racing from the room screaming, "They're wrong. Make them leave us alone. They're wrong. I know it. There's been a mistake. Go to some other house. Please don't let it be Billy," and her sobbing as she collapsed on the couch, beating at the cushions.

William managed to calm her enough so that they could follow the police to the hospital. But it was William who had to identify his son's body on the emergency room table. It was William who needed to fill out the necessary forms. It was William who drove them home, empty and cold. But, once home, it was Sarah who made the coffee. It was Sarah who then began to comfort William as the harsh reality finally sank in. It was Sarah who could share her feelings later with the family.

So we see how masculine and feminine grief can work together. It is when the grief doesn't mesh, when the couple isn't in tune with each other, that things go wrong with the marriage.

How does age contribute to outcome measures in bereavement in either sex? Few studies have examined age differences beyond conjugal bereavement. One might think that the older one is the more difficult the consequences. However, this is not always true. An early study by Ball (1977) comparing three groups of widows—younger, middle-aged, and older—showed that the youngest group suffered more symptoms than the others. They were the ones whose husbands had died suddenly, giving no warning. Sanders (1981), on the other hand, in a study to determine outcome in bereavement, used the same three samples. It was shown that initially younger spouses had higher intensities of grief. Yet, two years later they indicated a substantial improvement. They had been able to pick up the pieces of their lives more easily than the older widows. The following case study illustrates this situation.

Marion had just gotten her two older children off to catch the school bus. She was getting the youngest ready for kindergarten and her husband had already left for work. Suddenly, she heard a thunderous crash from the next block. Continuing with her own duties, she didn't react until she heard screaming and saw people running toward the sound of the crash. She later said that a cold chill ran through her as she grabbed her four-year-old and ran down the block. The ambulance had not arrived yet but it was easy to see that the two-car collision was deadly. It took a minute to see that her husband's car was smashed beyond recognition except for the license plate, which was the only way she could readily identify it. She screamed and ran toward the car but neighbors held her back. Her husband was dead and, as she said, her world ended right there.

Marion struggled with the horrible realization of the loss she had suffered. She felt that her body was empty and her broken heart was the center of all her pain. It gnawed at her constantly. Yet watching her children, confused and suffering their own pain, kept her aware that the need to help them was greater than her own.

Time was agonizingly slow for Marion. It was helpful to have the duties of the house, of her children's school, even the financial problems, although she had little ability to concentrate. Slowly, things began to take shape somewhere in the second year. During that time she began to gather the strength to think about her own life and to remember the legacy her husband had left her. Feelings of hope began to return—hope that she could still have a life once again. This is not to say that suddenly life became easier for her, but that, instead, the turning point had been met and her grief eased slightly. For widows in their younger years there was a promise of continuing experiences, a new life to look forward to.

For the older widows in the study, however, there were different feelings to deal with. Anxiety and loneliness were the primary conditions, together with feelings of helplessness. Health seemed poorer and the future was not as bright as it was for the younger widows. The results of this study, rather than seeing grief alone as the cause of their difficulties, pointed out that older women were plagued by other problems common among the elderly.

Interestingly, several of the older widowers, while they struggled with some of the same variables that caused problems among the older women, were able to move on with their lives more quickly. Within a year after their wives died, a number of the men had remarried. While marital satisfaction was not a variable examined in this study, one can surmise that loneliness was reduced in many cases. In one case, the husband made it clear that he wanted a quick replacement. This marriage unfortunately did not work out as well as it did for those widowers who waited a year or more before remarriage. It seems, however, that friends are more helpful in seeking out a possible companion for a widower than they are for widows.

Yet a number of researchers have determined that widowers have many more problems than do widows (Helsing, Comstock, and Szklo, 1981; Stroebe and Stroebe, 1983). Social support, where wives had always managed the social calendar, as well as the nurturing provided by these wives, had diminished. When these resources are no longer available, widowers often isolate themselves. In one case a widower living in a town not too far from his grown daughter became a recluse after his wife died, going out only to shop. He made it clear that he didn't need anything and wanted to be alone for a period. His daughter, very concerned by this behavior, talked to his neighbors each day to see how he was managing. When they didn't see him coming out on the front porch for the daily newspaper, they called him to see if he was all right. He told them that he was getting along fine. When asked if he would like them to bring him some fresh doughnuts, he agreed but told them to leave them on the front porch. This continued for about a week until one day he did not take the doughnuts in. Concerned, they called his daughter, who came immediately. They found him dead from an overdose of sleeping medication. He left a short note to his daughter telling her how sorry he was but that he couldn't face life alone without his lifelong partner.

An additional problem for older bereaved spouses is their frequent lack of skill in dealing with the problems of everyday living. Widowers lacked the ability to cook, shop, and clean the house, while widows felt a deficiency in making home repairs, and managing legal or financial affairs. These tasks were a source of frustration; however, when the bereaved learned to perform a certain task, they immediately felt better about themselves (Lund, Caserta, and Dimond, 1993). The authors found that, while older men and women differed in their lack of specific skills of daily living, they still were quite similar in their emotional, psychological, social, and health adjustments.

Lund and his group observed that, although support from others is extremely important, personal resources unique to each individual are what make the biggest difference in bereavement outcome. By personal resources Lund et al. referred to the ability to take control of one's life during the major adjustment following the loss of a spouse. Adjustment requires motivation, pride, flexibility, and, of course, some help from others. But all this requires time, because most of the problems of single living emerge slowly and appear without too much forewarning. In other words, life must be accepted and dealt with as each adjustment or resolution occurs. This is not a passive acceptance but one in which the grieving person sets about supplying answers to the problems at hand. In so doing the individual generates a degree of personal competence in managing the tasks of everyday living. The authors felt that this leads to positive self-esteem, which will result in a favorable bereavement outcome.

Gender differences across the life span do appear to exist in bereavement. These differences gradually shift as one moves from childhood to old age. The cultivation that comes from the layering of experiences where loss was the centerpiece teaches each person the importance of valuing moments, relationships, family. We begin life by being attached to one person, then two, and gradually a wide array of familiar and important people, animals, and things. Each creates a web of connections with friends and family members that grows steadily as one creates larger and more inclusive circles. Yet each connection must eventually be broken, separation suffered and dealt with. Grief, it seems, is no different at one level of life or another. Pain is still felt. With the accumulation of losses, while one doesn't get better at dealing with the pain, despite the gender, one suffers nevertheless in ways that are traditionally and culturally gender-biased.

---

*Catherine M. Sanders, PhD, is a psychologist in general practice and the director of The Center for the Study of Separation and Loss.*

# ELEVEN

# Revisiting Masculine Grief

*Terry L. Martin and Kenneth J. Doka*

M en and women are different. Exactly how and why has fueled debates among scholars, discussions on television talk shows, and arguments between couples. Lost in the controversy surrounding sex differences are sex similarities—men and women are probably more alike than they are different. Yet gender is often cited as the obvious explanation for observed differences between men and women who have lost a significant other.

Value judgments about perceived differences between male and female grievers have resulted in widely accepted assumptions about gender differences in bereavement. In particular, men are usually seen as "inexpressive," and therefore as having more difficulty responding and adapting to loss. Thus, the twin assumptions—that differences in grieving are determined by gender, and that women grieve more effectively than men do—influence programs and interventions for the bereaved. The *masculine grief* hypothesis directly challenges the aforementioned assumptions and offers an alternative to traditional interventions.

The theory of masculine grief originated from a desire to validate men's grief. When a female colleague told us that she, too, grieved in the way we had defined as *male* we were confronted with the reality that some women may grieve as most men do. Conversely, we reasoned, some men must grieve in a like manner to most women.

Since spousal loss has been the most intensively studied of all loss experiences—and more than 11 million of the 13.7 million widowed people in the United States are widows—the pattern of grieving associated with women has dominated the bereavement literature as the "norm." In this pattern, feelings are intense, overt, and shared with others. We refer to this predominate pattern as *conventional* or *feminine*.

## The Nature of Grief

We define grief as a form of psychic energy. This energy results from the tension created by the individual's strong desire to (a) maintain their assumptive world (Rando, 1993) as it was before their loss, (b) accommodate themselves to a newly emerging reality resulting from their loss, and (c) incorporate this new reality into their assumptive world. Grief energy is converted into the affective, cognitive, physical, and spiritual domains or modalities of human experience. Despite distinguishing each domain as a separate entity, in reality all of the domains are interrelated. For instance, the spiritual domain can consist of thoughts and beliefs (cognitive) as well as powerful feelings (affective). Likewise, contemporary views of the relationship between mind and body highlight the complementary nature of these various domains. How much energy is converted into the various domains varies among individuals and situations.

The expression or outer manifestation of the inner grief experience can be quite varied. Crying, sleep disturbances, loss of appetite, or searching behaviors are common expressions of grief. Other observable behaviors might include restless overactivity, social withdrawal, or a loss of interest in activities that the griever previously enjoyed.

The modalities of experience that are most useful in discriminating between masculine and conventional grief are the affective and cognitive. These modalities might best be viewed as lying along a continuum. Thus, the conventional griever invests more energy toward the affective end of the continuum, while masculine grievers allocate more energy towards the cognitive. For the conventional griever, the inner experience of grief consists primarily of profoundly painful feelings. These grievers tend to spontaneously express their painful feelings through crying. The conventional griever responds favorably to traditional, affect-intensive forms of intervention, such as the open sharing of feelings and group support. Conversely, masculine grievers convert most of their grief energy into the cognitive domain. Goal-oriented activity is usually the behavioral expression of the masculine grief experience.

The following cases are illustrative of the differences between conventional and masculine grievers. Susan was overwhelmed by unremitting, agonizing feelings when her fiancé was killed in an industrial accident. She cried openly and often. As the weeks went by, Susan found solace in confiding her feelings of loneliness, anxiety, and despair to a sympathetic and understanding neighbor. After suffering a panic attack, Susan entered counseling. Using the client-centered approach pioneered by Carl Rogers (1951), the counselor facilitated Susan's efforts to purge herself of her painful feelings by continually eliciting Susan's memories of her fiancé and supporting her in her need to cry. The counselor also referred Susan to a support group for survivors of traumatic losses. By the second anniversary of her fiancé's death, Susan felt back in control of her feelings and her life.

Rebecca's husband also died accidentally; he was electrocuted while helping his best friend install a satellite dish. Although she initially was shocked and overwhelmed by his death, Rebecca did not experience chronic agonizing or incapacitating feelings, nor did she have any particular desire to share her grief with anyone else. She dedicated herself to parenting her two young sons and comforting her husband's best friend. She ultimately, and symbolically, held the ladder for the friend as he completed installation of the satellite dish. At first, Rebecca's friends and family were concerned that she was "bottling up" her grief and would eventually "crash." Two years after the death, she had not crashed; instead, she remarried and eventually gave birth to twin girls.

Both Susan and Rebecca described their relationships to the deceased men as strong and affectionate. Though their experiences and expressions of grief were significantly different, they both adapted successfully to their losses.

## Mourning As Adaptation

*Mourning* often is defined in two distinct ways among death-related professionals. It is both seen as the culturally-influenced expression of grief, as well as an intrapsychic process which (a) enables the bereaved to relinquish their emotional bonds to the deceased, and (b) promotes healing by helping the bereaved to learn how to live in a world without their loved one.

We prefer to use the term *adaptation* (Silverman, 1986) to describe how an individual adjusts both internally and externally to a perceived loss. Initially, the bereaved attempts to adapt to the immediate and short-term demands of grief as it is experienced and expressed. In the long run, adaptation refers to the ongoing work of redistributing and channeling the energy created by the loss. Adaptation requires the individual to reformulate their definitions of who they are, what they have lost, and what constitutes their assumptive world.

How quickly and how well an individual adapts to the death of a significant other primarily depends upon the adaptive strategies chosen by the bereaved. These strategies enable the griever to influence both their inner experience of grief and their outer expressions of grief. Some strategies are effective for both conventional as well as masculine grievers. One such strategy involves "shelving" feelings in order to fulfill immediate responsibilities and later "dosing" (Shuchter and Zisook, 1993) those feelings at a more appropriate time and place. For example, grievers often encounter the immediate demands of making funeral or memorial arrangements. Those who are fortunate will be able to divert their pain long enough to complete the task at hand. Other strategies will be discussed later which seem particularly effective for either conventional or masculine grievers.

## Masculine Pattern of Grief

How does masculine grief differ from conventional grief?

### MODERATED FEELINGS

First, feelings seem to be muted or moderated in masculine grievers. This may indicate that masculine grievers view their losses differently from conventional grievers. For instance, masculine grievers might believe that they can control the outcome of the loss experience, that they will eventually master this crisis. Masculine grievers also value self-control; mastering thoughts, feelings, and behaviors are tasks familiar to the masculine griever. Finally, masculine grievers may be limited in their ability to experience extreme feelings, that is, they may be more oriented toward rational thinking and behavior. What may appear to be the deliberate blunting or suppression of feelings, may, in fact, result from the masculine griever's feelings simply being less intense.

We are not saying that masculine grievers do not have feelings about their losses; they do. Common feelings experienced by conventional grievers such as sadness, anxiety, and loneliness are often shared by masculine grievers, albeit at lower levels of intensity. Some masculine grievers find anger to be the most readily available feeling. Anger may be easier to express than other feelings. Other masculine grievers may use humor. The key point here is that masculine grievers can experience feelings without outwardly seeming to do so.

## FOCUS ON THINKING

Most masculine grievers deal cognitively with grief. Conceivably, this might indicate that masculine grievers convert most of the grief energy into thoughts rather than into feelings. Perhaps masculine grievers are more "attuned" to their thoughts rather than to affective cues. By contrast, conventional grievers are often first overwhelmed by powerful feelings, then seek an explanation for those feelings. Masculine grievers associate feelings with specific thoughts. Thus, they may be more adept than conventional grievers at managing uncomfortable feelings by using various cognitive techniques, including dosing and distraction. Although attempts at avoiding negative feelings have traditionally been seen as a recipe for emotional disaster, the importance of confronting feelings as a prerequisite for adjusting to loss has recently been challenged (Wortman and Silver, 1993).

The critical role played by cognitive processes among masculine grievers might also mean that these grievers possess a different worldview, one that emboldens them with a sense of control and a belief that they can master this crisis. Thus, for the masculine griever, losing a loved one, though painful, represents a challenge rather than a threat ("I can survive this," rather than, "I can't deal with this, now or ever"). To wit, the energized cognitive domain of the masculine griever frequently is manifested in goal-oriented behavior rather than expression of strong feelings.

## PROBLEM-FOCUSED ACTIVITY

When masculine grievers respond behaviorally to a loss, it usually involves immersion in some form of activity. For example, they may take legal or physical action in response to the loss. One man organized a class action lawsuit following the death of his 7-year-old daughter (and injury to several other children) while playing on a piece of defective playground equipment. "I didn't waste time crying for [her]," he said. "They took [my daughter] from me and I needed to make them pay." This man harnessed the energy from his rage and channeled it into action. Masculine grievers may also take active roles in the funeral and other related rituals. One poignant example involved a 14-year-old boy who, following the death of his father, adamantly opposed his mother's attempts to place his father's cremains in a purchased container. Instead, he spent several evenings at a friend's house constructing his own container of wood. Later, the boy and his mother placed his father's cremains in the container he had created.

Many of these problem-solving activities occur in solitude, while some involve the company of others. Another man, in response to his wife's demands, sought counseling after the drowning death of his 22-year-old son. He reported that his wife was upset with him because he had not wept since his son's funeral. She wanted them to share their loss and their grief with each other, activities he sought to avoid. The father became concerned that perhaps he was "blocking" his feelings and would have a "breakdown" unless he talked about his son and "got in touch" with his pain. Further discussion revealed that the man met weekly with a group of four other men to restore historic automobiles. Although his son was not discussed, he said, "I felt like the other guys understood me; this was the one time I really felt okay." For this man, being in the company of others who respected his need not to discuss his loss was comforting. He was relieved to discover that, for him, pursuing his hobby with his friends was an effective strategy.

### DESIRE FOR SOLITUDE

Masculine grievers tend to be reluctant to share their grief, especially in organized support groups. This aversion to seeking help may emerge from their desire to master their feelings, as illustrated by the following case. When a man's wife died after a long illness, the hospice bereavement worker called frequently to invite him to groups or to see whether he wanted counseling. He attended a group once, hoping to discuss the practical concerns he had in raising his two adolescent children. However, every time he tried to talk about his children, the group leader would interrupt and ask, "What about your feelings?" The man, quite frankly, was uncomfortable with the question. There were times (rare, to be sure) when feelings threatened to overwhelm him. Alone in his car he would put on a tape with "their" song, and he would shed a few tears. But most of the time he was focused on holding his job and raising his kids. In a similar case, a widow revealed how uncomfortable she felt with the intense feelings shared by members of a bereavement support group and the not-so-subtle pressure to share her own feelings. She did not return to the group. Instead, she began making weekly pilgrimages to her husband's grave. There, she found comfort in privately discussing the week's events with him.

## Strategies for Adapting to Loss

It is important to remember that the griever's choice of adaptive strategies may be influenced by temperament, particularly by important traits such as introversion/extroversion. Thus, shy conventional grievers may do best choosing mediums other than support groups for expressing their feelings. Likewise, gregarious masculine grievers might prefer the company of others, even though they don't discuss their feelings. Earlier, it was suggested that dosing painful feelings is an effective strategy for both conventional and masculine grievers. However, conventional grievers might be advised to use this technique with care—it should not be allowed to become a permanent way to avoid feelings that need expression. Other adaptive strategies useful to both kinds of grievers are bibliotherapy (Doka, 1990) or keeping a journal, as well as identifying key individuals who might supply support and/or companionship. Below, we have listed effective adaptive strategies for conventional and masculine grievers.

## Effective Adaptive Strategies for Conventional Grievers

- Joining support groups

- Identifying others in their environment as sources of support and understanding

- Allowing time for fully experiencing inner pain

- Openly expressing feelings

- Temporarily withdrawing from, or limiting, obligations that might interfere with their ability to experience and express their feelings

- Choosing other mediums for the expression of feelings (e.g., keeping a journal, bibliotherapy)

## Effective Adaptive Strategies for Masculine Grievers

- Shelving thoughts and feelings in order to meet obligations, then dosing them when it is appropriate

- Choosing active means of expressing grief (e.g., physical exercise, competitive sports, hobbies, creating a memorial)

- Using humor or other ways of expressing feelings (but managing anger and aggression)

- Seeking companionship (in lieu of support)

- Using solitude as a way of reflection, adaptation

- Bibliotherapy, maintaining a journal

The key point is that grievers choose an adaptive strategy that works for them, not for others.

## Interventions with Masculine Grievers

The masculine pattern of grieving has implications for planned interventions. First, if active interventions such as counseling are indicated, the counselor should carefully assess the effectiveness of the griever's adaptive strategies. It is of central importance that the counselor not prematurely identify a griever as masculine, when, in fact, that particular griever may be a conventional griever for whom the absence of any affective distress might be a powerful predictor of future complications.

Counselors can choose models of counseling and interventions compatible with the masculine griever. In particular, cognitive-behavioral approaches utilize techniques compatible with the masculine style of grieving, including cognitive reframing, mood monitoring, increasing pleasant events, and identifying and challenging dysfunctional thoughts. Similarly, current tasks models of loss (Worden, 1991) encourage problem solving, a task favored by the masculine griever.

When dealing with feelings, counselors and other helpers should find ways to allow affective expression in ways compatible with the griever's style, remembering that diminished feelings are a key element in the masculine pattern of grieving. For example, masculine grievers may find it more comfortable to discuss *reactions* rather than *feelings*. In fact, "pushing buttons" to elicit feelings should be used sparingly, if at all.

Counselors can encourage physical activity as an effective form of adaptation. Exercise, for example, is often used as an outlet for anger and aggression. Although running is a solitary activity suitable for some, others may choose weight lifting, or some organized sport. The playing field, bowling alley, golf course, or gym may provide opportunities for companionship as well as support.

Finally, hospices should consider tailoring bereavement support programs to meet the needs of masculine grievers. While the traditional support group may be unsuitable for many masculine grievers, other group activities may fill an important need. We would suggest offering groups organized around social activities and/or outings, fund-raising teams, structured discussion groups, and educational presentations. Additionally, many masculine grievers may wish to volunteer. Hospices might consider actively recruiting masculine grievers to provide services appropriate to their talents and capabilities—regardless of how long it has been since the death. Hospice personnel should recognize and respect the masculine pattern of grieving as genuine, and not an artifact of the "John Wayne" syndrome.

*Terry L. Martin, PhD, is Professor of Psychology at Hood College. He maintains a private practice specializing in grief counseling.*

*Kenneth J. Doka, PhD, is a Professor of Gerontology at the College of New Rochelle. Dr. Doka is the associate editor of* Omega, *and editor of* Journeys, *Hospice Foundation of America's newsletter for the bereaved.*

# TWELVE

# Developmental Perspectives on Grief and Mourning

*Charles A. Corr*

Developmental perspectives have only recently attracted much critical attention in relation to grief and mourning. This is somewhat surprising, since taking account of developmental perspectives is essential to a comprehensive understanding of bereavement. In fact, scholars, researchers, and clinical practitioners have for some time been impressed with the importance of understanding human beings and their behaviors from the standpoint of human development. Originally applied with greatest intensity to childhood, and later to old age, developmental perspectives have shown themselves to have value across the entire human life span. Hence, sensitivity to lifespan human development should be a part of any attempt to understand bereavement, grief, and mourning. The argument begins with a brief explanation of what it means to speak of a developmental perspective. Thereafter, developmental perspectives on grief and mourning are examined according to four principal segments of the human life span: childhood, adolescence, adulthood, and old age. The analysis of each of these four principal segments is organized around two central questions: (1) What are central developmental issues in each portion of the human life span? and (2) What are distinctive features of grief and mourning in each portion of the human life span? Each of these four segments can be read on its own, or all of them can be taken together (in any order) to obtain a broader developmental picture of grief and mourning.

## What is a Developmental Perspective?

The central idea behind all developmental perspectives is the realization that all human beings face certain more or less predictable tasks at various points in the course of their lifelong development. Perhaps the best known theoretical conceptualization of these normative tasks was offered by Erik Erikson (1963, 1968), who described human development in terms of three principal factors: eight developmental eras within the human life span; a predominant psychosocial challenge or conflict which serves to define the character of each developmental era; and a "leading virtue" in the form of a strength or quality of ego functioning which results from successful coping with the psychosocial challenge or conflict in each developmental era.

According to Erikson, there are eight developmental eras in the human life span: infancy, toddlerhood, early childhood, middle childhood, adolescence, young adulthood, middle adulthood, and old age. Each of these is a developmental era, that is a period or stage in human maturation which is set off from other developmental eras by its distinctive challenges or tasks.

Since human development may proceed at a swifter or slower pace in some individuals as compared to others, developmental eras are not strictly correlated with chronological age. Erikson himself did suggest some general comparisons between developmental eras and chronological age. But those who wish to understand human development in general or specific individuals in particular should always be cautious about applying developmental theory too rigidly or binding it too closely to chronological age. An appreciation of the difference between developmental and chronological perspectives is the first caution to keep in mind throughout this chapter.

Normative tasks that dominate and define each era in the human life span are identified in the sections that follow, along with the leading virtue or strength of ego functioning that individuals carry forward with them when they are successful in addressing an era's developmental tasks. But first it may be helpful to take note of three additional cautions regarding this work: (1) developmental perspectives are not equally well-formulated in all eras of the human life span—the current state of knowledge is simply more sensitive and more nuanced in some developmental eras than in others; (2) similarly, developmental perspectives are not equally well-developed for all subjects that relate to human life and behavior; and (3) changes in society, culture, and human life patterns are continually impacting both developmental perspectives and research in specific subject areas.

These three cautions can be illustrated in the following examples: (1) Development in the various eras of childhood has been more fully studied than development in young and middle adulthood; (2) only in the last 10-15 years has a reliable body of knowledge emerged in the field of adolescent bereavement, while a parallel body of knowledge for childhood bereavement is just now in development; and (3) the recent "graying of America" has led to a need for much better understandings of both development and bereavement in the *young-old*, the *old-old*, and the *very-old* (as these distinctions have emerged in the study of individuals who are 65 years of age and older).

One implication of these cautions is that it is not possible at the moment to set forth a developmental account of grief and mourning that is distinctive for each of Erikson's eight eras in the human life span. However, a review of the current state of knowledge on the subject of grief and mourning can be provided with regard to the previously noted four broad developmental periods: childhood, adolescence, adulthood, and old age.

# Childhood

## CENTRAL DEVELOPMENTAL ISSUES IN CHILDHOOD

In terms of developmental challenges, infants face the fundamental issue of establishing basic trust or mistrust. Much depends upon whether or not their proximate care providers and the world around them can and do satisfy their primary needs. Are they fed, cleaned, sheltered from the elements, and the like in ways that are both satisfactory and consistent? If so, Erikson believes that infants can develop a basic trust and the virtue of hope that may stay with them throughout the remainder of their lives. If not, Erikson believes that this developmental challenge, like any other normative task which is not fully accomplished in human development, will result in a sense of mistrust and will remain in whole or in part a task that needs to be addressed again in subsequent developmental eras.

For toddlers, the principal developmental issue to be faced is one of autonomy versus shame and doubt. As the developing child is liberated from the many close restrictions of infancy, he or she acts to become a self-governing agent, a law unto himself or herself. The "terrible twos," a period in which everything is "MINE!" (according to the child) and "NO!" is the response to all adult directives, is an era in which the young child is defining boundaries, both by assertion and by rebuke. A toddler who is successful in confronting this issue achieves the virtue of will or self-control; a toddler who is unsuccessful in meeting this challenge is likely to experience doubt as to the appropriateness of his or her actions and shame as to their consequences.

In early childhood, children typically become more focused in their behavior. Classically, these are the preschool years (although there may be some variation for children in various early childhood education programs), in which play becomes more complicated and is, indeed, the real "work" of the child. Successful development in this era meets the challenge of initiative versus guilt and develops the virtue of purpose or direction.

In middle childhood, which in our society usually includes the elementary school years, the developing child faces the issue of industry versus inferiority. Can abilities and energies be harnessed to increasingly complicated projects at school and at home in ways that lead to the virtue of competency? Or will the child feel inferior either in terms of personal beliefs about what he or she can achieve, or in terms of comparisons with peers?

## DISTINCTIVE FEATURES OF GRIEF AND MOURNING IN CHILDHOOD

At one time, scholars debated whether or not children were able to grieve after a death. Since it is perfectly obvious that most children do react to (i.e., grieve) death-related losses, the claim that they were not able to grieve must have been founded on erroneous presuppositions. Specifically, these included a faulty conception of children's understandings of death, a failure to distinguish between grief and mourning, and a lack of adequate models for childhood mourning. These three points guide the following discussion.

The concept of death is a complicated one. It appears to embrace a number of relatively sophisticated subconcepts. It may be that many children, especially those whose cognitive development is not far advanced, have not yet mastered the concept of death. Nevertheless, children do strive to understand what it means when a death occurs that is significant to their lives. That striving is the essential point to note.

Many bereaved children ask questions like: "Did I cause it?" "Is it going to happen to me?" "Who is going to take care of me?" These efforts to make sense out of the experience of death should not be dismissed lightly. To appreciate the meaning of these efforts and to gain insight into children's understandings of death, adults need to attend to the whole of an individual child's development (not just its cognitive components), and to that child's life experiences, individual personality, efforts to communicate or express grief, and ways of seeking support.

Children may not always think of death exactly as adults do; that does not mean that such children have no concept of death. They may have their own understanding(s) of death, some of which are perhaps not yet differentiated or not fully distinguished from other concepts such as travel or sleep. Nevertheless, most children from infancy on recognize and respond to the absence of the deceased and to their separation from that person.

Children may not express grief as openly or as consistently as most adults. The grief of children may be longer in duration and more intermittent in character than that of many adults. Grief in childhood may also be influenced by the ability or inability of a particular child to establish continuing bonds with the deceased person. And grief may have an impact on a child's development when it threatens the achievement of normative tasks in any one of the four eras in childhood.

Understanding childhood mourning is more difficult, in part due to the inapplicability of theoretical models arising from adult bereavement. Some theorists have posited that children were not capable of mourning until they had resolved prototypical challenges associated with separation from the opposite-sex parent that are assumed to define the onset of adolescence. But mourning can be understood in a simpler way as a process of trying to cope with stress. In this way, *grief* identifies an individual's response to loss, while *mourning* designates what that person does to try to cope both with the loss and with his or her grief reactions. From this point of view, children need not be excluded from the class of beings who make efforts to manage stress in their lives.

One way to think of mourning in childhood is to think of four tasks for grieving children: to understand and try to make sense out of what has happened; to express emotional and other responses to the loss; to commemorate the loss through some formal or informal remembrance; and to learn how to go on with living and loving. This is a modest but helpful account of cognitive, affective, behavioral, and valuational tasks. It is useful in guiding adults who seek to help bereaved children and can serve until a more adequate model of children's mourning is developed and put forth.

# Adolescence

## CENTRAL DEVELOPMENTAL ISSUES IN ADOLESCENCE

Erikson described adolescence as a developmental era extending from puberty to the early 20s in which the normative issue is one of establishing a sense of personal identity versus role confusion. In other words, the challenge is to navigate the changes involved in moving from being solely or mainly the child of others to being or becoming a person in one's own right. Successful maturation enables the adolescent to emerge from this era as a young adult with a more or less stable sense of identity and the virtue of fidelity, which can anchor relationships to self and others throughout his or her life.

Adolescence is a particularly good era in the human life span in which to illustrate how developmental theory has been enhanced since Erikson's original work. Following the work of Blos (1979) and others, it is now common to speak of three developmental sub-periods in adolescence: (1) early adolescence, in which the principal developmental task is decreased identification with or emotional separation from parents; (2) middle adolescence (or "adolescence proper"), in which the principal task is the development of a sense of competence, mastery, and control achieved through a "second individuation" process of reorganizing values internalized from parents; and (3) late adolescence, in which the principal developmental task is the formation of a stable character, making possible intimacy and commitment.

## DISTINCTIVE FEATURES OF GRIEF AND MOURNING IN ADOLESCENCE

The leading causes of death for adolescents in our society are accidents, homicide, and suicide. Each of these is a result of human action. In fact, adolescence is the only era in the human life span in which a natural cause does not appear among the three leading causes of death. Thus, adolescents who experience the death of a peer are very likely to encounter a sudden, unexpected, and traumatic death. Adolescents may also experience the deaths of significant individuals who are older or younger than themselves, including a family member or other adult, a sibling or friend, a pet, a celebrity or cultural hero with whom they identify, or even, in some cases, their own child.

There are, of course, differences related to gender, race, and other important variables that are significant in adolescent encounters with death. But even without drawing out such differences here, it is not hard to appreciate developmental difficulties that might be associated with any of the following scenarios of adolescent bereavement: (1) an early adolescent who is striving to achieve emotional emancipation from parents might experience complications in those efforts if a parent should suddenly die; (2) a middle adolescent who is seeking to achieve a sense of autonomy in the form of competency, mastery, and control might experience a substantial threat to newfound independence if a peer should die, particularly if that death were sudden, traumatic, and perhaps violent; and (3) a late adolescent who is working to reestablish intimacy and commitment with those who are significant in his or her life might experience frustration in that effort when the death of a person of a younger generation—a younger sibling, friend, or the adolescent's own child—thwarts their hope of interpersonal closeness.

The body of knowledge currently available on adolescent bereavement (Corr and Balk, 1996) suggests that adolescents are able to understand the concept of death and its implications, but may not have appreciated its personal significance until death intrudes directly on their lives. Adolescents all too often maintain a personal fable of invulnerability and immortality until such time as it is shaken, especially by the death of a person of their own age and/or similar circumstances. With respect to coping with death and grief, adolescents frequently do not have extensive experience with the demands of integrating those realities into their ongoing lives.

Researchers who have studied adolescent bereavement have focused on three key variables: self-concept, depression, and age. For the first two of these variables, it appears that low self-concept and preexisting depression may foreshadow difficulties in adolescent bereavement. With regard to age, older bereaved adolescents have been reported to experience more psychological distress and to be more likely to talk with friends, while younger bereaved adolescents experienced more physiological distress and were less likely to talk with friends. This seems to indicate that greater developmental maturity is associated with an ability to seek out social support. As a result, older bereaved adolescents experience increased, but relatively transient, psychological distress.

Perhaps the most important point about bereaved adolescents in general is their resilience in the aftermath of a significant loss. Bereavement during adolescence does not in and of itself predispose one to ongoing psychological difficulties. In fact, it may actually help many adolescents to become more emotionally and interpersonally mature, even if those gains are purchased at high cost, in the sense that bereaved adolescents learn that bad things can happen in life, that there are ways to cope with such encounters, and that persons should be valued more than they sometimes are while they are alive. Nevertheless, bereavement may be problematic for vulnerable adolescents by reinforcing conditions they bring to their experience that predispose them to difficulty.

Adolescent grief manifests itself in familiar ways, such as confusion, crying, feelings of emptiness and/or loneliness, disturbances in patterns of sleep and eating, and exhaustion. Still, expressions of grief may be actively suppressed or limited to brief outbursts because adolescents perceive their grief as unique and incomprehensible, may fear loss of emotional control, and often are greatly concerned as to how they will be perceived by others.

Grieving adolescents may be helped by their own personal belief systems, activities that reduce stress, support from parents, other relatives, friends, or professionals, or peer support groups which normalize grief reactions. Note, however, that adolescent bereavement may represent a "double crisis" because the situational tasks of mourning and the normative developmental tasks of adolescence are parallel in many ways. Compare bereavement tasks involving protest/searching, disorganization, and reorganization with accounts of developmental tasks in adolescence as working to establish emotional separation, achieving competency or mastery, and developing intimacy.

Even without additional complications such as those associated with trauma or suicide, the "double crisis" aspects of bereavement in adolescence may be especially challenging for those who typically cope with stress by concentrating on managing one crisis at a time. Yet helpers can be optimistic about anticipated outcomes for most bereaved adolescents, even as they should be sensitive to the complexities of the work involved in all adolescent bereavement and the special challenges faced by some bereaved adolescents.

# Adulthood

## CENTRAL DEVELOPMENTAL ISSUES IN ADULTHOOD

For young adults the principal developmental issue is one of achieving intimacy versus isolation. There are, of course, many forms of intimacy for young adults, but Erikson believed the virtue that defines each is affiliation or love. Erikson thought the young adult lacking intimacy would experience a degree of psychological isolation, perhaps even during the remainder of his or her life.

Middle adulthood is focused on the developmental issue of generativity versus stagnation and self-absorption. This is the era in which one has previously established and pursued one's adult goals— for example, in vocational, familial, or other terms—and now must determine whether or not there is more to achieve. Can one develop the virtues of production and care? Even though many goals have already been accomplished, can one continue to go forward either in familiar ways or perhaps in new ways, or is the present situation essentially all there is and all there will be?

Levinson (1978, 1990) argued that for both men and women there are "seasons" in adult life in the form of an alternating sequence of structure-building and structure-maintaining periods. This seasonal portrait of adult development includes boundary and internal transition periods, together with a midlife transition between young and middle adulthood. For Levinson, the main seasons of young adulthood are concerned with "forming a dream" and "settling down," while those of middle adulthood are concerned with resolving four principal polarities in the form of tensions between young/old, destruction/creation, masculine/feminine, and attachment/separateness.

## DISTINCTIVE FEATURES OF GRIEF AND MOURNING IN ADULTHOOD

In any given year, adults account for approximately one quarter of all deaths in the United States. For all segments of the adult population, both numbers of deaths and death rates rise rapidly during the years of American adulthood. Leading causes of death among young adults are HIV-related illness and accidents, followed by cancer, heart disease, and suicide. Generally, human-induced deaths are more prominent during the early years of young adulthood, while degenerative diseases rise in relative importance during the later years of this era. Thereafter, cancer and heart disease account for over 60 percent of all deaths during middle adulthood.

Clearly, changes in mortality patterns present situational threats to the normative patterns of adult development. The prominence in the early adult years of deaths associated with HIV infection, accidents, suicide, and homicide suggests potential intrusions on the developmental tasks of establishing one's dream and achieving interpersonal intimacy. Even when one dismisses these threats as involving causes of deaths which might be avoided in various ways, the growing dominance of degenerative diseases throughout young adulthood and especially in middle adulthood reminds maturing adults that internal and environmental factors associated with most degenerative diseases are not wholly subject to individual control. Middle adults are also likely to face a newly personalized sense of mortality as they encounter the deaths of peers, parents, and spouses, often for the first time in the life cycle and especially as a result of natural causes.

Adults and the elderly are the developmental groups to which most research on grief and mourning has been directed. As a result, their experiences have been the basis for most of the theoretical formulations in the field of bereavement. This work highlights the very broad range of grief reactions that adults may experience as part of their encounter with the death of a significant other. These components of adult grief may take the form of feelings and emotions, physical sensations, cognitions, behaviors, social difficulties, and spiritual searching. How grief will be experienced is very much an individualized phenomenon. But for most adults, grief reactions will be healthy, normal, and appropriate responses to loss. Accordingly, this chapter speaks of signs or manifestations of grief rather than "symptoms," as if grief were an indicator of disease.

As a general rule, adults are usually impacted most powerfully by the death of a child, a spouse, or a parent—in that order. This is consistent with the sentiment that "the death of my parent is the death of my past; the death of my spouse is the death of my present; the death of my child is the death of my future." That is, the nature of an adult's bereavement will depend primarily upon the meaning of the relationship with the deceased individual and the significance of the losses which that death entails. The challenge facing the bereaved adult will be one of building a life, of establishing new patterns without the deceased.

The work of coping with loss and grief, along with building a new life, is that of mourning. Whatever solace or comfort is to be achieved in the aftermath of an important death will depend upon the mourner's ability to integrate his or her experiences into some form of productive ongoing living. Each death and bereavement has its own particular characteristics, but scholars and researchers have sought to throw light upon adult mourning through three main types of theoretical frameworks.

One group of theoreticians has suggested a series of phases in adult mourning. The best-known example of this work (Bowlby, 1961, 1973-1982; Parkes, 1970, 1987) suggests a pattern of four phases: shock and numbness, yearning and searching, disorganization and despair, and reorganization. This is essentially a kind of psychic closing or defense against the initial impact of loss followed by phases that are, in turn, oriented to past, present, and future. Plainly, there is no rigid sequencing in these phases; any one of them may be experienced and reexperienced at various points in bereavement. They are, in fact, broad generalizations of common experiences in adult mourning.

A second way of describing adult mourning (Worden, 1991) speaks of tasks: accepting the reality of the loss, working through to the pain of grief, adjusting to an environment in which the deceased is missing, and restructuring the relationship with the deceased and moving on with living. This model stresses the active dimensions of mourning and proactive ways in which adults can influence their experiences of bereavement.

A third way of depicting adult mourning is to describe it in terms of processes. This is similar in some ways to task-based models, although processes may have an advantage in focusing on mourning dynamics rather than task outcomes. One process-based theory of adult mourning (Rando, 1993) points to six "R" processes: recognize the loss, react to the separation, recollect and reexperience the deceased and the relationship, relinquish old attachments to the deceased and the old assumptive world, readjust to move adaptively into the new world without forgetting the old, and reinvest. Another process-based theory of adult mourning (Stroebe and Schut, 1995) emphasizes an oscillation between loss-oriented processes which are involved in coping with loss and restoration-oriented processes which are concerned primarily with reestablishing a personal and social equilibrium or balance in ongoing living.

One central feature of all of these descriptions of adult bereavement is their caution in depicting fixed timeframes for mourning. Overly facile accounts of recovery, completion, and resolution are far too simple for the complexities of adult bereavement experiences. Insofar as the intensity and duration of active grieving does lessen for many bereaved adults over time, there is a sense that the mourner has moved forward in a process of realization. But there is another sense in which mourning is never finished. Here the experience of continuing bonds and a newly defined ongoing relationship with the deceased are part of a lifelong achievement of enriched remembrance.

# Old Age

## CENTRAL DEVELOPMENTAL ISSUES IN OLD AGE

In the era of the elderly which Erikson called "maturity" and others have called "old age," the principal developmental issue is that of establishing ego integrity versus despair. By "ego integrity" Erikson seems to have meant a sense of wholeness and completion, a conviction that the various pieces of one's life fit together and that the whole has been meaningful. Ego integrity is sought through a process of introspection, self-reflection, and reminiscence—a review of one's life in which the elderly person brings past experiences to consciousness, assesses or reinterprets them, and seeks to integrate them in a coherent and satisfying narrative.

Without being able to come to terms with one's past and successfully resolve earlier developmental tasks, Erikson believed that in old age one would feel disgust and despair because one would not be satisfied with what one has done with one's life and would not feel that sufficient time or energy remain to alter directions and compensate for the ways in which one has lived. With a sense of balance and harmony that ego integrity entails, it is thought that the elderly person achieves the virtue of wisdom: old conflicts are resolved and a new sense of meaning is achieved both as an accounting to oneself of one's past life and as a preparation for death.

Customarily, the elderly have been thought of as those individuals who are 65 years of age or older. As average life expectancy has increased, this is now the fastest-growing segment of the American population. Moreover, healthier lifestyles, better healthcare, and overall improvements in wellness have resulted in great diversity among contemporary elders. That has led to a perceived need to distinguish between the *young-old* (those 65 to 74 years of age), the *old-old* (those 75 to 84 years of age), and the *very-old* (those 85 years of age and older). Together with other refinements in research and scholarly thinking, distinctions like these are likely in the future to lead to a more nuanced developmental portrait of the elderly.

## DISTINCTIVE FEATURES OF GRIEF AND MOURNING IN OLD AGE

Elders, who constitute approximately 13 percent of the total population of the United States, currently experience approximately three quarters of all deaths each year in our society. Both numbers of deaths and death rates rise rapidly throughout this era. All five leading causes of death among the elderly are degenerative diseases: diseases of the heart, cancer, cerebrovascular diseases, chronic obstructive pulmonary diseases, and pneumonia and influenza.

There is widespread agreement in the literature that elders are significantly less fearful of death than younger persons. For elders who hold such attitudes, death may be a frequent topic of conversation and may be perceived as less threatening than debility, isolation, or dependence. Elders may have come to hold such attitudes because many of them have lived long, full lives, most have been conditioned to accept death as part of life through their experiences of the deaths of others, and some have come to view their lives as having less value than the lives of younger persons.

Still, there are many occasions when older adults encounter loss and bereavement in their lives. Not all of these are directly associated with death. But those that are may involve great distress. A further complicating factor is the likelihood of *bereavement overload*, a situation in which elders are more likely than others to experience deaths in such number, variety, and rapidity that they do not have the time or other resources needed to grieve and mourn one significant loss effectively before another occurs. Elders who face these experiences live with death as a constant companion.

The general patterns of grief and mourning experienced by older adults appear not to be altogether dissimilar to those witnessed in young and middle-aged adults. What is perhaps most distinctive is the nature of the losses and the circumstances of elderly grievers. For example, many elders live with the burdens of "little deaths" associated with illness, disability, and loss. These may diminish quality of life in many elders and render some unable to perform even the most basic activities of daily living. Some diseases manifest themselves mainly in physical ways (e.g., pain or loss of muscle control); others have important psychological (e.g., confusion), social (through loss of mobility or institutionalization), and/or spiritual (through questions about the meaning of life or the goodness of a universe in which such losses occur) implications. These implications may affect both the elderly person and those who love and care for that person.

Bereavement arising from the death of a spouse, life partner, friend, or other significant peer is common in older adulthood and is especially typical of elderly females in our society, who often outlive their male counterparts. These deaths may threaten a source of perceived meaning in one's life, take away companionship, and generate a number of important secondary losses.

As average life expectancy increases, elders are more likely to experience the death of an adult child. Such deaths are often perceived as a violation of what is assumed to be the natural order of things. Also, the death of an adult child is often associated with survivor guilt and with a wish to have died in place of the child. Further, how will the adult child's former roles now be satisfied? Who will care for the parent or help the elder as the adult child may have done? Will reduced social contacts or institutionalization now be more likely? How will a family legacy be carried forward? Will the elder experience added grief for the pain experienced by the spouse or children of the deceased adult child? Will the elder now be required to assume care of surviving grandchildren?

Bereavement resulting from the death of a grandchild or great-grandchild is also increasingly likely for older adults in our society. This can be a powerful form of bereavement for the elderly when there are special bonds of intimacy between grandparents and grandchildren. As in the death of an adult child, there are multiple dimensions to this sort of bereavement. The older adult grieves his or her own losses in this death, the losses experienced by the grandchild's parents, and the grandchild's loss. In addition to pain at such an "out of sequence" death, there may also be anger at parents who are thought not to have taken sufficient care of the grandchild, guilt at one's own presumed failure to prevent the death, and resentment at God for letting such a tragic event occur. Added complications may arise where there is unwillingness to acknowledge certain causes of death (such as suicide), a refusal to discuss openly the circumstances of the death, or tensions between surviving parents.

For many older adults, companion animals are objects of special care and affection. For the handicapped and for residents of long-term care facilities, as well as for many other elders, companion animals relieve loneliness, contribute to a sense of purpose, and enhance self-esteem. The death of an elder's companion animal highlights the fact that grief is mainly associated with the nature of an attachment, not with what might have been assumed to be the intrinsic value of the lost person, animal, or object.

## Conclusion

Developmental perspectives are among the many considerations that should be taken into account in efforts to understand an individual's grief and mourning or to help a person in coping with loss. Nevertheless, developmental perspectives should be regarded as essential to both efforts. Human beings are most alike at birth; they become increasingly diverse as they pursue the particular paths of their development and are impacted by their special life experiences. It would be foolish to think that an individual remains the same throughout his or her life, unchanged by developmental challenges and unaltered by the abilities which he or she has developed (or failed to develop) in meeting (or not meeting) those challenges.

Helpers who are sensitive to developmental perspectives will strive to appreciate this unfolding individuality in each person alongside whom they are privileged to walk for a little while. In so doing, helpers must listen actively to determine the distinctive features of each person's loss, grief, and mourning, together with their implications for ongoing lifespan development. Most often, active listening is best accomplished by attending to the verbal and symbolic communications of the individual, the overt content and the underlying significance of his or her expressions, gestures, and behaviors. Sometimes helpers need to ask bereaved persons to guide them as to the developmental implications of their grief and mourning. Always helpers can keep in mind that most human beings are able to successfully confront challenges and tasks associated with lifespan development and with death-related losses.

_____

*Charles A. Corr, PhD, is a professor in the Department of Philosophical Studies at Southern Illinois University at Edwardsville. He is a volunteer with Hospice of Madison County and a member of the Executive Committee of the National Donor Family Council.*

# THIRTEEN

# Helping Individuals with Developmental Disabilities

*Claire Lavin*

## Introduction

In the not too distant past this book might not have included a chapter on people with developmental disabilities because the need to address this topic would not have been identified. People with developmental disabilities were relatively invisible because many lived in large institutions. They were not encountered in schoolrooms, shops, or doctors' waiting rooms. They did not work in offices. They were never on television or models in the media. Many died in their teens or early 20s, with few living to experience the vicissitudes of illness and old age. While it was recognized that people with developmental disabilities experienced the deaths of parents and caregivers, they were often viewed as being incapable of understanding what had happened, as needing to be protected from the harsh reality, or even worse, as not suffering from the loss as did "normal" people.

Today, individuals with developmental disabilities live within the larger community. Some may live with their parents, some in group homes, and others with friends or spouses in homes of their own. They also live much longer, into their 60s and even well into their 80s. They attend school. They patronize dentists and doctors. People with disabilities are also visible in the media. Chris Burke, an actor who also has a developmental disability, was a key character on a popular television program.

Individuals with developmental disabilities live, laugh, love, and eventually must cope with illness and death, whether their own or that of those they love. Their disability is simply one of their attributes. Biklen (1989) notes that when defining themselves, people with disabilities frequently see themselves as ordinary and are surprised that others do not see them the same way.

People with developmental disabilities are a very heterogeneous group, as is the population at large. Differences in personality, culture, life experience, and environment cause endless variations in people with and without disabilities. The discussion in this article is based on research with groups of individuals and may not be true of a particular person.

## Definitions

The term *developmental disability* means a severe, chronic disability of a person five years of age or older which:

- is attributable to a mental or physical impairment or combination of mental and physical impairments;
- is manifested before the person attains age 22;
- is likely to continue indefinitely;
- results in substantial functional limitations in three or more of the following areas of major life activity:
  —self-care,
  —receptive and expressive language,
  —learning,
  —mobility,
  —self-direction,
  —capacity for independent living, and
  —economic self-sufficiency; and

reflects the person's need for a combination and sequence of special, interdisciplinary, or generic care, treatment, or other services which are of lifelong or extended duration and are individually planned and coordinated; except that such term, which applied to infants and young children, refers to individuals from birth to age five, inclusive, who have substantial developmental delay or specific congenital or acquired conditions with a high probability of resulting in developmental disabilities if services are not provided (Seltzer and Seltzer, 1991).

This definition indicates both that the individual has specific needs which will last throughout the lifespan, and that, with support, these needs can be met. Often, it is the reaction of society at large to the disability that complicates the individual's life rather than the disability itself. For example, a person with cognitive limitations may be perceived as unable to understand death, and therefore not in need of any assistance when a close friend dies. In reality the person can and does understand death and feel the pain of the loss.

Conditions resulting in a developmental disability include mental retardation, cerebral palsy, autism, neurological impairments, and epilepsy. Intellectual, social, and physical skills can range from above average to severely impaired. Some individuals are affected by a combination of conditions such as mental retardation and cerebral palsy, while others are affected by only one.

## Specific Disabilities

### MENTAL RETARDATION

Much of the philosophy, treatment, and research regarding developmental disabilities grew out of the field of mental retardation. Prior to the advent of intelligence tests, mental retardation was defined in terms of inability to meet the demands of a particular culture. Later, the individual intelligence tests developed by Binet and Wechsler to predict success in school were used as the means of determining retardation. The sole use of the IQ score as a classification device was discontinued through the efforts of the American Association of Mental Deficiency, which successfully advocated the addition of adaptive behavior to the diagnostic criteria.

In 1992 the American Association on Mental Retardation changed the definition and classification system to emphasize the level of services needed to help the person fully participate in the life of the community, rather than to simply describe and classify the person on the basis of his or her weaknesses. The new system defines mental retardation in terms of the following: age of onset of 18 or younger; significantly sub-average abilities in intellectual functioning; and related limitations in two or more adaptive skill areas. The person's strengths and weaknesses are described in terms of four dimensions: intellectual functioning and adaptive skills; psychological and emotional well-being; health, physical well-being and etiology; and life activity environments. A profile of needed supports across all four dimensions must be included. The new definition shifts the emphasis from what is wrong with the individual to ways in which the individual's strengths can improve their quality of life. (Luckasson, Coulter, Polloway, Reiss, Schalock, Snell, Spitalnik, and Stark, 1992).

The use of antibiotics has reduced deaths from respiratory causes, while advances in surgical techniques have corrected the heart abnormalities common to individuals with mental retardation. De-institutionalization has reduced exposure to infections and improved the overall quality of medical care. However, nearly all individuals with Down syndrome, a form of mental retardation, generally exhibit the signs of Alzheimer's disease, although not necessarily the behaviors associated with it. Hearing loss in this population can also begin as early as 20 years of age, and half of all individuals with Down syndrome will develop cataracts (Adlin, 1993). The longevity of individuals with mental retardation has greatly increased over the past 50 years. They are now more likely to experience multiple illnesses and losses during their lives.

## AUTISM

One of the most severe developmental disorders, autism has four diagnostic criteria: beginning before the age of three; failure to form social relationships; delayed language development; and stereotyped, repetitive patterns of behavior. Autism, first clearly defined by Kanner (1943), was interpreted in terms of then-current Freudian philosophy. Parents, generally mothers, were thought to have caused the condition, which was treated by psychotherapy or institutionalization. Later theorists stressed the neuropsychological basis of the disorder and the treatment shifted to a more structured educational intervention. In 1977, autism was designated as a developmental disorder and included in the Developmental Disability Act of 1977. The American Psychiatric Association, in its *Diagnostic and Statistical Manual III*, classifies autism as a pervasive developmental disorder. The rate of incidence is 4 or 5 per 10,000 and affects four times as many boys as girls (Schopler and Sloan, 1989).

Kanner originally thought that intelligence was normal in autistic children, but subsequent testing classified most in the retarded range despite unusual abilities in some areas. However, it is very difficult to test the intelligence of individuals with autism because of their severe language disabilities. The most debilitating aspect of autism is the inability to relate appropriately to people. Communication skills are very deficient in this population. However, in older adults these symptoms seem less severe and many are viewed as mentally retarded. Change is very difficult for people with autism and they respond best to preparation for even minor changes in routine.

## CEREBRAL PALSY

Cerebral palsy is a brain injury that affects individuals differently depending on the severity and type of injury. In 90 percent of cases cerebral palsy is linked to factors related to prenatal development or childbirth. The remaining 10 percent of cases are due to head trauma, infection, exposure to toxic substances, or child abuse and neglect. Cerebral palsy is characterized by the following criteria: resulting from injury to the brain; causing motor disturbance including paralysis, weakness, and lack of coordination; consisting of a cluster of symptoms; originating in childhood; and possibly linked to learning difficulties, psychological problems, sensory defects, convulsions, and behavioral disorders of organic origin. In addition, the condition is non-progressive, static, and not amenable to treatment (Overeynder, Turk, Dalton, and Janicki, 1992).

The most common form of cerebral palsy is the spastic type, in which body musculature is tightened. It primarily affects lower extremities and is generally mild or moderate in severity. Athetoid cerebral palsy affects the head and upper extremities and is characterized by involuntary irregular movements. Individuals with this condition are generally ambulatory but have problems with speech, hearing, and visual perception. Intelligence is generally unaffected. The poor speech of those with cerebral palsy may convince others that they are mentally deficient when this is not the case. Ataxic cerebral palsy is linked to problems with coordination and fine motor movements. It is generally found in conjunction with one of the other forms of cerebral palsy (Steppe-Jones, 1987).

With advancing age, individuals with cerebral palsy may become more prone to fractures and osteoporosis than others. Mobility problems may develop because of overuse of particular joints. As they age, individuals in this group have increased problems with speech and ventilation (Overeynder et al., 1992). Physical, occupational, and speech therapies, as well as computer technology, are used to mitigate the effects of this condition. It is estimated that about 500,000 persons in the United States have cerebral palsy, with a substantial number in their 50s and 60s and a smaller number in their 80s and 90s. Life expectancy mirrors that of the general population, except for a small number of individuals with severe impairment who are institutionalized (Adlin, 1993).

## NEUROLOGICAL IMPAIRMENTS

Many different conditions can cause neurological impairments. The central nervous system, which controls many of the functions of cognition, communication, mobility, and memory, is affected by some trauma or a genetic condition. Neurological impairments that are classified as developmental disabilities include severe learning disabilities, spina bifida, Tourette's syndrome, neurofibromatosis, and Prader-Willi syndrome. These conditions are more common among children and less common among older adults. Many of these neurological conditions are associated with early mortality.

Severe learning disabilities are the result of a central nervous system disorder and cause difficulty in processing and integrating information. Deficits affect academic learning and social skills. Spina bifida, or myelomeningocele, is caused by the failure of the spinal cord and vertebrae to develop properly during the prenatal period. The impact of spina bifida will vary depending on where the malformation occurs. Hydrocephalus may occur, resulting in perceptual, fine motor, and learning problems. In some cases, intelligence is normal and only mobility is affected. In other cases, retardation accompanies the physical problems (Kirk, 1989). Tourette's syndrome results in uncontrollable tics and involuntary speech. While intelligence may be normal, social acceptance is a problem. Neurofibromatosis is a condition in which tumors affect functioning. While intellectual ability may initially be normal, deterioration will occur as the tumors grow. Prader-Willi syndrome is a genetic defect generally resulting in obesity and mental retardation.

### EPILEPSY

Epilepsy is a disorder of the nervous system marked by abnormal electrical patterns in the brain that result in seizures, either mild or severe. In *grand mal* seizures, the individual suffers convulsions, muscle spasms, and loss of consciousness, but in *petit mal* seizures may simply seem to pause and stare into space. Severe seizures may result in brain damage and mental retardation. Only those who suffer from severe epilepsy are classified as having a developmental disability. Medication can generally control epileptic seizures. One of the implications of epilepsy for an aging population is the long-term effect of this anti-convulsive medication, which has been shown to increase the risk of osteoporosis (Kirk, 1989). The risk of fractures would be expected to increase with age due to this condition.

## Coping with Illness and Death

People with disabilities are like the general population in most respects. However, their disabilities affect their lives in a number of ways. Sensitivity to these differences can help caregivers respond appropriately in times of illness and loss. Research over the past 20 years has provided striking evidence that, with the proper supports, individuals with disabilities can live fulfilling and relatively independent lives. They can handle painful experiences and master abstract concepts of death and loss.

### LIMITED EXPERIENCE

Individuals with developmental disabilities may be ill-prepared to cope with death and loss because of limited prior experiences.

Developmental differences have traditionally triggered a very different set of life experiences from those of the general population. Many people with developmental disabilities have mental ages below their chronological ages; therefore, their personal autonomy and independence have been severely restricted as others make decisions for them. Many adults have guardians who oversee financial and living arrangements. Interactions with others have been curtailed, and social networks generally revolve around those of the family. While education may be in regular school or classes, the ultimate level of attainment may be low. Vocational opportunities are limited, as are housing options. Most individuals with developmental disabilities live at home with family caregivers. Others live in group residences under supervision of professional staff. Their choice of residence or roommate generally is made by professionals. Opportunities for marriage and sexual relationships are limited, as are those for having children. Independent movement is curtailed. Even leisure activities may be group rather than personal choices.

In a sense, individuals with disabilities become defined by the disability, which overshadows other aspects of their identity. They have few opportunities for making meaningful choices and becoming independent, self-directed adults. They approach middle and old age lacking many of the necessary experiences for accomplishing the tasks of this stage of life and dealing with its inevitable crises of illness and death.

People handle crises better when they are prepared. Attending wakes and funerals provides opportunities to see peers and family members survive one of life's most devastating experiences. For individuals with cognitive limitations, real-life experiences are particularly valuable in developing coping skills. However, all too often individuals with disabilities are denied these experiences. One individual spoke with pain five years after his beloved father's death. Now living in a group home, this middle-aged man with cerebral palsy and some cognitive limitations recalled clearly the phone call he received from his brother telling him of the death. He was not asked to be at the bedside; he was not asked to attend the funeral. He never had a chance to say good-bye. As he ages, this man will encounter additional losses of family and peers. He has yet to attend any mourning ritual or service, still grieves for his father, and is without support in coming to terms with this loss.

## OVERPROTECTION

The limited experience of individuals with developmental disabilities is linked to the fact that they are often overprotected. They have been perceived as fragile and unable to cope with the harsh realities of death and loss. Most live at home with caregivers who are fiercely protective of them and attempt to shield them and soften unpleasant experiences. For example, the fear that a child with disabilities might outlive them and face the world alone is the major worry of aging caregivers. Yet this fact often does not galvanize them into action. They fail to discuss the issue of their future death with their adult child. They also fail to make provisions for the individual, or if they do, often do not consult the parties involved. It is not uncommon for a sibling of an individual with developmental disabilities to learn after a parent's death that they have been named guardian, a matter that was never discussed. Even worse, the affected individual was never consulted about where and with whom he would prefer to live. It is important that parents prepare their children for the eventuality of their death. Questions such as, "Who will take care of me?" and "Where shall I live?" must be addressed. These questions make the grief reaction of the bereaved individual much more difficult. The impact of a parent's death can be devastating to an individual with developmental disabilities because it changes his or her life completely. An individual's residence, support network, and financial stability may vanish upon the death of the caregiving parent.

In some cases, family members may try to protect individuals with disabilities, restricting their access to medical information. This can also affect advance directives, or living wills. The ability of persons with developmental disabilities to contribute to or make such decisions should be evaluated. To the extent possible, they should be actively involved in making such decisions, and the decisions should be regularly reviewed by an ethics committee.

In the long run, overprotection results in harming, rather than helping, the individual. If illness strikes the individual with disabilities, caregivers may react by withholding information or reassuring them that everything is fine. However, honesty will help the individual deal with what is to come. Respect for the individual should ensure involvement in decision-making to the extent possible. To make informed decisions, they need to be given information and explanations about their conditions and the available choices.

Individuals with disabilities have a need for autonomy. They have formed their own advocacy organizations and are lobbying to have their needs met. They do not need overprotection. They need supportive adults to help them grow in independence. Interventions should be based on this principle.

## DISENFRANCHISEMENT

Doka (1989) has identified groups in our society whose grief is *disenfranchised*, meaning that it is not publicly acknowledged, socially supported, or openly mourned. In some cases, it is because the loss is not recognized. Persons with developmental disabilities can become very attached to roommates, housemates, friends, fellow workers, teachers, and other staff, whose constant turnover causes repeated losses. These losses are often unacknowledged.

Grief can also be disenfranchised when the griever is unacknowledged. This can be the case when the griever has developmental disabilities. It is assumed sometimes that the person with developmental disabilities does not experience the loss, as though they were impervious to human emotions. This assumption may also be due to the fact that their manifestations of grief cannot be understood by others. Individuals with developmental disabilities may use behavior rather than words to express grief. Ghaziuddin, Alessi, and Greden (1995) report that children with autism display grief through loss of interest in activities, withdrawal, frequent crying spells, and disturbed sleep and appetite. One young man displayed regression in terms of personal hygiene and became less cooperative three months after his father's death. Staff did not immediately recognize these behaviors as grief reactions, and so he grieved in isolation.

Individuals with developmental disabilities have also been disenfranchised from mourning rituals in the mistaken belief that they need to be shielded from the harsh reality or simply would not comprehend them. One supervisor of a facility for individuals with severe disabilities fought with her administrator to take residents to the cemetery when one of their peers died. While the administrator maintained that it wouldn't matter to individuals who had severe cognitive limitations, the supervisor's interpretation of their behaviors and reactions indicated otherwise. She prevailed and they were transported by van to bid farewell to their friend. Another resident of a different facility spoke of the disappearance of a peer from the home. He had died during the night and been spirited away. The man recalled, "I asked and asked; no one said." Eventually, the residents were informed of the death, but not until there had been widespread fear and speculation about the disappearance. No ritual for the residents allowed them to express the feelings of loss for their friend. A third group of residents told an even more poignant story. Excluded from funerals, they were later unable to even identify the gravesites so that they could pay their respects.

It is now recognized that even individuals with severe impairments react to the loss of caregivers and need special provisions to help them cope with the loss. One administrator of a large facility for individuals with severe cognitive impairments spoke of the changes in behavior among bedridden residents when a staff member left. They became irritable and unresponsive. Recognizing these nonverbal reactions to loss, she had staff increase the use of soothing massages and react to noncompliant behavior with understanding rather than anger.

## COGNITIVE FACTORS

Individuals with mental retardation form the largest group among those with developmental disabilities. By definition they have impairments; however, this does not mean that they are without cognitive ability. They can reason, comprehend, and remember, although they may do so in unique ways. Helping individuals with developmental disabilities cope with loss requires that intervention and support be based on their cognitive strengths. It is important once again to mention that some individuals with other disabilities may have normal or superior cognitive abilities, and this too must be taken into account in interventions.

Many individuals with cognitive impairments deal best with *concrete* rather than *abstract* learning. Philosophical discussions of death may have little meaning without concrete examples. Previously it was thought that individuals with mental retardation were not able to master the concept of death. Lipe-Goodson and Goebal (1983) found that their sample of adults with developmental disabilities were able to conceptualize death, with understanding increasing with age. They suggested that additional losses throughout life further developed the concept of death. Harper and Wadsworth (1993) reported similar findings. In fact, some of their subjects had an understanding of death beyond that predicted by cognitive theory. The researchers speculated that prior experience with funerals, wakes, and death had provided some subjects with a repertoire of understanding about death beyond expectations.

The concept of death incorporates three dimensions: irreversibility, universality, and the end of functioning. Many individuals with developmental disabilities do not see death in these terms. They view death as temporary and reversible. One resident of a group home kept asking, "When will he be back?" even though he had been told that his roommate was dead. Concrete experiences are needed to develop understanding. Having pets or plants that die offers a perfect opportunity to make the abstract concept of death more concrete and understandable.

Many individuals with retardation will also more quickly forget what is taught and require more frequent repetitions to reach mastery. Caregivers must not think that once a concept has been taught and apparently learned, they can consider their task completed. Frequent review and clarification are needed. Tasks and concepts should be separated into parts to be mastered one by one. Active involvement in role playing or art activities will help reinforce concepts. Individuals with developmental disabilities function best in structured, predictable contexts, and are uncomfortable with changes in routine.

Similarly, individuals with cognitive limitations learn best for a specific situation but have difficulty generalizing to new situations. While they may have been taught what to expect in the funeral parlor, they may not recall or transfer the information when they are actually there. Prior experiences in the room with a sensitive coach will facilitate transfer.

Individuals with cognitive impairments learn best with direct instruction. Less incidental learning occurs among those with cognitive limitations. Some people may learn how to act with a grieving individual by noting the behaviors of others or simply from television programs. For those with cognitive impairments, direct teaching of concepts is required. One woman was horrified at a wake when an individual with retardation asked loudly, "Why is he in that box?" A perfectly logical question for someone who had never been to a wake before.

Individuals with developmental disabilities function at a developmental level that is not consonant with their chronological age. They may see the world from an egocentric viewpoint, similar to that of a young child. Thus when a death occurs they assume they are to blame. When a caregiver attempted to engage an individual with developmental disabilities about the death of a friend by saying, "I understand that Sam died," the man withdrew, saying anxiously, "I didn't do it, I didn't." Some individuals may feel that their angry words or thoughts contributed to the death. One young woman did not understand the circumstances of her mother's death and persisted in saying to her housemates, "If I had been different she wouldn't be dead." This young woman's grief was so intense that she subsequently attempted suicide (Berman, 1992).

## RESTRICTED SUPPORT NETWORK

Studies by Edgerton (1991) of individuals with disabilities living in the community indicate that almost all depend on a support network. In times of difficulty some concerned adult will assist them. The majority of individuals with developmental disabilities live at home. As their family caregivers age, their support networks diminish. The aunt or cousin who formerly drove the individual to the doctor's office may now be infirm herself. For individuals with disabilities the family social network may be their only social network. When it diminishes they are left alone. It is crucial in times of illness and death that concerned caregivers provide support since it is unlikely that an extensive system exists.

Individuals with developmental disabilities are more likely to experience a major disruption in their lives as the result of a death, particularly of a caregiving parent. For many, the death means a relocation, the loss of a primary support system, and changes in vocational and leisure activities (Harper and Wadsworth, 1993).

## LIMITED COMMUNICATION

Many individuals with developmental disabilities have limited verbal communication skills. Their reactions to loss are the same as the general population: sadness, anger, anxiety, confusion, and physical pain. However, they may not express these emotions in socially-sanctioned ways. They may act out these feelings, becoming withdrawn or irritable and uncooperative. Caregivers may misinterpret these nonverbal expressions, when in fact they are expressions of grief. Rather than support the individual in their grief, untrained caregivers may react by treating the behavior with medication or by placing the individual in a more restrictive environment. Thus the individual with disabilities never learns to cope with grief. When a loss occurs again, the same negative cycle may occur (Harper and Wadsworth, 1993).

Years of saying "Yes" in an effort to please or avoid prolonged discussion may cause some individuals with disabilities to report that everything is fine during illness or loss. Misunderstanding a question, they may not ask for clarification because it makes them appear dumb. Caregivers who take such responses at face value may miss important information about the person's real reactions. It is helpful to ask the individual to explain things in his own words to check for understanding. The choice of vocabulary words is a key factor. When dealing with death, euphemisms such as *passed* may confuse those with limited vocabularies who take words literally. When dealing with illness, the *digestive system disorder* is better described as a *pain in your belly*. Walz, Harper, and Wilson (1986) report that professionals may not accept reports of pains from people with mental retardation, autism, or cerebral palsy.

There is a need for training of healthcare personnel. Wadsworth and Harper (1991) developed a training program designed to foster communication between individuals with mental retardation and healthcare personnel. Open, interactive communication shows respect for patient self-determination and fosters a cooperative relationship. Healthcare professionals have an obligation to tailor their communication to the needs of persons with developmental disabilities. All too often the professional addresses the caregiver without even making eye contact with the sick patient. Such disregard diminishes the person and interferes with good medical practice. The caregiver is not experiencing the symptoms, the patient is. Unless patients are helped to identify and describe what is occurring, how can they monitor progress or assess whether medications are having the desired effect?

## Developing Coping Skills

The autonomy of individuals with disabilities must be respected. Since individuals with disabilities are apt to have restricted social and support networks, concerned helpers may be needed to intervene during times of crises. However, assistance during a crisis is much more effective if individuals with disabilities have been prepared to deal with illness and death. Therefore, preparation will be considered first.

### PREPARE YOURSELF

It is crucial that grief counseling be provided to individuals with developmental disabilities, even though, as Deutsch (1985) indicates, caregivers feel inadequate dealing with death. Helping people with disabilities cope with illness and death can be problematic for caregivers because the task involves a type of double taboo: death and developmental disability (Harper and Wadsworth, 1993). The combination can seem overwhelming. Remembering that people with disabilities are more like than unlike the general population can make the task easier. Illness, bereavement, and grief know no boundaries in terms of age or functioning level.

Also, people are all relatively unprepared to deal with these eventualities. Both caregivers and clients will fare better if they engage in activities to prepare them to deal with these inevitable losses. To the extent that people have dealt with small losses and less painful deaths, they are better equipped to deal with more painful losses. Self-awareness on the part of caregivers is an important first step in helping others.

Feelings of inadequacy can affect the responses of staff at crucial points in the lives of individuals with disabilities in their care. Staff training can be of great assistance in helping frame appropriate responses to loss. Preparation requires a planned sequence of training activities for caregivers, as well as programs for individuals with developmental disabilities. These programs should be adapted for a particular site and implemented as part of the program. Kauffman (1994) cites this as an overlooked aspect of care. He advocates a needs-based program that is carefully taught and reviewed over a span of time. His training program for caregivers includes an introduction to the mourning process, special characteristics of people with retardation, grief reactions of the group (primarily behavioral), ways of helping clients deal with grief, staff awareness of their own reactions, relationships, loss, and human dignity, termination with clients, and working with families.

## EDUCATION PROGRAMS

Even before the onset of illness it is necessary to teach preventative care and to help persons with disabilities avoid chronic illness. The preventative program should include physical, psychosocial, dental, exercise, and nutritional components (Gambert, Liebskind, and Cameron, 1987). Individuals with developmental disabilities must also learn to recognize and report symptoms that might indicate serious illness. Staff need to be trained to identify signs of serious physical or emotional illness among individuals with disabilities. Frequently, changes in behavior or performance are attributed to the primary disability rather than any developing illness. In the case of individuals with Down syndrome, the onset of Alzheimer's disease may be mistaken for behaviors due to mental retardation.

Formal prevention programs should be provided for individuals with developmental disabilities. Exercise, diet, and nutrition are all topics that impact the health of individuals with disabilities. Edgerton, Gaston, Kelly, and Ward (1994) reported little understanding of the relationship between smoking, diet, exercise, and health among adults with developmental disabilities living in the community. As a group they did not understand when to seek health care, how to communicate to providers, or how to follow doctors' instructions. They received few usual services such as mammograms, pap tests, or annual physical examinations. In contrast, those in facilities had their healthcare monitored by others, and doctors communicated to the providers, not the patients. It is recommended that religious and service organizations serve as advocates to ensure that individuals receive needed medical services.

Similarly, agencies should provide programs that prepare individuals with disabilities to cope with death. In the case of a major illness or the death of a parent, caregivers are too caught up in the press of events to meet the needs of individuals with the profile detailed above. It is far better to put a structured program in place to prepare individuals with developmental disabilities to cope with these crises. Programs can include information about vocabulary, concepts, and behaviors. For example, when individuals with developmental disabilities view a movie in which someone dies, staff can elicit discussion about what happened, how survivors feel, cemeteries, and other related aspects of the situation. This may help not only to demystify these concepts and places, but also to teach critical concepts and standards of behavior. Group discussions and interactions on the topic of death and loss will both clarify concepts and provide support for grieving members.

Lavin (1989) has outlined a program involving pets, plants, and simple books that can be used to develop the concepts of death. Suggestions for preparing individuals for rituals of mourning are outlined for implementation long before a crisis occurs. Turner (1990) has designed an extensive educational program to assist clients with concerns about death and dying. Activities include listening carefully to individuals and then capitalizing on their needs to provide information or offer support. Structured activities include role playing, visits to mortuaries, noting deaths in nature related to the change of seasons, caring for animals, and drawing feelings related to death and loss.

## Suggestions for Caregivers

The grief process for individuals with developmental disabilities involves helping them to accept the reality of the loss and experience the pain in a safe setting. The loss may have a severe impact on the care and independence of the individual with developmental disabilities, who must also be helped to adjust to new relationships and perhaps living arrangements (Rothenberg, 1994). Kauffman (1994) points out that this grief is likely to be complicated by deep feelings of anxiety, dependency, ambivalence about the dependency, and fears of abandonment. Like any loss, the intensity of the grief reaction will be affected by a number of factors such as the relationship to the deceased and the circumstances of the loss.

The individual's prior experiences and coping skills, as well as the degree of formal and informal support available, will also affect grieving. His or her grief may be manifested in a number of ways general to all bereaved. This can include physical reactions such as headaches or other aches and pains. Emotional reactions, particularly anger and guilt, are also common. There may be cognitive reactions as well, including preoccupation with the person who died, distractibility, and confusion. There may be behavioral manifestations of grief: withdrawal and silence, hyperactivity or resistance to change, or even regression in previously mastered skills. Helpful interventions include exploring the person's feelings, giving emotional support, and providing information about the loss. It is critical that the grief of persons with developmental disabilities be validated.

A number of interventions are useful in assisting persons with developmental disabilities as they cope with grief.

1. Help individuals recognize and accept their feelings. Death will trigger buried emotions related to previous losses, abandonment, fears, and guilt. Individuals should have opportunities to discuss their experiences of grief in a safe, patient environment. Expressive therapies, such as art and music, can be very helpful in allowing persons who are less verbal to express grief. Empathy from a caring person provides a shoulder to cry or lean on and a heart that will understand their pain.

2. Help the person accept the reality of the death. It is critical that they are told the truth and involved in the process as much as possible. Here, euphemisms may confuse rather than develop understanding. Instead of saying, "He's living with God," express the fact that "He is dead." Explain the facts of the death as clearly and simply as possible. In the absence of facts, individuals will manufacture their own. Individuals with disabilities have the right to honest answers and to wrestle with the unsettling intimations of their own mortality that result from a death just as anyone else (Turner, 1990).

3. Participation in rituals helps individuals cope with loss (Doka, 1989). Persons with developmental disabilities should not be denied these opportunities. Offering a memorial service at the group home allows residents to express their feelings in community and say good-bye.

4. Using pictures and videotapes to recall the person is a helpful intervention as well, providing opportunities to discuss relationships, share feelings, and recall good memories. It also reinforces the fact that memories always remain. Other technology may also be useful. Deutsch (1985) suggests taping messages that the person may replay at will. For example, if that person believes that no one will care for him or her, it might be useful for that person to make a tape listing the people who still do care. In addition, the person should be prepared for and participate in any transitions that the death may bring.

5. Religion provides strong support for many in times of loss. Individuals with developmental disabilities should be encouraged to explore their spiritual beliefs and utilize their religious rituals.

6. Acknowledge the fact that individuals with disabilities may express grief nonverbally, even using disruptive or disturbing behavior. Respond with empathy rather than annoyance, and name the feelings behind the behavior. "You are angry because John died, and so you won't eat. You feel angry, angry, angry. And that's okay."

7. Be alert for grief reactions requiring psychiatric intervention. All too often behaviors are incorrectly attributed to the primary disability, rather than to depression in need of treatment.

8. Provide support that is now missing from the individual's life. One man with cerebral palsy had for many years depended on his brother for company and transportation to a favorite restaurant. This event was one of the high points of his life, and when his brother died it was no longer available to him.

9. Be an advocate for the individual to allow him to mourn and participate in rituals if others fail to recognize the need for him to do so.

## Conclusions

This discussion has emphasized the importance of implementing formal preparation programs for both individuals with developmental disabilities and caregivers to allow them to successfully cope with illness and death. The difficulty of grieving is compounded by the social experiences and cognitive characteristics of individuals with developmental disabilities. Disenfranchised and often misunderstood in the ways they express grief, individuals with disabilities need both a supportive counselor and an advocate who will fight to empower them to deal with life's crises.

---

*Claire Lavin, PhD, is a Professor of Psychology at the College of New Rochelle. As a clinical and school psychologist, she works with adults and children with disabilities.*

# FOURTEEN

# The World of the Deaf Community

*Frank R. Zieziula*

## Introduction

Hearing loss affects between 21 and 28 million Americans (about 10 percent of the US population). People with profound hearing losses, often referred to as deaf, number about 1.5 million. Over 75,000 children in the United States have a severe enough hearing impairment to necessitate placement in special education classes. In all, hearing impairment represents the largest disability within the United States. Further, profound hearing impairment is considered the most difficult of disabilities in today's world because of its direct impact on daily activities. The general public, as well as many professionals, continue to misunderstand the ramifications of hearing impairment and deafness on the psychological and social lives of people who experience this disability. We are also at a loss to understand how hearing impairment in general and deafness in particular affect the grieving process and how hospice workers, medical personnel, counselors, or clergy can best serve this community when they experience significant loss.

As this chapter was being written, I received a phone call from the director of a hospice in a major metropolitan area requesting information on how hospice can best serve members of the deaf community. This was the first time they had been approached by the family of a deaf terminally-ill patient. The director had specific questions about the Americans with Disabilities Act and deaf peoples' rights under the law. She wanted to know if the agency should purchase a Telecommunication Device for the Deaf (TDD), whether the agency could or should rely solely on this "new" phone relay system in the state. She wanted to know where in the community a person could take sign language instruction and what system of sign language the staff should be learning. This professional was unfamiliar with deafness, deaf people, and hearing impairment in general, and was desperately seeking information on how she and her employees could best assist hearing impaired people in the future. This hospice director is certainly not alone.

This chapter will give professionals who deal with loss and grief a better understanding of what it means to have a hearing impairment and how professionals can best serve this population of grievers. It will focus primarily on people with profound hearing impairment, since this group requires the greatest adjustments in the provision of services. First, it will provide a clear explanation of the nomenclature in the world of hearing impairment, which confuses so many people; second, it will provide a glimpse into the unique aspects of being a member of the Deaf community; third, it will present the languages used by different groups within the hearing-impaired spectrum; fourth, it will explore how deafness impacts the grieving process; last, and most importantly, it will offer suggestions to hospice workers, grief counselors, and case workers for improving services to people in the hearing impaired world and deaf community.

## Understanding Deafness

There is no universally accepted definition of a "deaf person." It was the National Association of the Deaf (NAD), a national consumer group, who in 1947 vehemently fought against a Federal definition of deafness and tax exemption for deaf people (similar to that which presently exists for blind people), because the NAD could not agree upon an acceptable definition and felt that the definition would stigmatize deaf people as "disabled" in the eyes of the hearing world. Therefore, definitions of deafness are left to professional groups and consumers to interpret as they see fit.

Audiologists describe a deaf person as an individual having a specific decibel loss across a continuum from mild to profound. Persons with a profound decibel loss are identified as *deaf*, while people with mild or moderate losses are identified as *hard of hearing*.

Educators classify deafness on the basis of the age of onset, with the age of two, a critical time in the development of language, being the criterion for *prelingual deafness* (before the acquisition of language) and *post-lingual deafness* (after the acquisition of language).

Linguists focus on the language used by people with a hearing loss and identify people who use some form of American Sign Language as *Deaf* (with a capital D, representing a cultural identity) and those who use the English language as the primary vehicle of communication as *hard of hearing, hearing impaired* or *adventitiously deafened*. The degree of hearing loss is not an issue in linguistic perception.

Social service personnel such as psychologists, professional counselors, and social workers define deafness from the perspective of a self-concept: Who do I identify myself to be? Definition of identity with the deaf world is based primarily on communication needs and social preferences, manifested in an identity with either the "deaf world" or the "hearing world."

The general public's definition of deaf people is most likely singular and is ascertained by exposure to people using sign language or to deaf celebrities. The public has been introduced to the beauty of sign language and fingerspelling by Academy Award winner Marlee Matlin, Tony Award winner Phyllis Frelich, and *Sesame Street* star Linda Bove. Yet the public has also identified deafness with the amazing lipreading and speech skills of Heather Whitestone, Miss America of 1995, and bodybuilder Lou Ferrigno, better known as "The Incredible Hulk." In addition, the public is exposed to deafness indirectly through modern technological advances such as closed captioning of TV programs and movies, and Telecommunication Devices for the Deaf (TDD). Further, the public identifies deafness through daily exposure to a growing gerontological population whose hearing losses are so profound that the sight of people with hearing aids is commonplace. The world of hearing loss received even more exposure when President Clinton, during a routine physical examination, was found to have a hearing impairment severe enough to limit some communication and therefore warrant the use of a hearing aid. Public exposure to the breadth of hearing impairment is evident, yet understanding what labels to use for people with this disability is muddled.

Hearing impairment is the most widespread disability in the United States. Whether mild or profound, this disability directly impacts communication between the hearing-impaired person and everyone else in their world for every waking, resting, and sleeping moment of the individual's life. The barrier to communication, most evident in an American society based on sound and successful writing and speaking skills, impacts every aspect of an individual's life, including childhood development, education, marriage, employment, death, and grieving.

This leads to definitions of deafness that combine issues of communication, self-identity, and cultural affiliation. The word *Deaf* (with a capital D) should be used to refer to a person who identifies culturally with the deaf world, and who communicates primarily with an American Sign Language system. Many people in this category are born deaf or became deaf before the age of two, and usually have a hearing impairment severe enough that normal communication cannot be heard.

The term *hard of hearing* should be used with individuals who primarily use sound to communicate. Some in this group may supplement their communication with signs or other gestural systems, yet many do not. They may use devices such as captioning chips in televisions, lighted door bells, hearing-aid dogs, and the like. Cultural identity, that is, feeling oneself to be a part of the hearing world or Deaf world, is not clear and may be situational, depending on the present needs of the person. *Adventitiously deafened* refers to a person who becomes profoundly deaf later in life, after the establishment of a communication system based on sound. A growing number of adults have become deaf due to accidents, progressive hearing loss caused by environmental noise pollutants, or for genetic reasons.

Communication can be varied, and cultural identification is some-times confused; within the last 10 years there has been a growing cultural identity among individuals who become deaf later in life. The Association of Late Deafened Adults (ALDA) is a national orga-nization formed to attend to the specific needs of this group. The term *hearing impaired* represents a continuum from mild to severe audiological deficit.

## Deaf Community and American Sign Language

There exists within the hearing-impaired world a distinct Deaf community made up of individuals who may have a profound hear-ing impairment and/or are prelingually deaf, and who may have a history of deafness in the family. This community has existed in America since the formation of the first permanent school for the Deaf in Hartford, Connecticut in 1817. By 1830, graduates of this school had formed an association with the intention of purchasing land from the federal government and establishing a "deaf state." A similar idea surfaced again in 1850. The idea of a distinct Deaf culture, based on a specific language system called American Sign Language, had a prominent ally in outspoken and respected Northeastern University linguist Harlan Lane (1984, 1988).

Yet it was not until a week in March, 1988, known in the Deaf world as the Gallaudet Revolution, that the Deaf community gained momentum and respectability in the hearing world. It was a week in which the primarily hearing board of trustees of the only liberal arts university for the Deaf in the world, Gallaudet University, attempted to appoint a hearing person as president. All previous presidents had been hearing. The appointment of a hearing president over two well-qualified deaf applicants inspired the students and faculty to a peace-ful, yet very powerful, revolution that resulted in the resignation of the new president, as well as the chairperson of the Board of Trustees. Dr. I. King Jordan then became the first Deaf president of the university. That event created a wave of Deaf pride that vibrated through all 50 states and garnered international attention. The words of Dr. Jordan were heard around the world: "We must insist that the enhanced attitudes toward deafness and deaf people become even more positive. We know this, and we can do this only by demonstrating that, given the opportunity, deaf people can do anything but hear" (Gannon, 1989, p. 174).

The revolution encouraged the discussion and clarification of what it means to be a Deaf person in our culture and in the world, which continue today. Not every person who is hearing impaired feels that they are members of the Deaf community; some people actually resent being viewed as such. Yet all would agree that, because of a number of important factors including language, sports, telecommunication needs, social clubs, theater, religious affiliation, school, housing, and values, a Deaf culture exists. This culture is alive and well and meeting the needs of its members. The pride of Deaf people is exemplified in the book, *Great Deaf Americans* (Moore and Panara, 1996), already in its second edition. The book chronicles the lives of over 75 Deaf women and men who have had a tremendous impact on our society in the arts, sciences, politics, sports, theater, education, and business.

The Deaf community's most distinctive cultural feature is American Sign Language, better known as ASL. The languages of people who are hearing impaired are often placed on a continuum, with ASL at one end and lipreading and verbal speech at the other end. The use of any gestural and verbal language systems is not dependent solely on the hearing loss of the individual, but on many factors, including when an individual became hearing impaired, parents' communication style, the communication philosophy of the school where the person was educated, and the individual's present environment.

In the Deaf community, ASL is the language of choice. It is estimated that up to 2 million Americans use ASL for everyday communication (Lane, Hoffmeister, and Bahan, 1996). ASL is the most widespread minority language in the United States after Spanish, Italian, German, and French (Lane et al., 1996). Its grammar and vocabulary are very distinct from English. Signed languages are not the same the world over; therefore, American Sign Language is distinct from other sign language systems. There is a great deal of controversy surrounding the issue of communication systems which *should* be used by Deaf people and communication systems which *should* be used in schools to educate Deaf people. Much of the controversy stems from the facts that ASL does not follow English syntax, it is used without speech, and there are many nuances of the language from one Deaf community to another. The controversy is compounded by the fact that it is a difficult language for many hearing people to use fluently, unless you are a CODA (Children Of Deaf Adults) brought up using the language.

Therefore, many hearing advocates opt for and encourage a gestural communication system (as distinct from *language*) known as *total communication* or *simultaneous communication*, which incorporates English language syntax and speech, along with gestural signs and fingerspelling. This combination of systems would appear to make most sense in an English language society. Would it serve the needs of both populations, the hearing world and the world of the Deaf? The answer is "No."

Total communication is certainly easier for a hearing population, or for Deaf people who became deaf after the age of language development, yet it is not the first choice for people who have not been brought up hearing sound and, therefore, without the English language system. English syntax is foreign to these Deaf people and very difficult to learn. The late 1990s (post-Gallaudet Revolution) has ushered in a new and stronger language movement within the Deaf community and among some professional linguists whose goal is to bring up Deaf children with bilingual communication (often known as a *bi-bi* approach). Its proponents believe that Deaf people should strive for competence in both ASL and English. They assert that the only way to accomplish this is to teach Deaf children in their primary language, ASL, and, through ASL, teach English.

## How Deafness Effects the Grieving Process

One of the most debated questions among professionals working with Deaf people is whether a psychology of deafness exists that so impacts the lives of people who are profoundly deaf that the disability itself alters the psychosocial development, behavior, thinking, and feelings of Deaf people and results in lifestyles that are very unlike normal hearing peers. Hilde Schlesinger (1978), one of the pioneering psychiatric researchers of Deaf children, asked, "Does the absence of early auditory stimulation, feedback, and communication in itself create a propensity toward (these) behavioral and achievement patterns, or does early profound deafness elicit particular responses from parents, teachers, siblings, and friends that contribute a particular set of cognitive and behavioral deficiencies?" (p.20).

The answer, like many answers in a complex world, is "Yes and no." It is within this nebulous response that an understanding of how deafness affects the grieving process can be discerned.

The study of the psychological development of people with hearing impairments shows that deafness does not alter basic psychological and social needs, drives, and ambitions. There has been no research to date that has shown Deaf people to be unlike hearing people in their need for survival, self-worth, companionship, their fear of death, their striving to understand the meaning of life, and their desire for a future legacy. That is clear.

Yet it is also very clear that for people born with a severe hearing impairment or those acquiring a severe hearing impairment before the age of two, loss of auditory stimulation causes a very different kind of experience of another's presence. Those experiences alter, in some fashion, all developmental aspects of a person's life, but most importantly, styles of interaction. Much of the interaction of Deaf people is impacted by the negative preconceptions and misunderstandings that so many adults have toward disabled people in general and Deaf people specifically. These interactions can understandably give rise in Deaf people to feelings of mistrust, anger, and skepticism regarding the behavior of hearing people, and may result in weakened ego development. Some evidence for this last assertion is found in studies of Deaf children born to Deaf parents, compared to Deaf children born to hearing parents (Meadow, 1972, 1980; Lou and Charlson, 1991). Deaf children born of Deaf parents are more confident, exhibit a greater love of self, accept their deafness, are assertive in fulfilling their needs, and are simply more happy growing up compared to Deaf children born of hearing parents. For a variety of reasons, ease of communication and acceptance of deafness being primary among them, Deaf parents and hearing parents interact differently with their Deaf children, resulting in differences in development of the children.

It would be incorrect to believe that Deaf people develop or have in common some deafness-related "personality flaw." Worse, it would be unfair to believe that Deaf people are a psychologically homogeneous group, based simply on impaired hearing. Many past studies have attempted to prove just these assertions, only to be later proven false (Pintner, 1933; Levine, 1956; Mykelbust, 1964). Deaf people are as heterogeneous as the majority population. Yet the impact of the lack of auditory stimulation, combined with a primarily foreign language-oriented world and negative attitudes and stereotypes toward people with disabilities in general and people who use a visual gestural language system specifically, does affect how a Deaf person will feel and think. Further, all these experiences affect how a Deaf person attempts to satisfy their needs in a primarily hearing world. The differences in interaction, coupled with the actual physical limitation of not receiving auditory input, give a preliminary indication of the distinctiveness of Deaf people's process of grieving, and more importantly, the role of helpers in assisting a Deaf person through the event(s) and the psychological aftermath.

Regardless of theoretical orientation, experts agree that a significant loss results in a natural pattern of grieving that includes a number of psychological processes: responding to the event by emoting or other activities; comprehension and assimilation of the event(s); adapting to life without the person or loss object; coming to terms with the event(s); and continuing one's existence as a changed person. Deafness impacts all aspects of grieving. An understanding of this impact is crucial in providing direction on how caregivers can best support a Deaf person or person with hearing impairment living through a serious loss.

All people react to loss through emotions or other physical and cognitive activities. Deaf people are no different. There is the great example of a Deaf man, Abel, grieving the sudden loss of his only son in the classic novel of a Deaf couple, *In This Sign*, by Joanne Greenberg (1970):

Abel, freed of the body he would protect even in death, seemed
to go mad. The onlookers stood back staring, amazed at the extrav-
agant noise of his wildness. Everything he could not hear himself
was loosed from him. He turned from the group of them and ran
to the street door, kicking it closed; he kicked at the wall, pound-
ed it, ran to the stairs and kicked at them, pounding on the rail and
then at the steps with his fists; then he ran back to the door and
opened it again and smashed it closed; back to the wall to pound
and kick, bellowing all the time in his horrible voice. Back and
forth he ran from wall to wall while the witnesses stood stiff in the
uproar. They did not notice the dead boy now, only the man, as
they waited, terrified of what he might do. Soon his voice warped
and broke, but his mouth was still open—he didn't know that
there was no sound coming. Back again he went to smash at the
patient wall, one side then the other, until he was too tired to go
on. Then he stood, sweating, breathing loudly, clicking his tongue
against the roof of his mouth, impatient to begin the rage again.
His hands were swollen, and there were bruises beginning
from the beating he had given them. The police had come then,
and they had taken statements and made their useless notes.
(p. 99-100)

Abel's reaction exemplifies the emotional torture that a Deaf
person experiences with the loss of a child. The nature, variety, and
intensity of feelings is no different from those experienced by people
with hearing. Yet the manifestation of the emotions may be associated with the hearing loss. Abel's anger at losing a son needs to be
expressed externally, visibly, and with passion. His response is a traditional masculine one, yet possibly also a manifestation of the frustration of the silence of a Deaf person and the need to bring out, in
the only way possible, his pain. Do Deaf people cry? Certainly. Do
Deaf people wail in ways which make some hearing people uncomfortable? Certainly some do. Do Deaf people have an opportunity to
convey their emotional turmoil to loved ones and friends around
them? Many do not. And the fact of the inability of many hearing
people to understand the communication of Deaf people alters the
grieving process by making it more difficult for Deaf people to
express what is inside.

The need for survivors to comprehend and assimilate a loss is also complicated by the issue of communication. Most information regarding a loss is gained by verbal communication, often lost or misunderstood when two different language systems are being used. Yet the solution is not as simple as hiring an interpreter to meet the needs of the Deaf griever. There is very often a mind-set on the part of many hearing people, including professionals, that Deaf people, those with a "disability," will not be able to comprehend complicated messages, and therefore should receive only the basic information of what has happened or what is to follow. Equally destructive is the attitude that communicating with the Deaf person may involve more time and effort that one wishes to expend.

I once worked with a Deaf couple in their early 70s, one of whom had terminal cancer. Their entire extended family was deaf, including two married children and four grandchildren; only the wife of one of the sons was hearing. The family was very close and, as a family unit, decided to utilize hospice. From the initial meeting with the hospice team, communication was an issue both from the perspectives of the staff and the family. The hospice team wished to communicate to the family through the hearing daughter-in-law, because that was the easiest and most economical approach. The family demanded that hospice personnel communicate directly with them by using a qualified interpreter. Once the hospice hired an interpreter and, more importantly, changed its attitude and agreed that communication was a key issue with this family, all parties involved were satisfied.

There are a number of ramifications of deafness for a Deaf survivor as they adapt to life without the deceased. Most Deaf people marry Deaf partners. In the death of a spouse, a Deaf person not only loses a wife/husband, the mother/father to their children, a lover, friend, and companion, but also a cultural and communication partner. A senior Deaf professor of mine died recently, leaving a widow of 40 years who also was deaf. She has a beautiful family of four children, all of whom are hearing, 10 hearing grandchildren, and many Deaf and hearing friends who love her dearly. Yet at her husband's memorial service, what tore at the mourners' hearts were the stories about how the couple had traveled together in their retirement years: how they were able to rely on each other to decipher the communication and quirks of the hearing world, how they took solace from each other when they were isolated on a tour because they were "different," and how they were still able to enjoy the richness of their travels because they could rely on one another.

Lastly, the process of grieving includes coming to terms with the event and continuing one's existence as a changed person. These processes are made more difficult by the fact that one has a profound hearing impairment. Growing up deaf can require a dependency on others for a variety of needs, including communication, information, and networking with the hearing world. Entitlement schooling, rehabilitation services, special medical care, and segregation of services are part of the culture of individuals with disability in the United States, including many Deaf people. Growing up, though, most Deaf people shed an entitlement persona. They become independent, self-sufficient citizens living successfully not only within their Deaf culture, but in society generally. Yet a serious loss can rekindle behaviors and feelings of dependency.

I worked with a young Deaf couple whose nine-year-old Deaf daughter died with no warning of an undetected heart ailment. Both parents were products of an archaic residential school environment, where for years hearing professionals not only took responsibility for the education of Deaf children and Deaf young adults, but went too far, in many cases, by not involving Deaf people in decisions about their lives. In the case of these wonderful parents, they were able to shed the learned dependent behaviors of the past, becoming independent, self-sufficient members of the larger society while maintaining close ties to the Deaf community and pride in Deaf culture.

When their only child died, each parent separately expressed guilt that they had not been responsible enough to care for a child. They recalled their residential school, where they were made to feel unable to attend to their own needs and make decisions for themselves. Each expressed discomfort when many people were willing to "do for" them. Dependency issues, decision-making concerns, questions of self-worth brought on by the nature of their daughter's death, and the behavior of loved ones following the death all needed to be discussed and worked through before the couple could come to terms with this tragic event and continue on their path of an independent lifestyle.

The uniqueness of grieving among Deaf people can also be viewed in terms of the disability itself. Do Deaf people, in their own unique way, grieve the loss of their hearing? And, if so, will this loss affect all future losses? The answers we have been provided are inadequate. Most writings on the subject utilize the Kübler-Ross model (1969) of experiencing loss, more appropriate for dying people than Deaf people. No research has been conducted to date to determine if this model of grieving fits this specific loss. I suspect it does not. People born deaf or who become deaf in the early stages of life do not overtly grieve over their loss of hearing. Their hearing parents may, but they do not. When asked, most Deaf people are happy with their deafness. It is not uncommon to hear a Deaf couple express a wish to have a Deaf child. Deafness is natural to them, a positive cultural identity. Dr. Ken Moses, a psychologist whose own child is disabled, has written and spoken extensively on parents' reactions to having a disabled child. Dr. Moses (1991) talks about hearing parents who give birth to a deaf child experiencing grief over the loss of "the dream of a normal child" and how difficult this grieving process may be for the remainder of a hearing parent's life.

Another population who experience grief in a different way are late-deafened people, whose unique needs have only recently been recognized. In a research study (Zieziula and Meadows, 1991), people who had experienced late deafness spoke with researchers at length about their loss experiences. Three themes were identified through the stories of the participants. First, all participants described a complex array of emotions, depending on the new life situations they faced after becoming deaf: disbelief, shock, anger, hopelessness, depression, anxiety, guilt, awkwardness, boredom, acceptance, and hope. The second theme was the difficult adaptation to secondary losses. In addition to the loss of the ability to hear, participants identified other losses in their lives: significant relationships with friends and colleagues, social activities like music and theater, and status in work, which were distinct from the loss of hearing, but just as powerful. Third, participants felt confusion over identity: whether to identify as a Deaf person or with the hearing world. In general, participants felt they accepted their physical hearing loss within two years following the loss. Although all participants eventually reached a point where they could acknowledge their deafness, many expressed a greater concern because significant others had problems accepting their physical and social conditions. Some participants stated that their parents and spouses have never accepted their disabilities.

## Suggestions for Successful Service to the Deaf Community

For individuals and agencies who wish to best serve Deaf and hearing-impaired individuals and their families, following are suggestions based on these guiding principles. First, professionals should be sensitive to the cultural history of Deaf people; second, professionals should find ways to meet the variety of communication needs of all members of this population; and third, professionals should be aware of and have a working relationship with local and national resources that specialize in serving the needs of people with hearing impairments. With these principles in mind, here are some practical recommendations for all professionals.

*Be aware that all hearing-impaired people are not alike.* Members of the Deaf community, people who are hard-of-hearing, individuals who are late-deafened, individuals who are deaf-blind, and people with serious hearing difficulties have unique needs and backgrounds like all minority populations. Do not assume that every person with a hearing impairment or, for that matter, every Deaf person identifies with the Deaf community. Do not assume that every Deaf person uses ASL or any specific sign communication system. An initial meeting with the client will clarify their background and the best way to serve their needs. Some pertinent information is: the communication system the client is comfortable using (both expressively and receptively); the degree of deafness of the individual; the age at which the deafness occurred; the educational background of the person; who else in the family is Deaf; the self-identity of the Deaf person; how you can best contact the person at home; and the kind of interpreting services needed, if any.

*Make your office communication accessible.* Each office should be equipped with a Telecommunication Device for the Deaf (TDD), an inexpensive piece of hardware and one of the strongest ties to the home of a Deaf person. Make sure you advertise the availability of a TDD for clients with hearing impairments. Use of a TDD is not limited to the Deaf community. Most hard-of-hearing and late-deafened people have them in their homes and offices. All states have implemented a hearing impaired "relay telephone service" for use by people with hearing difficulties. For Deaf people, this is the communication strategy of second choice, since it relies on a third person for communication. Yet be aware of this service and how to use it.

*Be fluent in basic sign language.* The best strategy with a Deaf person is direct communication, and knowledge of sign language and fingerspelling is key. A vocabulary of 100 signs, along with a working knowledge of the manual alphabet, can be very comforting to a grieving Deaf person. This basic knowledge should never replace the need for an interpreter where fluent conversation is needed and a Deaf person's primary communication system is ASL.

*Be cognizant of office environments and personal habits.* Office and meeting room lighting, as well as peripheral noise, are often not attended to. Well-lighted rooms are extremely important for visual communication. Peripheral noises, such as soft music or office chatter, may interfere with hearing aid use. Eliminating as many of these environmental distractions as possible will enhance communication with a person with a hearing impairment.

*Personal habits should be reviewed.* For example, it is not a problem for hearing people to understand the communication of a person who is chewing while talking. Yet it can be a cause of great frustration for a Deaf person who is trying to lipread. To a certain degree, all Deaf people observe lip movements for cues to what is being said. Talking with hands on one's mouth or covering one's mouth can impede communication. In group settings, do not talk with your back turned to the Deaf individual. When using an inter-preter, do not talk to the interpreter rather than to the client. Instead, face the Deaf person and speak directly to her/him. Ignore the interpreter and concentrate on communication with the client.

*Be aware of interpreting resources in your community.* Before a client walks into your office, their communication needs should be identified. It is very uncomfortable for a Deaf person to show up at the first meeting with a counselor and not be able to interact in a satisfactory way. Ask about the communication needs of the Deaf person when the appointment is scheduled. If interpreting is required, make sure that you choose an interpreter who is certified by the Registry of Interpreters for the Deaf (RID). If an interpreter can-not be located through the yellow pages or professional networking contacts, ask the client for a suggestion of a RID-certified person or call the closest school for the Deaf in your area and ask for a referral. Do not ask the Deaf person to bring a family member or friend with them for interpreting purposes.

*Be knowledgeable about the Americans with Disabilities Act (ADA).* Be aware of the legal rights the ADA provides for Deaf people. It is equally important to know what accommodations and services must be provided to be in compliance with the law. In providing grief counseling to a Deaf person, the question of who pays for interpreting services is always raised. It is in the best interest of the community at large and Deaf people specifically to provide for open communication in all meetings and services. Yet the law, when written, was cognizant of the needs of private practices and provided great latitude for small businesses that could not operate if required to provide certain ADA services. Likewise, volunteer, non-profit organizations whose services are offered free-of-charge are not oblig-ed to pay for interpretation services if the cost would cause undue hardship. Anyone who provides social services and is committed to opening services to all disabled people should become familiar with the provisions of the ADA. A great deal of information is available through Federal government offices as well as the Internet (see http://www.gsa.gov/staff/pa/cic/fedprogs.htm).

*Make meetings and group services accessible to Deaf people.* Do not assume Deaf people are aware of your services. Advertise in magazines and newspapers read by the Deaf community, as well as to social and religious organizations frequented by Deaf people. A local chapter of the NAD can be helpful in locating appropriate conduits for advertising. Make sure your announcements to the general public welcome people with special needs and announce if interpreting services (ASL, signed English) will or can be provided.

*Include members of disability groups on your advisory boards.* Empowerment is a key tenet of the Deaf community. Deaf people are capable of speaking eloquently for themselves and the variety of hearing-impaired people they may represent. It is a powerful symbol of empowerment to request that a Deaf person serve on an existing advisory board. While this may be time consuming and costly (when interpreting services need to be contracted), it is the best way to involve the Deaf community and assure that Deaf clients will use an agency's services.

*Caption media materials.* Federal law requires that all television sets larger than 19 inches sold in this country be installed with a computer chip that allows for closed captioning. Professionals developing media materials should make the effort to have them captioned so that they are accessible for people with hearing impairments. Better yet, captions can be supplemented by sign language, and Deaf people can be part of the content of the video. A good example is Heritage Hospice of Danville, Kentucky (1996), which produced a video, "Neither Silent Nor Alone," explaining the concept and services of hospice to the Deaf and hard-of-hearing communities. The video uses both captions and sign language.

*Be aware of resources available for clients and professionals.* Many national and local organizations exist that serve the needs of the diversity of Deaf people. These organizations are divided into two groups: those that serve the Deaf or hard-of-hearing or late-deafened consumers and those that assist professionals to better serve all hearing impaired people. These groups can be valuable for information and as resources to help find contacts in your area. There are also outstanding written materials available to learn more about the lives of Deaf people.

*Provide service with a "can do" attitude.* The most important suggestion for counselors and professionals involved in grief work with Deaf people is to have a positive "can do" attitude. Deafness does not present an insurmountable obstacle to proceeding through the grieving process. Attitudes based on pity or dependency do not serve the interest of the Deaf mourner.

*Editor's note:* The organizations referred to in this chapter are included in the Resource List.

---

*Frank R. Zieziula is Professor of Counseling at Gallaudet University. He is director of a masters degree training program in counseling with deaf people, and director of the Association for Coping With Loss.*

# FIFTEEN

# Sexual Orientation and Grief

*Ron E. Wilder*

Even dying is not enough to end the discrimination that gay men, lesbians, and bisexuals face every day. In fact, this discrimination often escalates at the end of life, when loved ones are most vulnerable. There are many factors that contribute to this, but more often than not friends and relatives do not know what to say or do to help a gay man, a lesbian, or a bisexual work through the loss of someone they love. Until the onset of the AIDS epidemic, the literature on grief and bereavement revealed little about the loss of a life partner or a loved one in gay, lesbian, or bisexual relationships.

Over the past decade studies have been conducted on the grieving process of gay men who have lost loved ones due to AIDS. There has still not been any extensive research conducted on the loss of a lesbian lover due to breast or ovarian cancer, on the loss of a gay male lover due to prostate cancer, or on the loss of a lover due to natural causes in a gay or lesbian relationship. The literature is just not there.

Faced with anti-gay violence, AIDS, and disease, the issue of mortality is, unfortunately, often on the minds of gays and lesbians. Yet with so much grief and so many problems facing the gay and lesbian community, the "normal" issues of loss and grief are often overlooked. In fact, the death, dying, and bereavement issues facing gays, lesbians, and bisexuals as they get older have been almost completely ignored.

## What is Sexual Orientation?

Sexual orientation is one of the four components of sexuality and is distinguished by an enduring emotional, romantic, sexual, or affectionate attraction to individuals of a particular gender. The other three components of sexuality are biological sex, gender identity (the psychological sense of being male or female), and social sex role (adherence to cultural norms for feminine and masculine behavior) (Garnets et al., 1991). Three sexual orientations are commonly recognized: homosexual, attraction to individuals of one's own gender; heterosexual, attraction to individuals of the other gender; or bisexual, attraction to members of both genders. Persons with a homosexual orientation are sometimes referred to as gay (both men and women) or as lesbian (women only). Persons with a heterosexual orientation are referred to as straight.

Sexual orientation is different from sexual behavior in that it refers to feelings and self-concept. Individuals may or may not express their sexual orientation in their behavior (Garnets and Kimmel, 1993). How a particular sexual orientation develops in any individual is not well understood by scientists. Various sources have been proposed, including genetic or hormonal factors and life experiences during early childhood. However, many scientists share the view that sexual orientation is shaped for most people at an early age through complex interactions of biological, psychological, and social factors.

## What is Grief?

In *Dying: Facing the Facts* (1995), Therese A. Rando defines grief as "the process of experiencing the psychological, behavioral, social, and physical reactions to the perception of loss." She goes on to explain that this definition has five important implications:

1. Grief is experienced in four major ways (sorrow or guilt, anger at or preoccupation with the deceased, confusion or physical symptoms, social withdrawl or increased use of psychoactive substances);

2. Grief is a continuing development involving many changes over time;
3. Grief is a natural, expected reaction;
4. Grief is a reaction to all types of loss, not exclusively death;
5. The experiencing of grief depends on the individuals' unique perception of loss, regardless of whether the same perception is held by others (a desirable, but not necessary, condition).

This definition of grief will be used to explore the specific factors influencing grieving in the gay, lesbian, and bisexual community.

## Grief in the Gay Community

The Gay Community is not a specific place. Despite a shared sexual orientation, people in the Gay Community are not always cohesive and mutually supportive. In these gay, lesbian, and bisexual communities there is grief at all levels: among individuals, within groups, and pervasively throughout the community. The symptoms of *loss saturation*, grief from multiple losses, in the community closely parallel the impact of grief on individuals. Most symptoms can be attributed to the emotionally and physically draining nature of grief, the lack of acknowledgment and support in the grieving process (*disenfranchised grief*), and feelings of helplessness, rage, and survivor guilt.

One outcome of the AIDS crisis that has helped the members of the gay, lesbian, and bisexual community has been an awareness of the need for mourning rituals. Whereas the concept of a memorial service is not new, many AIDS memorials have become highly personal (sometimes theatrical, sometimes political, and sometimes humorous) in ways far removed from traditional observances. AIDS memorials often came about due to the need to have a ritual for the deceased's "gay family" apart from their "straight family." Invariably, these memorials have emphasized the person's gayness, loving relationships with members of the same sex, and the connection with the gay, lesbian, and bisexual community.

These rituals should not be limited to AIDS-related deaths. There is a need to remember and celebrate the struggle to develop a gay/lesbian identity, and its attendant connections. Lovers, ex-lovers, and friends can share and remember. It has often been necessary to create specific rituals for this purpose.

## Grief and Coping After a Life Partner's Death

Just as in a heterosexual relationship, a gay or lesbian relationship grows and lasts, and the initial exhilarating feeling of being in love settles into a comfortable familiarity, with a shared intimacy and private jokes about mundane things. For lesbians and gay men, this can be doubly wonderful because it represents the right and ability to love fully and deeply in spite of overwhelming odds.

The research on stress has consistently reported the death of a close relative, especially a spouse, as the most stressful passage in life. The partner who confirmed the ability to love and be loved is no longer there. This is true in a general sense for gay as well as straight people, although there are important differences.

First, joining your life with a lover is a significant developmental step for many lesbians and gay men. It confirms the ability to love, despite having grown up thinking it is wrong or will never happen. Unlike heterosexuals, when gays and lesbians present lovers and lives shared together to the world, it is an act of pride and identity. This is as true in the supermarket check-out line as it is on a visit to Aunt Harriet or Uncle Ted.

To lose a spouse is devastating to anyone. But for lesbians and gay men, the loss of a life partner also entails the loss of a built identity, both individually and as part of a lesbian or gay couple. For those who are not *out* (living a life that shows others that they are gay or lesbian) to family or co-workers, the loss can be especially hard because it is not fully shared. Expressions of sympathy and respect are not forthcoming. The silence is difficult because it doesn't acknowledge that the center of one's life is missing.

All too often, even to those who are out, the straight community doesn't acknowledge or recognize the full importance of the loss.

This discrepancy is reflected in practical matters, such as company bereavement leave policies, as well as in personal ways, such as silence from extended family or an expectation that one should be "moving on" more quickly. It can be subtle, as when co-workers don't know what to say, or when they casually and thoughtlessly talk about their marriages in a way that would be more appropriate with a straight widow or widower. In part, this reflects society's general discomfort with death. But the lack of recognition also reflects homophobia. There is a scene in *Torch Song Trilogy* (Feinstein, 1979) when the character's mother is angered at his equating the loss of his partner with the loss of her husband.

> **MA** Wait, wait, wait, wait. Are you trying to compare my marriage with you and Alan? Your father and I were married for 35 years, had two children and a wonderful life together. You have the nerve to compare yourself to that?
>
> **ARNOLD** That's not what I mean, I'm talking about loss.
>
> **MA** What loss did you have? You fooled around with some boy...? Where do you come to compare that to a marriage of 35 years?
>
> **ARNOLD** You think it doesn't?
>
> **MA** Come on, Arnold. You think you're talking to one of your pals?
>
> **ARNOLD** Ma, I lost someone that I loved very much...
>
> **MA** So you felt bad. Maybe you cried a little. But what would you know about what I went through? Thirty-five years I lived with that man, he got sick, I brought him to the hospital and you know what they gave me back? I gave them a man...they gave me a paper bag with his watch, wallet and wedding ring. How could you possibly know what that felt like? It took me two months until I could sleep in our bed alone, a year to learn to say "I" instead of "we." And you're going to tell me you were "widowing." How dare you!

**ARNOLD** You're right, Ma. How dare I. I couldn't possibly know how it feels to pack someone's clothes in plastic bags and watch the garbage pickers carry them away. Or what it feels like to forget and set his place at the table. How about the food that rots in the refrigerator because you forgot how to shop for one? How dare I?

Nothing quite prepares a person for the sudden realization that one's lover is no longer physically in the world. Even when there has been preparation for the death, as with AIDS and other prolonged illnesses such as breast cancer, it is impossible to be fully prepared until it happens. Some people feel tremendous grief and sorrow. Others feel nothing at first. It is important not to judge an immediate reaction as the full response to the loss; bereavement is a process rather than an event. One common feeling is dissociation, a feeling of not being in the real world. The loss of a part of oneself, the part that joined with another as a loving unit, is akin to having an amputation. Actually, the business side of death (attending to funerals, notifying friends and family, dealing with estates) often provides a needed focus for the grieving person. Many people are amazed at the survivor's ability to attend to these matters. It makes sense when it is realized that this is a way of still caring for and about the lover who died.

A whole host of feelings gradually emerge. Grieving is as unique as the individuals who experience loss, and varied emotions come up differently for different people. Depression and sadness over the loss are universal; however, for some it is a constant feeling, while for others it is intermittent. Numbness and dissociation occur frequently as well. There can be a sense of living in two worlds, the everyday world that goes on and one's own private world of grief.

It is common also to feel angry, angry at your lover for leaving you, angry at the world for not caring enough, angry over AIDS or breast cancer or heart disease. The anger may be clear and direct, or it may direct itself at other people or seemingly unrelated things.

None of these feelings is wrong. They are all reactions to a profound loss. It is not unusual for combinations of feeling to arise at different times. If the depression deepens, causing more serious dysfunction, a support group, a therapist, or possibly a psychiatrist may helpful. But depression and impaired functioning are normal after a death, and may persist for some time.

The bereaved get repeated messages from concerned friends and family to "move on." It is very appropriate to need a period of time to "hold onto" the person who has died. Some people talk to their lovers when they are alone and missing them. Others have dreams in which the lover is still alive. It is important to give special recognition to things that recall the loved one: a special dish or a favorite CD. Although these rituals may evoke pain, they also value the person who has died, and focus on his or her life rather than solely on death and loss.

It can be helpful to reach out to others who have also lost important people in their lives. They often can be the most understanding. This shared experience is why bereavement groups have proven so helpful, especially in the case of AIDS-related deaths. Many gay, social service, and religious organizations sponsor bereavement programs. If a group is not gay- or lesbian-specific, find out if it is at least gay-sensitive (friendly to gay people and their sense of personal loss). It is our jobs as caregivers to be able to reach out and help gay, lesbian, and bisexual people who are suffering from grief. Caregivers need to be able to accept these people simply as people that are grieving the loss of someone, and not let it matter that the loved one was the same sex. Caregivers need to be sensitive to the fact that these people have to do battle every day in the normal world just because they are gay, lesbian, or bisexual, and be aware that they need just as much (if not more) assistance in the grieving process.

Although it is small comfort at the moment of loss, the old dictum that the intensity of grief diminishes over time is true. But it is usually a much longer period of time than expected. A loved one who dies is never truly forgotten. Love was a reflection of growth and development for each individual and as a couple. There is added significance for those who have had to overcome homophobia and fear to find a measure of acceptance in a loving relationship. The loss will be felt periodically, and also unexpectedly, tempered but not eliminated by the knowledge that to have loved is also to have become a part of another, a full person with the human right to have genuine and caring love in your life.

At present there are still limited resources which directly address the specific stresses of loss which are related to sexual orientation. Specific organizations, such as the Whitman-Walker Clinic (Washington, DC) and Gay Men's Health Crisis (New York) are sources of information and support regarding grief in the gay, lesbian, and bisexual community.

---

*Ron E. Wilder is currently the administrative officer of the American Psychological Association. He directs a program responsible for graduate students and their affiliation with APA, and is on the Board of Directors of the Association for Death Education and Counseling.*

# SIXTEEN

# Cultural Aspects of Peer Support: An Examination of One Program's Experience

*Bonnie Carroll*

M ilitary service is a profession of arms, a tradition as old as civilization; for as long as troops have been rallied in defense of nations, soldiers have died on the field of battle. This service has been idealized and these deaths romanticized. In 1000 BC, Homer wrote in *The Iliad*, "A glorious death is his, who for his country falls." Six hundred years later, Sophocles spoke this way of death in battle: "It is the brave man's part to live with glory, or with glory die."

Two Federal holidays, Memorial Day and Veterans Day, honor those who have served and died in the national defense. There are even terms to refer to this loss that are different from any other sort of death experience. Those who have died in the military have *given their lives in service to their country* or they have *made the ultimate sacrifice.*

In an age of high-tech weaponry and remote control warfare, it is easy to forget that those in uniform are training with high-powered weapons loaded with live ammunition, flying supersonic aircraft in high-speed maneuvers, and operating heavy equipment in less than ideal conditions. These training activities are inherently dangerous, and casualties do occur. In the event of casualties, the military has well-honed regulations to deal with the disposition of the deceased service member and take care of the family in the immediate after-math of a military death, seeing to all administrative matters in an efficient manner and providing benefits for next of kin.

What is not addressed in military regulations or directives is the emotional fate of the loved ones left behind. Military culture has developed a ceremonial way of bidding farewell to comrades who have died a *glorious death* and bringing closure to units that must continue to fly and fight. The families and friends grieving the death of a service member are included in the final tribute, a funeral or memorial service filled with military tradition: presentation of a care-fully folded American flag, firing of a 21-gun salute, the mournful sound of taps echoing across rows of white headstones. And then they are left to grieve the death alone.

Those who raise their hand and pledge their life "to protect and defend" do so knowing the dangers and risks. However, those who say "I do" at the altar, or who are born into a military family, or who see their child off to Basic Training, do not make that same pledge. Yet they are a vital part of the military team. They grow up in base housing, move from assignment to assignment, live for letters from overseas, wait through long deployments, and build a life around the service of their loved one. When a death occurs, their grief is com-plicated by their own loss of lifestyle and compounded by history's view of death in the armed forces.

A noted bereavement specialist was addressing a room full of military survivors at the Tragedy Assistance Program for Survivors' (TAPS) annual national seminar. Every one of the attendees had been directly affected by the death of a loved one in the armed forces, whether they had lost a spouse, sibling, child, parent, or friend, and was connected by no other bonds than the military and the loss.

When the lecturer offered very sound, albeit generic, advice on coping with the death of a loved one, he told the group, "You don't have to make any major decisions in the first year." Hands shot up and knowing glances were exchanged around the room. *Ah, but in the military, moving is a way of life and you must leave base housing after the death of a service member if you are the "dependents."* Then he offered the next good, standard piece of advice, to "lean on your circle of friends." Again, hands shot up and people nodded at each other. *That circle of friends will disappear almost immediately when you move away, as you must when someone dies on active duty, and if you remain in the community around the military base where the death occurred, within two years every single person who was there at the time of the death will have transferred out, leaving you alone and stranded.* The point here is not how difficult those military survivors have it when a death occurs; rather, it is how wonderful that knowing nod was in a room full of people who had finally found others who really understood.

This holds true for children as well. Two six-year-olds, who had each lost a father in the same Air Force plane crash, were talking animatedly about what they had overheard the grownups saying regarding their crash and their dads' cause of death. These children shared the same fears, talked through the difficult information which they had found particularly puzzling, and found that they were not alone. They were going through a loss that to the military was tragic, to their teachers was horrifying, and to their young friends was incomprehensible. However, in that childlike conversation, they found a link to each other, an "understanding nod" that told them that they were going to be okay.

That's the secret of support groups which deal with specific types of loss experiences. You take your broken heart and wounded spirit and lean over the proverbial backyard fence with a cup of coffee in your hand and talk to a fellow survivor about the things you could not share with anyone else on earth. In the case of a military death, that could be burnt dog tags, burials at sea, or bombs exploding. Subjects, certainly, that no one else wants to hear about! And even if out of morbid curiosity, a sense of duty, or long-standing friendship they listen, they certainly cannot relate and jump up at just the right moment exclaiming, "That's it! That's exactly precisely absolutely what I felt/wondered/thought!"

The experience can be very healing. Proof that you're not crazy; or, if you are, that you're not alone in your insanity. These fellow military survivors are the ones who understand that Memorial Day and Veterans Day are now sacred holidays, not just long weekends for vacationing. These are the people who stand a little taller as the flag passes by in a parade. Or who feel tears well up when taps is soulfully played on a lone trumpet. It's a sad, sacred fellowship of those who have been there and who *know*. It's not a club you want to join, but it's one you surely don't want to be alone in.

In America, the power of the support group is recognized; each type of experience is unique and only those who have walked that path can empathize, understand, and have the "moral authority" to relate. When someone dies in a jet fighter crash and someone dies in a shooting at the local convenience store, the end result is the same. A knock on the door and word that a life has ended all too soon. For those left behind, the world has stopped turning. Yet look at the experience of the two families in the weeks to come. The homicide survivors will likely have considerable contact with the police, and if the killer is apprehended and convicted they will face months and possibly years of court trials, sentencing, newspaper stories, eventual parole hearings, and coping with the injustice of it all. They will also grieve the loss of security. Imagine being killed buying bread at the neighborhood market. A loss of faith in humankind, that another human being, a total stranger, could do this. And they will learn more about the legal system than the average American learned during interminable months of *People v. O.J. Simpson*.

Why do these families find tremendous comfort in groups for homicide survivors? And why could they not relate to those suffering an equally tragic sudden death in the armed forces, or in a drunk driving crash, or of a heart attack? The type of support that is so vital to healing can only be found in those who share the elements unique to each cultural loss, and who have lived the nightmare of that specific type of death.

A mother who had discovered her precious baby dead of SIDS several years before was introduced to another woman who had just recently experienced the same tragedy. Off in a corner, the first woman asked breathlessly, "Did you find the baby? Was he blue? Did you try to save him? Did people make you feel guilty? Did the police question you? How is your marriage now?" Questions fired off in rapid sequence, and eagerly answered. At last, a chance to say, "Yes!

He was blue and it was awful. People did make me feel guilty, without meaning to! And the police did question me and it was horrible! And they tried to be nice but they also asked those questions. Of me, his mother! And my marriage *is* suffering, but I don't want anyone to know, and I don't know what to do." The first woman had no professional training, but her understanding, her nod, if you will, was all it took to remove the heavy weight of guilt and burden from her new-found friend, just by letting her know she was not alone and giving her a safe environment to share the pain.

When military survivors attend a community grief support group, they often find themselves quietly sitting in the circle thinking, "But John didn't die quietly in his sleep after a long illness: the crash was violent and sudden. He didn't live well into retirement: he was killed suddenly at age 24. I may never know the results of the Air Force investigation, it's all private: I don't have the trial and all that disclosure. I can't relate!"

These groups may offer consolation but not true validation. They can explain the grieving process in general terms, provide a safe and loving environment to talk about death, and give people a chance to come together. But how much more powerful was that brief conversation with the two mothers, exploring things that no one else would, or could, talk about; or the children sharing the details of their fathers' deaths in the same crash; or the homicide survivors, sitting outside the courtroom, sharing rage and fears and anxious moments over the fate of the killer. Only one who has walked that painful road can truly empathize, or have the moral authority to say, "I understand!" And that knowing nod is a powerful comfort and healer.

Each loss has a unique language, culture, and journey. The words are unique, the culture a part of our very individual souls, and the road mapped only by those who have walked it before and have it carved in their hearts.

In talking to a group of survivors about the value of the support group for those affected by a death in the armed forces, former Chairman of the Joint Chiefs of Staff General John Shalikashvili said:

I have been wondering since I heard about TAPS, why is it that the military never created something like this? And then it became patently clear to me that there's no way to organize something like this in the military. What would we do? Have lieutenant so-and-so, or sergeant so-and-so, call you and talk to you? A young man or woman who simply cannot share your experience? It can't be done. It can only be done by people who have walked this very difficult road before you, and who are now willing to devote their energies and their caring and their heart, to take your hand and say, "Walk with me, I can help you."

Time and time again, military survivors who find this support group echo that very sentiment in their own experience. The widow of a Navy pilot who crashed at sea was asked by a local support grief group what had helped her cope. She remembered, "Nothing anyone said would have made me feel better. What I needed was someone who had been there before me. Ironically, that friend came in the widow of the F-18 pilot whom my husband had done Search and Rescue for, not six months earlier." A total stranger, yet someone bonded to her because she understood, she spoke the language, lived the culture, and traveled the road before her.

A young fiancée shared a similar story. She was living a dream life: well-educated, employed, and finally ready to start a family on a solid foundation. She met the man of her dreams, a Navy instructor pilot, but months before their wedding day, on Valentine's Day, 1995, those hopes and dreams crashed with him into the Gulf of Mexico. Her "peer support" came from his Squadron, who shared her pain in mourning a friend, a fellow aviator, and colleague. She recounted:

Certain items, although precious before, become more treasured in the aftermath of traumatic loss. It's as if you've lost everything else and these few things are all you have left. They are evidence of the life you once knew, the life you desperately want back. Loss in the military accentuates this like no other. You have not only lost the one you love but also a way of life. A camaraderie, a culture, an attitude. Reminders of this can be painful, but they help us realize the significance our loved one played in the lives of others.

The Rangers of Training Squadron 28 at NAS Corpus Christi were an immense support to me after David's accident. Their mere presence gave me strength to face each grueling day, each difficult ceremony. On a bright, typically windy day in Corpus Christi, the Commander of the Squadron called me aside. Without fanfare or ceremony, he quietly gave me a most precious gift: Framed in gold was a picture of two Navy T34C aircraft in flight over Corpus Christi Bay, the same area where David had trained, taught, and tragically died. The skyline of the city in the background, the image of the Carrier Lexington below.

The picture was surrounded by a blue mat covered with hand-written memories and stories of squadron members about my beloved. Most were simple but spoke volumes to me. The most common observance was that David always had a smile on his face and brought out the best in those around him (something I knew already, but it was nice to know others did, too!). Each had his own little story, and it all came from the heart. This picture and the signatures that surround it remind me of the reason David was so proud to be a Naval Aviator and Officer. Its meaning to me is far reaching. It gives me the honor of knowing that others were touched by him and that he lives on in the minds and hearts of those who knew him. It also lets me know that they thought enough of our relationship to bestow upon me such a lovely remembrance. It was a bond we shared, a loss only we could understand.

When a military survivor hears of a crash, explosion, or incident similar to the one that has claimed their loved one, their first reaction is often panic. They can still vividly remember when they were first told of the death, still feel the shock and disbelief, the pain, the fear, the sense of being lost. But now there is a way to reach out, to comfort, and to act. Through peer support groups, survivors reach out to let the grieving family know that they are not alone, that there is a support system, that someone understands and can honestly relate to the things they will be going through.

One young widow who reached out in just this way met another survivor for lunch. While they had little in common on the surface, they shared a deep bond. One was 23, the other 33. One had four children, the other had none. One was married for a year and a half, the other for 13 years. When they met, the only thing they knew they had in common was the loss of their husbands in military accidents. They talked for three hours that afternoon, and their friendship began. They laughed and cried, were able to share their grief, their memories, and their hopes for the future. Their friendship moved beyond being widows. As the first survivor related, "She's not my 'widow' friend, she's my *friend*. She has helped me so much. And I've helped her. I would never have called her if it hadn't been for my association with TAPS. Although our friendship came out of tragic circumstances, it is a friendship that I truly cherish."

Another young widow described her loss and her first connection with the peer support group as follows:

> My husband, a Marine Corps Captain, was killed just a couple of weeks before ending his deployment in Japan when his FA-18 plane crashed off the Korean coast. During my emotional roller coaster, searching for answers, comfort, or even peace, I read the Survivors' Handbook that the Navy had so insightfully prepared. At first, I thought, "survivor of *what?*"

> Still in shock, only weeks after the devastating news, I found a small excerpt about the Tragedy Assistance Program for Survivors. Not knowing what this organization was all about, but desperate for answers, I called. Within a half hour, the phone rang and I heard the warm, caring voice of a fellow survivor; a call filled with empathy, needed advice, and, most importantly, information.

> Knowledge is the power behind strength and that's what this group stands for. TAPS is a group of caring individuals united by their loves ones' ultimate sacrifice. They are ready and willing to take on new challenges; whether you need a listening ear, a shoulder to cry on, or information regarding your personal situation. The military lifestyle shelters us from the civilian sector, creating a huge struggle for those affected by a tragic military death.

This phone call was one of the most empowering conversations I've ever had. A total stranger relating, sharing, and guiding me during this crisis. I was amazed there were others like me, people caught in this web of confusion, all of us desperate for answers, dealing with the same difficult issues. Most military families live far from their friends and other relatives, leaving a void with little support. The fragile uncertainty of what happens next with your health insurance, finances, use of base facilities, and housing adds to the uphill battle of acceptance. The grief that follows a military death is compounded by so many other extenuating circumstances. Those words from the survivors gave me the strength to endure, the power to move on, and the knowledge to succeed in starting my new life.

Cultural differences take many forms, and in the microcosm of the military another subset of survivors went largely unnoticed, unrecognized, and unsupported for a quarter of a century. That is, until TAPS counselor Sally Griffis took her own personal tragedy, the death of her husband in Vietnam, and dedicated her life to researching this loss, providing a link for others, and in doing so, healing her own heart and the hearts of thousands of women who have borne the burden of unrecognized grief.

In 1970, one day after Sally gave birth to her second child, her husband Bill was killed in Vietnam. The pain of his death has never gone away. According to her, "It has blended into the fabric of my life, creating a complicated pattern of bereavement, courage, strength, and joy." Twenty-four years after his death, she decided to pursue a doctorate in psychology. While reading literature on Post-traumatic Stress Disorder, she found little research concerning the wives of Vietnam casualties. She wondered about the other widows of that war, who had been young women often left with infants to raise alone, their grief experience complicated by an unpopular war in a nation torn apart. She longed for that knowing nod, that honest empathy. She found no research on this specific loss experience. It was as though the widows, numbering approximately 18,000, had no voice, no recognition, no acknowledgment. There was nothing to let them know that they were not alone, that they shared a common bond with thousands who were desperately struggling to cope and heal all across America. Sally dedicated her research and her life to exploring this unique aspect of grief in the military, and has found that our nation is dotted with shared experiences that can heal only when validated by another who has been there and who can ease the pain by truly understanding it.

Unlike the war widow, much has been researched and studied about Vietnam-era victims of Post-traumatic Stress, and the *walking wounded* from war. We have been fascinated by veterans and Post-traumatic Stress, their long-term emotional suffering and their coping mechanisms. Yet the missing piece, which often comes in the quiet conversations of vets meeting at the Wall, or in the back rows of Memorial Day ceremonies, or in that knowing nod when service in Southeast Asia is recognized, is the profound power of peer support.

Scott Robart shares his memories of a friend lost in the war, and in doing so, passionately shares the perspective echoed by thousands of veterans who are coping with the loss of friends in Vietnam.

> I often see Richie Forte in my mind. Nothing has dimmed the memory of his smile and the sparkling eyes so common to those vibrant young men, some only in their teens. Because he lives only in my mind, he looks exactly like he did when I saw him last, at Newton High School in June, 1966.
>
> To be honest, Richie and I were not *close* friends, we were just *good* friends, so I lost contact with him until January, 1969, my third year in Vietnam. I was reading a worn and muddied copy of *Stars and Stripes* in a place called Bao Loc, and my eyes fell on his name under the heading Killed in Action. "Richard J. Forte, Newton, Mass., December 23, 1968."
>
> Although some time has passed since that day, my friendship with Richie continues to urge me to speak of him. I used to let him through the one-way doors of the old North High School. He would occasionally remind me how beautiful he thought my girlfriend was. Perhaps most importantly, in those days filled with raging hormones and total uncertainty about life, he'd sometimes refer to me as being cool. We never exchanged a harsh word. He never criticized anything close to me, nor I to him.

Richie's death came as a shock to me. His was the closest death I was to experience from the tragedy that was Vietnam. His loss continues to play a role in my life, sometimes soft and plaintive, like a spring rain.

Through the 70s, Richie was never far from my mind as many of us veterans worked for our country's extrication from Vietnam. He was my strongest connection to the concept of losing more "Richies" over there. His memory provided a critical, personal connection to the issue.

When the Vietnam Veterans' Memorial was dedicated in Washington, I participated in the reading of names. They were to have been read in public at the site, but the politics of the day prevailed and the reading was relegated to a small chapel at the National Cathedral. I went to the chapel the day before I was to take my turn, and heard Richie's name being read as I took my seat. I was stunned by the coincidence. A hand reached out to mine and someone asked, "Are you okay?" I fell to my knees and began to sob, unable to explain.

Through Veterans Days and Memorial Days, anniversaries of the fall of Saigon and other days in between, I have continued to think of Richie. Every time I go to Washington, I stop at the Wall, where I am reminded of the terrible cost of the war by the engraved names of over 58,000 "Richies." It's an incredibly powerful experience.

I always find Richie's name and think what a waste his death was, and how much more painful his loss must have been for those who were closest to him. Have they managed somehow to forget when I have not? I don't think so, yet part of me wishes they had, for it hurts me to think of the pain they must continue to feel.

If I could locate Richie's parents I would want them to know that there are others who had relationships with Richie whom they may be unaware of. That there are others who still carry memories of him, keeping him alive in a sense. That even though it was 28 years ago, I continue to remember their son with fondness, and his loss with an intense lament.

Each person lives in a unique culture defined through jobs, friends, experiences, neighborhoods, faith, families, and education. Only those who have lived those shared experiences can speak the unique language, understand the inside jokes, and move comfortably within the group. These become vital connections when the stakes are raised to coping with a death. At a time when the world has stopped for one among them and things seem their darkest, it is those who share the deep bond of a common culture who rally to provide support and comfort. No amount of counseling can match the validation of the knowing nod; and while peer support cannot replace professional therapy, it can complement it and provide a safe harbor in rough seas.

---

*Bonnie Carroll is President of Tragedy Assistance Program for Survivors (TAPS), a national non-profit organization providing services to those who have suffered the loss of a loved one in the Armed Forces.*

# PART IV

# Making Sense Out of Loss

How then do we use knowledge of individual and cultural differences in loss to assist those struggling with grief? The chapters in this section assist both in identifying critical sensitivities and in suggesting basic counseling approaches.

One critical area is ethics. One of the dangers of cultural relativism is that it challenges the notion of ethical imperatives or even standards of care. For example, in North American culture, individual autonomy is highly regarded. Critical to a system of care, then, is a patient's right to know about his or her condition and care options, and therefore, to participate in decisions about care. But among many groups there may be a pervasive need to protect the patient, or even not to share bad news. How does one balance these conflicting needs? Price's chapter, aptly titled "Deciding What Is Right When We Are So Different," explores the ethical dilemmas that arise from Tolerance. In reviewing a series of cases, he affirms that tolerance of other perspectives is a critical ethic, but often, other principles, too, will need to be applied in ethical decision-making.

Neimeyer and Keesee offer an integrative model that in many ways represents a new wave in our thinking about grief. In this model, the central process in grief is reconstructing meaning in the face of loss. As their chapter shows, this sort of approach is extremely useful, for it allows us to acknowledge the many ways in which an individual's unique attributes, cultural identity, and spirituality may influence both the meaning of the loss and the ways one seeks to redefine the world in the face of that loss.

While Neimeyer and Keesee emphasize theory, the chapters of Ellis and Zulli stress techniques. Ellis' chapter provides a broad overview of the essence of counseling diverse groups of people. He reminds us that counselors and caregivers need to look toward themselves, acknowledging their own values and beliefs. For example, many counselors may value emotional expressiveness much more than cognitive reconstruction. They may affirm individual autonomy more than familial or communal solidarity. They may relate better to clients who are open to self-disclosure. They may see insight as a goal of counseling, rather than assistance with day-to-day functioning.

All of these values may limit interactions with clients who have different values or perspectives. For example, a cultural group may not value self-disclosure or emotional expressiveness. And such an approach can fail to validate certain grieving styles, such as masculine grieving. In many cultural groupings, family or communal solidarity ranks before individual autonomy. In some populations, such as lower socio-economic groups, practical advice may be more appreciated than personal insight (Sue and Sue, 1990). And any counselor's style of communication may or may not fit with what is needed or valued by a particular client.

To Ellis, acknowledging these differences is the beginning of effective counseling. He reiterates other points stressed throughout this volume: There is no magic way to bridge the individual differences that may divide us; rather, what counselors need is to examine these differences carefully, to be willing to journey together. At times this merely means actively identifying and surmounting mistrust, recovering from gaffes that will occur in cross-cultural communication, and using a variety of styles, approaches, and sensitivities.

Ellis also reminds us of the key traits counselors should possess: flexibility and sensitivity to the many losses individuals experience. He notes that many individuals, when they experience one loss, may be aware of other unresolved losses. The meaning of one loss may be tied to others. The counselor's gift, then, is to allow individuals to prioritize and explore these losses, knowing that these priorities may change in the counseling process.

Ellis' chapter reminds us, too, of three essential aspects of sensitivity. The key to assisting clients is not in attempting to master another culture—that is simply too complex. Rather, it is a sensitivity to information, to ask questions rather than assume answers.

Caregiving is also about taking risks. We dare to reach out, to enter into a relationship, to learn together. So often, as other chapters reflect, a person from a different culture may not be approached by caregivers who feel unsure or want to respect the other's autonomy. Indeed, by reaching out, one runs the risk of rejection, but that is preferable to the risk that a patient or client may feel abandoned.

And that reinforces the need for a third skill. Sue and Sue (1990) state that among the critical skills of a counselor working with diversity are "recovery skills." Recovery skills are simply techniques that allow us to move forward, even after an awkward gaffe. It can be as simple as an acknowledgment of the mistake, an apology, an honest confession of misunderstanding, or a processing of the failed interaction. Such skills spare the counselor the burden of perfection. As such, they allow risk.

Zulli's chapter reminds us of an interventive strategy that can speak to many, regardless of individual differences. Ritual itself is universal. Some of the earliest evidence reminds us that even prehistoric humans had rituals to assist them as they coped with dying and death (Mumford, 1961). Rituals are powerful, Gennep (1960) reminds us, because they are liminal, that is, they speak to us simultaneously at a conscious and unconscious level. Zulli, then, offers sound suggestions for empowering individuals to use rituals as they cope with loss. One advantage of living in a culturally diverse society is that we have the ability to see varied rituals and traditions. Counselors or other caregivers may feel free to share alternate rituals with clients, providing them with additional options for creating their own meaningful rituals.

Finally, in the last chapter in this section, Smith reiterates the message that counselors and caregivers should look to themselves. His metaphor of the wounded healer is a critical reaffirmation that by acknowledging our common hurts we have the potential of transcending individual differences.

# SEVENTEEN

# Dimensions of Diversity in the Reconstruction of Meaning

*Robert A. Neimeyer and Nancy J. Keesee*

B ill and Martha sought therapy one year to the day after the death of their son, Michael, age 22. From his youth Michael had suffered from a severe and life-threatening asthma, from which he died during his junior year abroad. With Bill's stoic support, Martha tearfully described how "everything special about our family died with Michael," leaving them ordinary people, trudging dutifully through ordinary lives, with two other ordinary sons.

In part, Michael's "specialness" derived, ironically, from his illness, because, as Martha stated, "having a chronically ill child gives a focus to your life that few other things can." But it soon became evident that Michael's unique role in the family went beyond the intense mutual bond he formed with his devoted mother; he was also the conduit for other family members to relate to one another, the bearer of the loftiest ambitions to excel and explore the world, the one who subscribed to *U.S. News*, *National Geographic*, and *Smithsonian* magazines, and the one who injected his political and cultural sensibilities into the otherwise local conversations among family members.

Martha's response to his death was to cling tightly to his memory, resisting Bill's insistence on redecorating Michael's room, to the point of wishing that she could "have him encased in glass and lying on his bed," so that she could feel closer to him in his "shrine." In contrast, Bill felt compelled to "formulate plans for the future," and "find ways to control the kind of thinking that creates depression." Both spouses urgently sought spiritual responses to the unanswerable question of "what made Michael get asthma," and both sought solace through carrying his pens, briefcase, and other cherished possessions. But each ultimately attempted to adapt to the wrenching loss of their son in ways that presented them with very different challenges.

While Bill acknowledged the desperate insufficiency of his efforts to "adjust to reality by using the power of positive thinking," Martha conceded that her "refusal to deal with Michael's death prevented her from dealing with his life." Each was feeling increasingly estranged from the other, stuck in a cycle of grieving that seemed unable to move forward. I was left wondering how I could support them as individuals, while simultaneously helping them recover a sense of intimate collaboration in grieving their son's death in ways that seemed irreconcilably opposed.

My only contact with Mayumi, a first-generation, 40-year-old Japanese American widow, took place in the emergency room of a large metropolitan hospital. Since her husband's apparently accidental shooting death two years earlier, Mayumi had become increasingly depressed and immobilized. Neither the prescription medicines she had come to rely on to dull her pain, nor the support of friends and family members compensated for what she had lost, and she described herself as "empty" and "without value." Although she was an intelligent and capable woman, she had become dependent on her eldest son to make decisions about the most minute aspects of her life, even though he ultimately squandered the family's resources on fast cars and needless luxuries while her most basic financial needs went unmet. Her ER visit was precipitated by a suicide attempt through drug overdose, a "failed" act that compounded her shame and sense of dishonoring her family.

Mayumi's manner of coping with her grief expressed her culture as much as her personality, and her inability to reengage life in the wake of her loss reflected her traditional conception of widowhood;

in Japanese, the term for widow, *miboujin*, is literally translated as 'she who is not yet dead.' This seemed an apt description for the loss of moorings for her identity following her husband's death, so that her own death seemed the only logical solution to her predicament. As I prepared to entrust her inpatient care to a European American male psychiatrist, I worried about how much of her experience as a Japanese American woman would be pathologized (perhaps as a "dependent personality") or missed entirely by the medical establishment, and how she might be further estranged from potential sources of help by the imposition of Western norms for grieving.

If the process of grieving is examined in the concrete particulars of people's lives, the boundaries of popular grief theories are immediately tested, with their simplifying assumptions about stages of emotional adjustment to loss and universal tasks to be mastered by the bereaved individual. Instead, the intimate details of people's stories of loss suggest a complex process of adaptation to a changed reality, a process that is at the same time immensely personal, relative, and inevitably cultural. This chapter will reflect on these complexities, adopting as a starting point a view of grieving as a process of meaning reconstruction, with special emphasis on its diversity rather than sameness across persons and groups. It will therefore review a few basic propositions of the meaning reconstruction model, and follow this with a consideration of three factors: culture, gender, and spirituality, that contribute to the form and shape of this meaning-making in the lives of those who have lost.

## Grieving as a Process of Meaning Reconstruction

In response to the growing dissatisfaction with traditional models of mourning, a "new wave" of grief theory is emerging, one that is less the product of any particular author than it is the expression of a changed *Zeitgeist* about the nature of bereavement as a human experience (Neimeyer, 1997b, 1998). Among the common elements of these newer models are:

(a) skepticism about the universality of a predictable "emotional trajectory" that leads from psychological disequilibrium to readjustment, coupled with an appreciation of more complex patterns of adaptation (Attig, 1991; Corr, 1993),

(b) a shift away from the presumption that successful grieving requires "letting go" of the one who has died, and toward a recognition of the potentially healthy role of maintaining continued symbolic bonds with the deceased (Klass, Silverman, and Nickman, 1996; Stroebe, Schut, and Stroebe, 1998),

(c) attention to broadly cognitive processes entailed in mourning, supplementing the traditional focus on the emotional consequences of loss (Horowitz, 1986; Janoff-Bulman, 1989; Viney, 1991),

(d) greater awareness of the implications of major loss for the bereaved individual's sense of identity, often necessitating profound revisions in his or her self-definition (Attig, 1996; Neimeyer, 1997b),

(e) increased appreciation of the possibility of life-enhancing "post-traumatic growth" as one integrates the lessons of loss (Tedeschi, Park and Calhoun, 1998), and

(f) broadening the focus of attention to include not only the experience of individual grievers, but also the reciprocal impact of loss on families (Gilbert, 1996) and broader (sub)cultural groups (Nord, 1997).

These trends sketch the outlines of an alternative model of mourning, one that argues that meaning reconstruction in response to a loss is the central process in grieving (Neimeyer, 1997b; Neimeyer, Keesee and Fortner, 1997). In keeping with the broader constructivist approach to psychotherapy from which it derives (Neimeyer and Mahoney, 1995), this approach is informed by a view of human beings as inveterate meaning-makers, weavers of narratives that give thematic significance to the salient plot structure of their lives (Neimeyer and Stewart, 1996).

Innovating upon culturally available systems of belief, individuals construct permeable, provisional meaning structures that help them interpret experiences, coordinate their relationships with others, and organize their actions toward personally significant goals (Kelly, 1955). Importantly, however, these frameworks of meaning are anchored less in some "objective" reality than in specific negotiations with intimate others and general systems of cultural discourse.

One implication of this social constructionist view is that the themes on which people draw to attribute significance to their lives will be as varied as the local conversations in which they are engaged and as complex as the cross-currents of broader belief systems that inform their personal attempts at meaning-making. A further implication of this view is that people may feel varying degrees of authorship of the narratives of their lives, with some having a sense of deeply personal commitment to their beliefs, values, and choices, while others feel estranged from those beliefs and expectations that they experience as imposed upon them by others in their social networks or by communal ideologies.

In keeping with this general thesis, loss is viewed as an event that can profoundly and sometimes traumatically challenge one's assumptions about the world (Janoff-Bulman, 1989). For Mayumi, her husband's violent death not only deprived her of her life partner, but undercut her sense of cosmological balance in which her life had meaning principally to the extent that it supported and was sustained by his. In the cruel emptiness brought about by his absence, she struggled futilely to find some alternative framework for living, seeking out a dependent relationship with an undependable son, which was nonetheless coherent with her cultural assumptions about the appropriate roles of men and women.

Often, the sustaining assumptions that are violated by the death of a loved one are more subtle, functioning as "virtually automatic habits of cognition and behavior" that regulate our daily lives (Rando, 1995). In the case of Bill and Martha, for example, many of their day-to-day conversations, aspirations, and even disagreements centered on Michael and his "special" involvements, so that his death left them with few workable means of connecting with an anticipated future, with a preferred identity as a family, or with each other.

One of the key deficiencies in traditional models of grieving is their implicit presumption of universality: the idea that all or most bereaved persons respond similarly to loss at an emotional level. In contrast, a meaning reconstruction view emphasizes the subtle nuances of difference in each griever's reaction, so that no two people (even husband and wife, as in the case of Bill and Martha) can be presumed to experience the same grief in response to the same loss (Gilbert, 1996). Instead, each person is viewed as the constructor of a different phenomenological world and as occupying a different position in relation to broader discourses of culture, gender, and spirituality. This assumption of the radical incommensurability of grieving across persons challenges professional caregivers to approach bereaved individuals from a position of "not knowing" (Anderson and Goolishian, 1992) rather than presumed understanding, necessitating means of accessing each bereaved person's unique experience without the imposition of "expert" knowledge (Nadeau, 1997).

A third feature of a constructivist approach to loss is the conviction that grieving is an active process, however much bereavement itself was unbidden. While the choiceless nature of the loss can leave people feeling like pawns in the hands of some larger fate (Attig, 1991), bereavement in fact thrusts survivors into a period of accelerated decision-making. Martha and Bill faced myriad decisions about which of their son's possessions they would keep and share with others, how and whether to redecorate his bedroom, and whether to seek therapy to assist them in reorienting to a world transformed by his loss. At a very basic level, they even confronted the choice of whether to focus their attention on the loss itself (doing the grief work of sorting through the turbulent feelings triggered by his death), or on the restoration of their lives (through a practical focus on adjustments needed to reengage their occupational and social worlds) (Stroebe et al., 1998). Viewing mourning in this way encourages caregivers to assist bereaved individuals in identifying conscious and unconscious choices which confront them, and then helping them sift through their options and make difficult decisions.

Finally, as implied by both of the vignettes with which this chapter opened, the reconstructive processes entailed in grieving cannot be understood as taking place within isolated subjectivities divorced from a larger social world. However private our grief, it is necessarily linked with the responses of others, each constraining and enabling the other. This was perhaps most obvious with Bill and Martha, who attempted to remain "in control" to avoid further "burdening" one another. But it was also true of Mayumi, who struggled to find a place for her distinctively Japanese sense of loss in a European American culture that provided her little validation or understanding for her predicament. Ultimately, reconstructing a world of significance in the wake of bereavement is more than a cognitive exercise; it also requires survivors to recruit social support for their changed identities (Neimeyer, 1997b).

Having provided a thumbnail sketch of a meaning reconstruction approach, we will turn to a brief consideration of three dimensions, culture, gender and spirituality, that contribute in their own ways to the individuality with which people process the significance of losses in their lives. In touching on these three areas, we will draw particularly on recent qualitative research on bereavement, which lends weight to both a meaning reconstruction model and its distinctiveness for different persons and groups.

Highlighting qualitative rather than quantitative research on death and loss is not intended to diminish the important role played by more conventional statistical methods in theory building. Indeed, their refinement and extension have been promoted in a number of other contexts (Neimeyer, 1994, 1997a). However, we believe that there are aspects of human meaning-making that require a closer engagement with the data of experience than statistical procedures permit, and therefore have begun to extend our own research beyond our clinical work to study a broader range of persons struggling to reconstruct their lives in the wake of loss (Neimeyer et al., 1997). In citing qualitative studies on the role of culture, spirituality, and gender, we hope to build a bridge between these efforts and our own, although we acknowledge that a thorough review of such research is beyond the scope of this brief chapter. Instead, the intent is merely to point toward the utility of focus groups, grounded theory, narrative analysis, and ethnographic research in enriching our appreciation of the subtlety and range of personal adaptation to loss.

## Cultural Dimensions of Grieving

Of the various dimensions of human experience that contribute to the diversity of meaning reconstruction in response to loss, culture is perhaps the most encompassing. Yet because it surrounds us like an atmosphere, providing us with a sustaining communal repertory of interpretations, beliefs, and social roles, its effects on styles of grieving may often be invisible, at least for those who live within the frame of reference it provides. The inclusiveness of culture also makes it difficult to tease out separate contributions, distinct from those made by spirituality, gender, and other dimensions that shape our accommodation to loss. Indeed, culture in some sense even subsumes these other dimensions, insofar as gender arrangements may differ markedly in different cultural settings, and a given culture, broadly defined, may offer multiple forms of institutionalized religion that present competing claims regarding the meaning of death in human life.

Cultural contributions to meaning-making begin at the rudimentary level of language, which subtly configures the experience of death and bereavement through its structure as well as its content. Indeed, some scholars have held that the tendency in many cultures to speak of the dead as if they have a continuing existence derives from the generalization of linguistic forms adapted to speak of living, present entities (Haussaman, 1998). For example, Martha tended to seek consolation in her stated belief that in death, Michael "was released from the suffering of his asthma," a commonplace remark that nonetheless implied his continued existence as someone who was asthma-free.

Even the basic terms in which bereavement is depicted in different languages give a different connotation to the experience; contrast the Spanish translation of grief as *aflicción*, 'affliction,' with its implication of misfortune and injury from some outside source to be suffered passively, with the English term *grieving*, with its more internal and potentially active connotation. Such usages, taken up almost unconsciously, indirectly configure the meaning of mourning and even the experience of oneself as a survivor in ways that are rarely appreciated. This was vividly illustrated in the case of Mayumi, whose status as a *miboujin* seemed to confer upon her the existence of a shadow figure from the point of her husband's death until her own.

At a more concrete level, cultural beliefs and practices concerning death also frame the meanings individuals construct of the loss experience. Braun and Nichols (1997), for example, conducted focus groups of Asian Americans from four distinct cultural groups (Chinese, Japanese, Vietnamese, and Filipino) in order to elucidate the philosophic resources and practical customs with which each group characteristically responded to death, memorialization, suicide, euthanasia, and a variety of related topics. Their results make clear the considerable diversity among these groups, as well as the evolving nature of cultural beliefs and practices as successive generations become more assimilated into mainstream American culture.

The focus group members also provided insights that could improve a caregiver's understanding of the cultural frame within which a bereaved person is seeking to adjust to loss. For example, as a first-generation Japanese American, Mayumi's inability to organize an appropriate Buddhist pillow sutra for her husband, given the tragic circumstances of his death, contributed to her sense of guilt and may have complicated her grieving by denying her a supportive role in the journey of his soul from this life to the next (Goss and Klass, 1997). Moreover, the generally compassionate and permissive Japanese attitude toward suicide could have made this seem like a nobler and less pathological response to her situation than it may have been for a European American facing a similar crisis.

Finally, in addition to recognizing the role of subcultural and ethnic factors in death, dying, and bereavement (as illustrated in Dula's (1997) moving portrayal of the life and death of an elderly black woman in the rural South), it is important to acknowledge the role of popular culture in shaping both private grief and the collective response to public losses. The latter was exemplified by the incredible outpouring of public grief over the death of Princess Diana, which triggered shock, outrage, and sadness on the part of millions throughout the world. The subsequent funeral procession, memorial ceremonies, speeches, and media coverage also provided a powerful example of the healing power of public recognition of pain and fostered greater awareness of our shared need to make sense of a senseless death and to memorialize the life it ended.

## Spiritual Dimensions of Grieving

Like culture, from which they can be only inexactly distinguished, religious and cosmological beliefs can play a profound role in our response to death and loss. Indeed, contemporary theorists such as Becker (1973) have suggested that a primary function of religion is to help contain our terror of death by providing an interpretive frame within which it can be viewed. In traditional religions like Orthodox Judaism, this frame can extend to the prescription of elaborate rituals of mourning for both the bereaved individual and the community, effectively conferring on mourners "pre-packaged" temporary identities that sustain them through the role transition instigated by loss (Wolowelsky, 1996).

As constructivists, we are especially interested in the ways in which individuals selectively appropriate religious themes that have personal significance, in the process of configuring a spirituality that might or might not resemble the formal religion in which they were raised. As was true with Bill and Martha, who sought answers to the urgent but elusive question of why Michael had to be born with a life-threatening illness, many persons are forced to re-examine their personal spirituality at the point of profound loss. Braun and Berg (1994) conducted a grounded theory analysis of this experience by carefully interviewing 10 bereaved mothers and then coding their responses according to emergent themes. They identified three distinct phases of meaning reconstruction: discontinuity, disorientation, and adjustment, and found that the majority of the mothers reinterpreted the meaning structures they held prior to their child's death in order to give it significance. One of their more provocative findings was that those women who could not place the loss of their child within their preexisting framework of spiritual beliefs had greater difficulty adjusting to the loss, whereas those who could assimilate the death as orderly or divinely ordained fared better in the wake of the loss.

Milo's (1997) research on the experience of bereaved mothers of children with developmental disabilities adds detail to this depiction of the meaning reconstruction process. Complementing a standardized quantitative grief assessment with intensive, semi-structured interviews, she found that these mothers groped their way toward several different explanations in order to find a special meaning for the life and death of their children. For example, several of the mothers spoke of the child's birth and death as purposeful, intended by God to foster the mother's spiritual growth, a theme also identified in another case study of the mother of a young boy with congenital heart problems (Neimeyer et al., 1997).

Other participants in Milo's study found meaning through less obviously spiritual, but deeply personal strategies, including the orchestration of a beautiful, peaceful, or intimate death for their child, resorting to "downward comparisons" to families even less fortunate, or even having recourse to a grim sense of humor. Like Braun and Berg, Milo also found that mothers who could incorporate their child's disability and death into their preexisting beliefs adapted to these losses more readily.

Importantly, however, these constructions were not necessarily cosmological in their meaning; they could as easily express a deeply held secular philosophy of life. For example, one mother who was a social activist had accepted that the world was imperfect, that everyone had pain in their lives, and that one's task was to ameliorate it whenever possible through involvement and advocacy. A similar range of conventional and unconventional philosophical schemas was noted by Richards and Folkman (1997) in their qualitative analysis of the spiritual themes in interviews with gay men whose partners had died of complications due to AIDS. Thus, the process of personal reconstruction following a loss can be facilitated by having recourse to humanistic as well as explicitly theistic beliefs, underscoring the need to respect the individuality of meaning-making for each survivor.

## Gender Roles in Grieving

In an attempt to emphasize the relational context of loss, family theorists sometimes speak of "family grief," or the violation of a "family's assumptions," when confronted with the death of one of its members. Yet, constructivists like Gilbert (1996) have noted that families, per se, do not grieve or hold beliefs, only individuals do. Therefore, different family members may react quite differently to the same objective loss, as a function of the different meanings they attach to it, their differing positions in relation to the deceased, their respective roles in the family, and, most relevant for the present discussion, gender differences in grieving.

Traditional grief theories have been founded on the experiences of bereaved women, and hence have emphasized a "feminine" style as the "healthy" way of responding to loss. From this perspective, theorists and clinicians have stressed the value of emotional expression and self-disclosure, and have typically distrusted "intellectualization" and coping with grief through immersion in activities rather than the seeking of social support. Yet, as Martin and Doka (1996) point out, this may amount to little more than a prejudice against "masculine" styles of grieving, in which thinking often precedes feeling, and active problem-solving takes the place of discussion of feelings with others.

In the preceding case examples, this difference in grieving style was illustrated by Bill and Martha, who attempted to give meaning to Michael's life and death in ways that were only partially overlapping. Martha's response to her son's death was to attempt to foster an intense affective sense of his presence by spending time "with him" in his carefully preserved bedroom, frequently visiting his grave, and sharing her tears and feelings openly with others. For his part, Bill was more self-controlled and reserved, voicing only mild "irritation" about his son's need to "push away from all authority figures" as he sought adult independence from his father's guidance. To a greater extent than his wife, Bill also tried to confront and solve the practical problems engendered by his son's death, including the disposition of his property. Despite their shared sadness, Martha and Bill's divergent styles complicated their mourning, as Bill felt distressed and helpless in the face of his wife's seemingly endless pain, and she questioned his empathy for her and his love for Michael in his abrupt attempt to reorganize their lives. Their differing needs also complicated our counseling, which ultimately took the form of separate cognitive therapy for Bill, and more metaphoric, evocative exploration for Martha, before bringing them back together for joint sessions. Such flexibility in grief therapy may be essential to meet the needs of bereaved persons who mourn in a masculine or feminine style, whatever their biological sex (Martin and Doka, 1996).

In addition to considering these broad distinctions in coping styles associated with gender, it is important to examine the specific meanings attached by partners to their ongoing relationship in the wake of loss. Hagemeister and Rosenblatt (1997) contributed a poignant account of this aspect of meaning reconstruction in their grounded theory analysis of 24 couples, two thirds of whom reported a significant break or decline in their sexual relationship following the death of a child. What proved critical in accounting for changes in their sexual contact were the sometimes divergent meanings attached to intercourse by the couple. For example, a number of the spouses acknowledged that they avoided intercourse for a long time after the death because it symbolized how the child had been made, while others withdrew from sexual contact because it signified pleasure, which seemed incompatible with mourning. Still others sought out intercourse specifically because it meant another chance to have children, or because it represented a reaffirmation of the relationship and reconnection to life. Significantly, husbands and wives consistently differed in some of the meanings attached to sex, with men more often experiencing physical intimacy as a source of comfort and connection, whereas women were more apt to interpret their partner's advances as intrusive or selfish. This pattern was also evident for Bill and Martha, as he complained of feeling "cut off from her as well as Michael," while she felt he was placing unfair sexual demands on her when she had "nothing more to give." These discrepancies deserve attention in the counseling context, as they can contribute to the pursuit of extramarital affairs in an effort to feel wanted by someone, or escape the problematic meanings associated with sexual contact with one's spouse (Hagemeister and Rosenblatt, 1997).

Finally, it bears emphasis that culturally prescribed gender roles can be experienced as oppressive or constraining by both sexes. In our case illustrations, this was most evident in the passive and dependent script for widowhood offered to Mayumi, but it can apply equally to European expectations for strength and stoicism on the part of male grievers, who may disregard or suppress aspects of their own reactions in order to comply with these role requirements. Thus, the extent of congruence between gender expectations and personal predilections is important to assess in the course of grief counseling.

## Interactions and Conclusions

While we have focused on the separate impacts of culture, spirituality, and gender, it is worth noting that meaning reconstruction following a loss is made more complex and idiosyncratic not only by the above dimensions of diversity but also by interactions among them. For example, in our earlier case study, the grief reaction of a woman whose two-year-old son eventually succumbed to congenital heart problems was shaped in part by the ambivalent spiritual significance it had for her (Neimeyer et al., 1997). Jacob's death, for her, represented not only a cherished opportunity to develop a depth of character for which she yearned, but also a stern attempt by a patriarchal god to break a "matrilineal pattern of female unconsciousness," represented by her mother and herself, before this pattern was passed on to her surviving daughter. Thus, Kerry's deeply personal cosmology represented the confluence of a spiritual quest for meaning in her son's death and a gendered conception of a somewhat retributive male deity that was deeply inscribed in her culture. Likewise, the interaction of cultural expectations, gender roles, and spiritual beliefs presented distinctive challenges for Mayumi's postbereavement meaning reconstruction, particularly in an alien American setting that offered few means of support other than readily available medication. Thus, understanding the unique predicament of individual grievers requires caregivers to tease out the many threads of personal and social construction that are woven together to make up any given person's tapestry of loss.

Grieving persons are active agents in negotiating the course of their post-bereavement adjustment, whether such dimensions as culture, spirituality, and gender seem to facilitate or impede their attempts at reconstructing a life worth living. Ultimately, such broad dimensions are forms of socially available discourse offering myriad potential meanings of loss, upon which individuals selectively draw as they configure a new sense of self appropriate to their changed world.

---

*Robert A. Neimeyer, PhD, is a professor in the Department of Psychology at the University of Memphis. He is the editor of* Death Studies *and series editor for the Taylor & Francis* Series on Death, Dying, and Bereavement.

*Nancy J. Keesee is currently completing her doctorate in Counseling Psychology at the University of Memphis, and a clinical internship at the Vererans Administration Medical Center. She is interested in working with bereaved and traumatized persons upon graduation.*

# EIGHTEEN

# Deciding What Is Right When We Are So Different

*David M. Price*

"What should I do?" This is the basic form of an ethical question. Its variations are legion:

"Should I reprimand that child?"
"How should I break the bad news to her?"
"Is it my responsibility?"
"Who should decide?"
"Are we obligated to attend?"
"How far ought we to go?"
"What does it mean to be a 'good mother' in this instance?"
"What's right?"
"Whose rights are more important?"
"Who should get to do what to whom…under what circumstances…with what safeguards?"

Everyone faces ethical questions each day. No kind of decision-making is more universal: in our work lives, in our family lives. As citizens, neighbors, customers, lovers, and friends, moral decision-making is what distinguishes us as human beings. Only humans appear to deliberate or argue about what is right. This capacity for principled action is what makes us distinctively human.

It is also what makes us most individual. We are at no time more truly ourselves than when we struggle to clarify what we ought to do. Though the activity of moral discernment is universal, we are scarcely uniform in our starting points or means of answering moral questions. Our basic assumptions and our ways of discerning are conditioned by culture, by social class, by religious heritage, and by life experience. Even as we differ across a wide range of social variables, we differ in our moral presuppositions and habits of mind about moral questions. Both literally and figuratively we "come from different places."

America is somewhat self-consciously a creation of immigrant streams from many different points of geographical and ethnic origin. This diversity has been both a strength and a weakness, a source of pride and an occasion for shame. We have rhapsodized about the "Melting Pot" and mounted signs reading "White only" and "No Irish need apply." Ambivalence about difference is part of our national character.

In recent years, the national community and many local communities have grown more tolerant of differences, if not always enthusiastic about them. We now seem more aware of diversity, and by and large we have embraced tolerance, at least as an abstract concept. Our official stance, repeated in laws and corporate policies, is pluralism, *affirmation* of our diversity. We require tolerance and encourage celebration. It would seem that at no time in our history has there been a greater awareness that our neighbors are different from us and that we are richer for that fact.

This attitude shapes and colors the behavior of most Americans most of the time. Tolerance helps answer questions about how we respond as caregivers to issues of loss and grief. Tolerance (and its enthusiastic cousin, celebration of diversity) has emerged as a moral touchstone when we are confronted with difference in our clients, coworkers, or neighbors. Challenged to respond appropriately, but unsure what that means in a novel situation, responsible caregivers can remind themselves of the value of tolerance and even appreciation of cultural, ethnic, and religious diversity.

Though not commonly cited as a basic moral principle applicable to healthcare decisions, it is clear that Tolerance functions as an ethical principle, an abstract concept, held in high regard by many, if not all, Americans and firmly enshrined in our formal pantheon of values. Thus, when we, as a community or as individuals, worry about how we ought to behave in the face of cultural difference, we refer for guidance to Tolerance as a moral benchmark.

Current bereavement literature reflects these attitudes. Popular theorists and teachers emphasize that, while grief may be a universal process, its particular forms are learned behavior and that we learn how to express our grief in our own cultural and subcultural environments. Accordingly, it is the advice of all mainstream grief experts that professional and non-professional caregivers alike should be sensitive to and respectful of the variety of ways in which people acknowledge and accommodate loss.

Of course, it is not that simple. There are two ways in which problems persist after one has acknowledged Tolerance as an ethical principle. One is a common ethical challenge: a perceived clash of two principles, both of which appear to be morally compelling. This is the "damned if we do, damned if we don't" kind of dilemma. The other way in which it is not enough to merely acknowledge that one ought to be tolerant is that it is not always clear what it means to be tolerant (or appreciative of differences) in particular instances. In this kind of dilemma one is not caught between two competing obligations; rather, the problem is one of ambiguous application of the general ethical principle. In short, Tolerance is only one of many applicable ethical principles and it is not necessarily obvious what Tolerance entails in concrete situations.

Newark, New Jersey, is a community with a high incidence of heterosexually transmitted HIV infection secondary to intravenous drug abuse with contaminated needles. Tragically, this means that Newark also has a high incidence of children who acquired HIV perinatally from their infected mothers. This translates to a large number of school-aged children with active disease whose parents are either dead or incarcerated for drug-related crimes. Many of these children are in the custody of their grandmothers.

Despite inevitable variation within this population of custodial grandmothers, there is a strikingly common subtype. She is Black, church-going, determined to do the right thing as she sees it, loving but firm, trusting in the Lord but not very trusting of The System. Professional and paraprofessional helpers are part of The System. She values our technical capabilities, but she does not imagine that we know much about raising children in her circumstances.

This grandmother type tends to pose a particular problem for health professionals who share with her the responsibility for the care of children with AIDS. The focus of the problem is that she typically insists that we not disclose the diagnosis to her grandchild, even as that child survives to 10, 12, 14 or, occasionally, 16 years of age. This withholding, with its inevitable evasions and deceptions, is counterintuitive for most modern health professionals of any discipline. Moreover, when these health professionals think carefully about it, they often conclude that Grandma is wrong. Whether on grounds of a supposed obligation to tell the truth, even to a minor child with limited independent autonomy, or on grounds of benefit to the child through an enhanced therapeutic relationship, most professionals think that these grandmothers are ill-advised to insist on keeping the truth from their infected and sometimes terminally ill grandchildren.

Quite clearly, this is a culture clash, whether it is seen as a clash between a White, upper-class culture and Black, lower-class culture, between professional culture and street culture, or between liberal humanism and traditional, religious, African American maternalism. Faced with this kind of culture clash, most American health professionals, at least those in or trained in non-sectarian institutions (whether public or private), are guided by that hallmark virtue of the modern American public faith, Tolerance. At the very least, Tolerance is recognized as an important principle in the resolution of the ethical dilemma regarding disclosure of diagnosis.

As we debate the question of whether it is proper for us to accede to the grandmothers, we typically accord Tolerance the status of what lawyers call a "rebuttable presumption." In other words, we will regard Tolerance as an authoritative guideline which, though it may be overcome by stringently argued considerations, may not be simply ignored or dismissed. Even for those who place a high value on Tolerance, it is not always clear what it means to be tolerant in situations like those posed by the grandmother who insists that her pubescent, HIV-positive grandchild should be denied knowledge of why he or she is so often sick.

Does Tolerance require acquiescence in all matters of culturally mediated divergence from professional practice? Clearly not. Few, if any, professionals would perform or participate in ritual clitoridectomy in the name of cultural sensitivity and tolerance. On the other side of the spectrum, only the most arrogantly ethnocentric would object to the bedside prayers of the patient's spiritual advisor, no matter how eccentric the patient's belief system.

For thoughtful people, the hard cases are the gray-zone cases, those lying along the spectrum rather than at its extremes. The African American grandmother is fiercely devoted to the care of her dead child's child, grateful for our medicines but distrustful of our notions about child rearing, pious and conscientious but also independent and self-reliant. She poses a dilemma in that we think she is ill-advised in her own behavior and not really acting in the best interest of her ward. Moreover, we rather resent her insistence that we conduct ourselves in ways that we are convinced are professionally substandard.

On the other hand, for all our obligation to this child's well-being, *she*, not we, is the primary caretaker and the central guarantor of whatever quality of life and chance for normal development our medicines may permit. Furthermore, though sometimes vexing, these grandmothers elicit deep respect from most of us. We are acutely aware of just how bleak the prospects would be for this set of Newark youngsters if it were not for these resilient, middle-aged women who have accepted, along with the grief of losing their own children, a second round of child-rearing responsibility.

If it is not always clear what Tolerance entails in specific instances, it is often similarly unclear how to reconcile faithfulness to competing or apparently competing principles. If we frame the same dilemma in terms of a "Catch 22" conflict between our obligation to respect the grandmother's convictions and our obligation to do our best for the child, it is not obvious how to satisfy both obligations. Conceived as a classic clash of moral principles (Autonomy vs. Beneficence), one would presumably work Tolerance into the analysis both as a component of the Autonomy principle and as a consideration in calculating the overall good of a child whose well-being is largely dependent upon the zeal and strength of character of a grandmother.

If we frame the "grandmother dilemma" in terms of a clash of rights, we may feel that we are on more familiar ground. One can frame the issue as a conflict between the child's right to know and the grandmother's right to raise her child as she sees fit. One can also cast the dilemma as a conflict between the grandmother's right to insist on the terms of a plan of care (or right to informed consent) and the professionals' right to practice according to accepted standards.

Americans love talking about rights. Given a choice, many of us instinctively prefer to see conflict in terms of rights. Of course, this phenomenon is of a piece with our love-hate affair with the Law, particularly with the courtroom. In its most profound and dignified sense, our preference for rights talk and legal metaphors is based in our nation's self-conscious founding as a community to be governed by law, rather than by royal families or landholders or priests. In any case, a rights debate or legal analysis is rarely sufficient. Practical, clinical dilemmas are frequently informed, but rarely resolved, by a legal (rights) discussion.

The issue of whether professionals should accede to the grand-mother's insistence on non-disclosure of a child's HIV diagnosis can scarcely be complete and rigorous without addressing the questions of rights that it raises. The civic and clinical virtue of Tolerance has an important place in law and public policy. Yet, much of what is relevant to sound decision-making will not be mined with the tools of "rights" or the categories of law. These are insufficient to discerning the well-being of a school-aged, Black child living with HIV in the Central Ward of Newark, New Jersey, in the custody of a determined, pious, Baptist grandmother because his or her parents are dead from the complications of AIDS.

Helping professionals may experience moral dissonance among themselves, as well as between themselves and clients. Indeed, help-ing institutions may "come from different places" ethically. Each institution has a unique culture, and those cultures can clash when the institutions share responsibilities, especially when the circumstances are unusual. In one such instance, a plan of care for a profoundly ill woman which was worked out in a hospital met with passionate disagreement from the staff of the nursing home in which she had resided for several years. What was thought to be a completely appropriate and politically correct decision in one care setting was regarded as a shocking violation from the social and cultural perspective of another health care organization in the same community.

Mrs. Albano was an eighty-something resident of Mt. Sinai Nursing Home. She had a medical history of hypertension, diabetes, peripheral vascular disease leading to gangrene in one foot, and organic brain disease so advanced that she was unable to sustain herself through oral feeding. Mrs. Albano was admitted to the hospital for the third time in one year. As her acute symptoms were brought under control, her attending physician sought consultation from the hospital's Ethics Committee. He questioned whether it was proper to surgically implant a feeding tube in a patient who was judged by a neurology consultant to have virtually no chance for recovery "to a sentient state." This decision, ordinarily made by a patient through an advanced directive or by a close family member on the patient's behalf, was referred to the Ethics Committee because Mrs. Albano had no such directive and had not been visited by any relative in years. Meanwhile, the nursing home had insisted that she not be transferred back without a permanent feeding device.

The hospital Ethics Committee was able to contact a sister in a distant state who, because of her own poor health, had not been able to travel. The sister was unable to recall any specific statements by Mrs. Albano regarding her preferences about end-of-life care, but nonetheless said that she "cannot imagine" that Mrs. Albano would wish to be kept alive in a profoundly demented or permanently nonresponsive state. Because of this sister's lack of recent involvement, the Ethics Committee conducted its own review of the case. The committee, consisting of a nurse, a physician, a chaplain, and an ethicist, observed that:

- The sister, though out of touch by virtue of their mutual illnesses and geographical separation, appeared to be a caring and able surrogate. A diligent search did not uncover other family members willing or able to participate.

- State and Federal law clearly regards artificially delivered hydration and nutrition as a medical intervention which, like any other, is sometimes indicated and sometimes not.

- There is no reason to conclude that a person in Mrs. Albano's condition would have any experience of distress were feedings to be withheld.

- If Mrs. Albano were to receive continued nutritional and other life-prolonging support (e.g., antibiotics), she would likely continue to develop infections arising from the lungs, gangrenous foot, urinary tract, skin breakdown, or other sources and would be subject to continuing interventions of highly questionable net benefit.

Accordingly, the Ethics Committee recommended the following plan of care for Mrs. Albano:

- Palliation (comfort, hygiene, and dignity) as the sole goal of therapy.

- No artificial nutrition or hydration delivered by any route or means.

- No antibiotics or surgical intervention except as justified by comfort or ease of care.

- Medications for symptom relief, as necessary.

- Return to nursing home and no rehospitalization except as justified as a comfort measure.

Before arriving at these recommendations, the Ethics Committee had phoned staff members at Mt. Sinai Nursing Home. Those staff members had expressed dismay that the hospital staff was even contemplating withholding life-sustaining treatment. Two things in particular seemed troublesome to them. One was that they felt like family to Mrs. Albano; in fact, like the only effective family she had. The other was that they assumed that decisions of this sort should be made with due regard to *halakhic* perspectives, that is, in the light of Jewish law. (Whether Mrs. Albano, once married to an Italian Catholic, had lived as an observant Jew was never explored by the Ethics Committee.)

In response to both these concerns, the hospital's Ethics Committee invited the Mt. Sinai chaplain, Rabbi Feldman, to participate in the deliberations. The rabbi proved rather unfamiliar with the relevant medical considerations, but listened carefully and, when invited, went to Mrs. Albano's bedside for a specific review of all of her problems and the medical and nursing implications of each. He then discussed this information in a telephone consultation with a respected Orthodox rabbi who had recognized expertise in medical treatment decision-making according to Jewish law. Rabbi Feldman called the next day to report that, on the basis of the information presented, Jewish law did not require insertion of the gastrostomy tube.

Nonetheless, staff members at the nursing home, meeting with the attending physician, made clear that they wanted Mrs. Albano back on full life support and that they would take her without the permanently implanted feeding tube upon which they had previously insisted. The attending physician acceded and Mrs. Albano was returned to the care of the nursing home staff.

A member of the Mt. Sinai staff subsequently wrote to the hospital's Ethics Committee that he and his colleagues had not been afforded opportunity to represent Mrs. Albano's interests and wishes. A member of the Ethics Committee responded in writing, both to present a somewhat different perspective on the process and to propose a follow-up meeting to afford better communication. His letter included the following paragraph:

Perhaps what we have here, in addition to the usual problems with inter-personal and inter-institutional communication, is a difference of cultures. In the hospital, we are rather self-consciously bound by our understanding of the main currents of American law and ethics. Those currents emphasize the right of self-determination, with the correlative right of families to make those determinations when individuals are disabled. By contrast, as I understand them, the main currents of Jewish law and ethics are more communitarian, accord a more prominent place to authority and are, thus, less inclined to inquire about or be bound by expressions of individual will or private values. While I know that (Mt. Sinai) does not claim a "religious exemption" and regularly honors advance directives, I suspect that the institutional culture of our two facilities may diverge somewhat on these (and perhaps other) matters. To the extent that this is true (if it is true at all), it follows that we need to be even more conscientious about good communication.

A reasonable lesson to draw from the two detailed case studies in this chapter is that we should expect ethical differences as a fact of life. Being alert to such differences means that we are less likely to either paper them over or to withdraw in confusion and embarrassment when they surface. That, in turn, will help us to be more efficient and more successful participants in the scores of ethical decisions that we are called upon to make every day.

Awareness that we "come from different places," ethically and otherwise, fosters respect for and even occasional delight in those differences. Genuine communities of caring tend to be those which both tolerate and celebrate our differences.

---

*David M. Price, MDiv, PhD, teaches professional ethics at New Jersey Medical School and is the hospital ethicist at St. Barnabas Medical Center. He is a founding member of the ethics committees of several hospitals, nursing homes, and a hospice.*

# NINETEEN

# Multicultural Grief Counseling

*Richard R. Ellis*

This chapter examines some of the factors affecting how people from a variety of cultures live with their losses and their grieving, and basic considerations for those who do grief counseling. Cultural diversity is a dynamic concept. Some of the material herein is based on my own experience as a grief counselor in the New York City area and as a professor who trains and educates grief counselors, other counselors, and counseling psychologists. Other material is taken from clinical experiences, research, and the scholarly work of others.

My favorite resource on multiculturalism is *Kiss, bow, or shake hands?: How to do business in 60 countries* (Morrison, Conaway, and Borden, 1994). Think about this question: What is an appropriate nonverbal greeting to someone of your culture who is unknown to you? If you are even moderately familiar with a given culture, the answer comes easily. But what about greeting those from other cultures? The book's title tersely suggests the problem and the book itself proceeds to instruct the reader about social customs of many different cultural groups. Greetings certainly lie on the surface of human interaction, where we can present our genuine selves or our facades and exercise our least risky outward behaviors. Nevertheless, greetings create lasting impressions, and poor first impressions tend to resist the effects of ensuing positive interaction.

# A Multicultural World

There are approximately 200 different countries in the world today. Together they comprise thousands of different societies. Rosenthal (1997) relates that each of these societies is unique in terms of culture, language, religion. Scholars do not agree conceptually on whether to include language or religion under the rubric of culture. Some argue, for example, that because the same language and the same religion can be found in similar forms in a variety of cultures, scholars should treat them separately. The Random House *Dictionary of the English Language* (1987) lists as its sixth meaning of culture a definition taken from anthropology: "the sum of ways of living built up by a group of human beings and transmitted from one generation to another" (p.488). Another definition comes from Parkes, Laungani, and Young (1997): "The primary features of a culture are...1. A past history...; 2. Dominant religion with salient beliefs and activities...; 3. Set of core values and traditions...; 4. Regulated social systems...; 5. artifacts unique to that society, e.g., literature, [fine and performing arts]" (p.14-15). The authors also include a set of secondary features. I prefer an inclusive definition, because clients who describe their cultures usually include ethnicity, race, religion, and language.

Multicultural counseling, according to D'Andrea and Daniels (1995), "...refers to a process in which a trained professional from one cultural/ethnic/racial background interacts with a client of a different cultural/ethnic/racial background for the purpose of promoting the client's cognitive, emotional, psychological, and/or spiritual development" (p.18). This definition seems to meet our need regarding multicultural grief counseling.

While culture is the product of a society, individuals develop a personal worldview. Scholars have variously defined worldview as the way one thinks the world works, and the basis for decisions and perceptions of one's relation to the world. Sue and Sue (1990) point out that worldview does correlate with cultural background, reflecting the effects of race, ethnicity, social class, and gender. A worldview is the product of heritage and life experiences. An individual holds a worldview that guides thoughts and behaviors even if it is not articulated. The counselor and the client each arrive at the grief counseling session accompanied by his or her individual culture and worldview.

The variation in expressed preference for disposition of the deceased's body provides examples of the effect of culture upon a griever's worldview. For an Orthodox Jew, cremation is never permitted, yet among Conservative and Reformed Jews cremation or burial are both acceptable. At one time among Christians cremation was viewed negatively; today Christians may be cremated or buried. Other examples abound. Some cultures tolerate autopsies, others have strong prohibitions against any violation of the body. In most cultures widows must provide for themselves while in others, the brother of the deceased must take the widow into his home as his second wife. The frustrations arising from a conflict between local laws and customs and the griever's attempts to behave responsibly are windows into the client's worldview. The grief counselor assists the client in exploring these frustrations.

## The Grief Counselor

The North American counselor arrives with a set of skills, knowledge, and attitudes based on Western European psychology or worldview. The same influences may be seen in the development of grief counseling, a fairly recent specialization in the profession of counseling. Underlying the practice of counseling are great bodies of empirical research and scholarly literature, numerous professional organizations, and a large number of colleges and universities offering undergraduate specializations in counseling for behavioral science majors, as well as graduate programs in counseling and counseling psychology. In contrast, grief counseling can claim only a small body of empirical research, a growing body of scholarly literature (including a large number of clinical reports and recitations of personal experience), a small number of professional organizations, a small number of college and university faculty members teaching related courses, and one or two Masters degree programs. Corr, Nabe, and Corr (1997) caution us that, although an acceptable degree of development in our current knowledge has occurred since the 1970s, there are still gaps in the literature (e.g., cultural differences in death-related experiences).

A few people seem to have been born with the requisite personality, intelligence, and compassion to be an effective counselor—caring but not suffocating, warm but not overpowering. The difference between these "naturals" and the professional counselor is training and education. The effective professional has studied the research and scholarly literature on personality and counseling theories; received an orientation to the profession of counseling; examined, under faculty supervision, his or her own attitudes toward others and their worldviews; studied and observed the dynamics of human behavior of individuals and of small groups; and engaged in extensive supervised practica in both individual and group counseling. They know, for example, not to tell a client what to do. They know how to be empathic while maintaining a professional relationship with the client. They can articulate their own stance as a counselor.

In addition to the skills of an effective counselor, the grief counselor possesses something more: the specialized study of thanatology; observation of the dynamics that occur in the face of death and bereavement; and, most important, the supervised assessment of his or her own personal attitudes, feelings, and beliefs about death, dying, and bereavement. The client deserves a counselor who will not be an impediment to her or his grieving. Untrained grief counselors usually have no awareness of their being an obstacle to client progress.

Presently there are approximately 250-260 grief counselors in North America who have been certified by the Association for Death Education and Counseling. Although more people are being trained in grief counseling, and more meaningful research is being conducted, the need for additional attention to multicultural issues persists. Those who train and educate grief counselors need encouragement to provide greater emphasis on sensitivity to multicultural issues, increased opportunities for trainees to develop more sensitive responses, and a greater depth of knowledge in cultural issues.

Trainees need to assess and articulate their own worldviews. This process can reveal flaws in their thinking and gaps in their knowledge. However, an increased awareness of multicultural issues alone is insufficient until the grief counselor translates that awareness into effective interaction with the client. When that translation occurs, Grieger and Ponterotto (1995) believe that there is "...greater client willingness to return for counseling, satisfaction with counseling, and of self-disclosure" (p.403).

## In Place of the Counselor

Shamanism exists today in many cultures. Native peoples who adhere to at least some of their cultures' traditions find many reasons to turn to shamans or healers. A shaman acts as an intermediary between the natural and supernatural worlds. The society attributes to the shaman mysterious knowledge and the capability of curing illness, foretelling the future, controlling spiritual forces, and apprehension and understanding of informative vibrations from the souls of natural objects and phenomena (Lee and Armstrong, 1995). There is evidence that the practices of shamanism go back tens of thousands of years. Lee and Armstrong (1995) tell us that *shaman* is a term anthropologists apply to people dubbed "...witch, witch doctor, medicine man/woman, sorcerer, wizard" (p.442). Throughout time people have turned to the shaman for relief from stress, as well as for resolution of situational and developmental problems.

There are counselors, therapists, and other mental health practitioners who pursue the goal of helping people resolve their developmental and situational concerns and problems. Lee and Armstrong (1995) remind us that the idea of community-recognized experts intervening in the lives of others has its roots in cultures predating the United States. Those interveners were and are the healers. The communities perceive them as possessing the knowledge, wisdom, and skills to help others. Some traditional healers engage in Western European mental health practices. (See Lee, Oh, and Mountcastle, 1992; and Vontress, 1991, for discussions of indigenous models of intervention.) Part of the success of Western European mental health practitioners and traditional healers today derives from the power and authority clients attribute to them. We should also include among today's healers those who practice medicine, nursing, and other aspects of healthcare.

The relevance for grief counselors of even a brief discussion of shamans and healers is that many Native peoples, even those who seem to hold little if any connection to their cultural traditions, in times of stress and loss feel compelled to seek the help of a traditional magic man or woman (Lee and Mountcastle, 1992). Bereaved Native peoples may also seek the help of a grief counselor. It is of paramount importance for the grief counselor to be aware of the availability of shamans and healers, their importance to traditional Native peoples, and the strong possibility that the grieving Native person is or will be seeking traditional help. The grief counselor should accommodate the desire of a Native person to have both a grief counselor and a shaman.

Members of Western European cultures and those who have adopted these cultures tend to believe that things are *either/or*—for example, either true or false, good or bad. It is unacceptable for a grief counselor to subscribe to this dualistic belief. The more difficult belief to hold, but one certainly more beneficial to grieving clients, is that a thing can be *both*. The grief counselor has to become comfortable with the concept of *both*, regardless of one's native or adopted culture. When a client feels devastated, usually in the early period of bereavement, he or she cannot imagine feeling alive. The client's belief is in either/or. At different times parts of one (feeling devastated) or the other (feeling alive) will dominate. Neither is likely to disappear entirely.

## Some Examples

What follows are brief sketches which illustrate grief issues for some members of selected cultures, which provide opportunity to call attention to specific points about grief counseling. Of course, some of these points are also relevant to other cultures, but the examples here may be sufficiently unfamiliar to most readers as to warrant closer attention. I caution against generalizing to a cultural group the characteristics, behaviors, and needs of individuals in these sketches. The temptation is to make generalizations, but the danger is that they can quickly become misleading stereotypes.

## Hmong

The Hmong are an ethnic minority in Burma, China, Laos, Thailand, and Vietnam. During the political crises in Laos during the 1960s and 1970s, the US backed the army of the Royal Lao government. In 1975 the government changed, and many Hmong had to flee. The largest number of Hmong refugees outside Asia are in the US. In 1990 there were about 120,000 Hmong scattered throughout the US, but concentrated in California's Central Valley and in Minneapolis-St. Paul. There are several Hmong subgroups.

From Bliatout (1990), a Hmong born in Laos and living in the US, we learn about the deeply-rooted, complex intertwining of Hmong religion with beliefs about death and afterlife. A basic Hmong belief is that both spiritual and physical worlds coexist. A variety of spirits—good, bad, ancestor, and house—inhabit all of nature and influence human lives.

Family health, safety, and prosperity depend upon proper burial and ancestor worship. Bliatout (1990) provides a wonderful description of the beliefs and customs for pre- and post-burial rituals and related activities in Hmong culture. The rules are quite numerous, precise, and mandatory, and consequences for not obeying them are severe. For example, one rule prohibits a Hmong to die in the house of someone else, especially if there is no spiritual or blood relationship between them. Breaking this rule unleashes the anger of the house spirits, who withdraw their protection from the homeowner's family, thereby causing illness and even death. The details to which a bereaved family must attend are numerous. Grief counselors unfamiliar with Hmong life may underestimate the importance of these beliefs and practices.

Hays and Kalish (1995) provide insight into the difficulties Hmong face in the US. While it may be possible in this country to maintain most Hmong funeral customs without enraging the spirits, local law enforcers may be less than sympathetic to sacrificing animals, firing cannons, maintaining horses in the yards of the deceased, or walking to the graveyards in large processions. Some Hmong living in the US have adopted Christianity. When it comes time to bury a loved one, though, some who had adopted a new religion will struggle with whatever remains of their ties to the old traditions. The authors remind us that too few people working with dying and grieving members of minority groups have sufficient knowledge of the cultural expectations of those groups. Grief counselors need detailed information and a breadth and depth of knowledge appropriate for working professionally with the cultural groups their practices serve. It is unethical to engage in counseling practices for which one is not prepared.

## Women in rural Brazil

Western European grief counselors and other practitioners generally agree that the death of a child can be one of the most wrenching losses. Evidence of this thinking appears frequently in the literature. However, it is not a universal truth. There are places where parents and families exhibit signs of indifference to child death.

The anthropologist Scheper-Hughes (1995) writes about her observations of mothers in northeastern Brazil, where impoverished communities abound, who experience a child's death. One such mother is Nailza. Some of Nailza's children died almost immediately, some lived one or two months. A daughter, Joana, lived to be baptized in church at about age one. Against the advice of her elders, Nailza allowed herself to love the child. At age two, Joana died. In tones ranging from wistful sadness to remonstrance and anger, Nailza spoke to dead Joana. Soon Nailza was again pregnant and her happiness returned, but a son was stillborn. She and Scheper-Hughes dug a shallow grave in an area behind the house where pigs and goats foraged. Nailza seemed to accept the reality of "...another little angel gone to heaven" (p.42).

In communities in northeastern Brazil where food is scarce, families make certain that the healthy, sturdy members get what is available (Scheper-Hughes, 1995). They see no reason to put a sickly, weak member ahead of others, especially if that member is a baby. A family wastes no resources on those who are about to die. The older members try to socialize the young women to shed no tears for their "Angel-Babies." Scheper-Hughes suggests that as the families conserve their resources in hope for survival, perhaps they similarly husband their emotions.

What thoughts do the above two paragraphs stimulate? The mixed messages the Western European mind detects may, indeed, suggest that the women are not indifferent. The temptation may be to reject those parts that do not fit neatly into what one "knows." What, then, about the remaining parts? Can we accept that the socialization of the women is successful, that they avoid most of the misery of grief?

When cultures clash, sparks can fly. In counseling grievers perhaps we can examine those sparks to understand their origin, substance, and power to illuminate. The grief counselor cannot permit his or her own culture to disallow expression of the other. Encourage expression. Work to achieve empathy, the ability to experience the world as another does, while remaining yourself. The idea of remaining yourself eliminates the prospect that one can or should be *one* with the other. Incredibly, there are some counselors who believe they can and should achieve that oneness. Other common fallacies are that the grief counselor should take the client's tears away, or resolve the client's grief, or always make the client as comfortable as possible. We cannot do these things. Clients do their own grief work. It is theirs, not the grief counselor's.

### Biracial/Multiheritage

Discussions about multicultural counseling often refer to the grief counselor as someone from one culture and the client as someone from a different culture. In most instances this is accurate. However, either or both of the parties might be a member of a group not yet mentioned: biracial. Kerwin and Ponterotto (1995) report that a biracial person usually is described as a first-generation child of parents each of a different race or races. Multiracial is a term sometimes used interchangeably with biracial. However, Root (1992) notes that multiracial more appropriately means a person of two or more different heritages.

Several of my multiracial clients have found it highly irritating that demographic information forms had no place for them to check except *other*. Their own category deserved recognition. In October 1997 the Federal government did recognize this problem. Policy now allows the individual to check as many categories as needed to indicate the appropriate multiculturality. More than an irritation is the loss of one's grandparents. Biracial clients have described a feeling of painful loss because one set of grandparents refused to have contact with them or their parents. The grandparents do not accept the multiracial marriage. In this case client grief can become complex because the grandparents are living but not available. A grief counselor needs to be aware that these and similar losses can impede the grieving of future losses.

Biracial/multiheritage clients have come to me for grief counseling because a parent was dying and they were in conflict as to which rituals to follow when death occurs. For example, one client recently embraced a religion which neither parent espoused. The client wanted her deceased mother to be buried according to the tenets of her new religion. She believed this would ensure that her mother would be waiting for her. The father and other family members had different plans. It would be a mistake for the counselor to take one side or the other. Instead the counselor should help the client explore facets of the issue and their meanings for her. These issues make decisions difficult; decisions are even more difficult when all persons involved are also trying to deal with their losses. Further, time often pressures these decisions. Grief counselors having a need for help can consult with a funeral director, who usually has experience in these matters. As another example, a client came to me because his father was gravely ill. With the realization that the parent really was going to die, the client began discussing his life experiences as a biracial man, the concerns he has handled well and those he has not handled so well. Until that time, he could always rely on the strength of his father. I learned that I did not need to reply to everything he said. He did not need me to echo him, or to suggest alternatives, or to make supportive statements. He needed me to listen to him attentively, to be there with him as he struggled to find the sense of who he was after his father was gone. It was only in the last few sessions that he wanted to include me in active dialog.

All of my biracial clients were clearly proud of their heritages. All of them had some ambivalence. All had not only a primary loss (the deceased) but with it secondary losses (e.g., a mentor, personal champion, best friend) and related issues and concerns from the past.

When you become aware of those losses, work with the client to determine which need resolving; then have the client prioritize them from most to least difficult. The process is best explained to clients before they are asked to set the priorities. Do not be surprised if the client changes the order of priorities as you work along. The underlying premise here is that unattended losses of lower priority are distracting to the client and may impede work on the loss of highest priority.

## Closing Comments

It is apparent that living in today's world can at times be stressful. When those times link together we can feel chained to things beyond our control. DeSpelder and Strickland (1996) sum up our plight cogently:

> In confronting stress, we must recognize that it involves loss and grief. In the modern era, relentless and rapid change continually transforms the familiar into the new, bringing about a variety of social displacements that affect health and well-being and create occasions for grief. (p.547)

They add that we try to adapt to those losses when, instead, we should take time to mourn them. Our mourning renews our passion for living which, in turn, allows us to consider our finiteness and impermanence. "Making room for death awakens us to our life in the flesh." Stress "...can be a signal that calls us back to ourselves" (p.548).

The examples in this chapter include circumstances of inherent stress. I have worked with a number of individuals who left their native regions, where they were of the majority group, to live here in North America. Each presented symptoms of the effects of stress, some from recent loss. All were quite surprised to find that they had been carrying considerable stress prior to the death of their loved one. Grief counselors need to be aware that bereavement does trigger thoughts, concerns, and memories of other times, as well as conflicts. It is not unusual for one or more of those recollections to be of unresolved losses.

It is important for grief counselors to be attentive and sensitive to the client's thoughts, beliefs, values, and practices relating to religion, religiosity, and spirituality. Assume nothing. Until you learn from the client, do not assume he or she has a sustaining faith, or harbors no religious thought, or is angry with a supreme being. Years ago I was counseling a religious leader who was dying. In my assumption that he had a good relationship with his God, I said something like, "I imagine that your faith is very helpful to you now." He immediately raised up from his pillow, pointed at me, and yelled, "Do you think I have no fears?" Faulty assumptions are the land mines of counseling.

Grief counselors, your work is there to do. My hope is that you will become a culturally responsive grief counselor. Grieger and Ponterotto (1995) tell us that acknowledging, showing interest in, demonstrating knowledge of, and expressing appreciation for the client's culture constitute cultural responsiveness. Research findings clearly indicate that cultural responsiveness adds substantially to counselor credibility. This positive effect is manifest in clients' engagement with you in their grief work.

Counselors, the word is: homework. Do your homework to achieve awareness about cultures other than your own. But please know that this is not the end of your task. Awareness is a good thing, but it is insufficient. Give your awareness life. Express it positively through your attitudes toward, acceptance of, and compassion for those with whom you would work.

---

*Richard R. Ellis, EdD, is a professor in the Department of Applied Psychology, Graduate Programs in Counseling & Counseling Psychology at New York University.*

# TWENTY

# Healing Rituals:
# Powerful and Empowering

*Alice Parsons Zulli*

R itual is sacred. Rituals can help to restore a sense of balance to life. Although many of us create ceremonies or rituals for one occasion or another, few understand why rituals help in adjusting to change. Even fewer understand the power of ritual to strengthen the bonds that connect us. Caregivers can influence the grieving process through ritual, customs, and traditions, and they can be sensitive to, and draw from, diverse cultures to create therapeutic rituals.

It is natural to express ourselves with physical actions. Death and grief are experiences that may make us feel helpless or out of control as emotional and physical energy is thrown out of balance. Rituals or ceremonies link physical and mental expression in a way that allows us to express and act out feelings and beliefs.

It seems that nobody teaches us how to die or to companion someone who is dying, or how to grieve or help those who are grieving. Much of what we know about dying and grieving we have not been taught explicitly, but have "caught" from culture, religious beliefs, and family traditions. Caregivers must incorporate ritual to teach and mentor those who are embarking upon the journey of dying and grieving.

Rituals empower people emotionally, mentally, and spiritually. As medical treatment has broadened in scope and capability, cure has tended to predominate over care. But when cure is no longer a possibility, care can be offered in the most meaningful ways. This is the time for a support system that encourages living to the fullest in the time that remains. Rituals can be created to heal the mind, heart, and relationships as patients and families deal with this crisis that involves them all. The uniqueness of human beings clearly shapes the dying process and, therefore, how it will vary.

Caregivers can begin mobilizing patients' and family members' energy for grieving, an extended process that begins with diagnosis and goes on after death. Families begin by mourning the loss of their hope for a cure. Caregivers can begin at this time to strengthen communication among family members in the hope of assisting family members in sharing their pain and sadness.

Ella and John had been married 57 years. They sat together, holding hands, as the doctor gently told her that her shortness of breath was caused by the growth of tumors in her lungs. Together, John and Ella told their four daughters the sad news.

Six weeks prior to Ella's death, her daughters began collecting scraps of fabric from the sewing room where Ella had spent hundreds of hours creating warm, colorful quilts. In the hospital room they arranged the scraps in an album, allowing Ella to reminisce about each piece as they wrote the memories on three-by-five cards and inserted them next to the fabric. Ella, John, and their daughters spent many happy hours completing the album.

The inevitability of Ella's death was very sad for John and his daughters, but they faced this loss and responded to it well. They were able to cry openly over the impending separation. They were able to honor their emotions and send messages to each other of recognition and understanding. Each was able to grieve in his or her unique way, and they allowed the pain to remind them who Ella was and what she meant in each of their lives.

A ritual is simply a function for getting in touch with that which brings wholeness and meaning. Other ways to extend a person's presence beyond death include videotapes, audiotapes, albums, memory quilts, poetry or novels depicting the person's journey of dying, or memorial funds or plaques. Healing rituals empower the dying and the bereaved to move from the fragmented, alienating, and disorienting consequences of change to a renewed sense of wholeness.

Memories play a prominent role in healing for bereaved people. Those who have experienced a death often feel as if something is missing from their lives, a part taken from the whole. The world they assumed to be safe has been shaken. Initially, memory serves as a stabilizing anchor so that the bereaved can begin to let go, a bridge between life as it was and life as it is now.

What ritual and celebration accomplish is to affirm an interconnection between our lives and the lives of others. As the bereaved move on to establish new connections, thus enlarging the web, new roles and new sources of gratification become available.

A good illustration is the Jewish custom of naming a person after someone who has died, symbolizing the perpetuation of the dead person's life. Another Jewish tradition, or ritual, dictates that at least four times a year memorial prayers be said in the synagogue for the dead and that a memorial candle be lit in the home for each deceased family member. On these occasions, the living again remember the dead and the meaning of their lives.

Caregivers in all cultures are in a position to offer healing to the bereaved through ritual. Bereaved people often have a strong desire to maintain their attachment and relationship with the deceased loved one, while society often demands rapid closure. The death of a significant person in our lives leads to a series of losses and changes in status and social network. Is it not asking too much of the human psyche to process the multiple losses and changes in so short a time?

The bereaved need basic help and support regardless of the duration of the grieving process. They need people who will listen and care. There are many groups and organizations where the bereaved can find comfort, acceptance, and a place to tell their story. With the support of compassionate listeners the stories begin to spin a web of healing. As feelings are expressed, the bereaved see that there can be a future without the deceased. They find role models in those who have successfully connected with their changed lives.

In her bereavement support group, Marie talked about the death of her young husband. She related how much pleasure she derived from the Mexican American tradition of spending time sitting at the graveside, often accompanied by her children and other family members.

Another group member expressed personal distaste at the idea of this ritual, but Marie explained that in her culture families often gather together, sitting by an immaculately tended grave, sharing memories and showing respect for the person who died. This tradition helped to include the children in healing rituals which they could understand, like drawing pictures and tying them to balloons to send "up" to the person who died.

In its best form, this ritual is a wonderful way for family members to help each other through a time of intense pain. Marie felt strongly that it helped her move through the painfully long hours, surrounded by loving companions.

After the sudden and unexpected death of her husband, Janis, a gifted artist, created a series of twelve paintings entitled *Widow's Journey*. Janis set out to paint a self-portrait as a way of working through and expressing her terrible emotional pain, but as the weeks passed she was driven to further expression of her internal rage and sadness. Eventually, she realized she had created a painting for each month of her first year of mourning. The first was blobs of paint thrown on the canvas, mostly black, brown, orange, and deep red. As the months passed and she created more paintings, the blobs began to take the form of a woman in great agony and despair. By the twelfth painting the colors were lighter, and emotional healing began to appear. Her face became more recognizable, though pain lingered in her eyes. This pain can still be seen, but to a lesser degree.

Artwork and journal writing are two powerful examples of creative self-expression, but may not appeal to everyone. Many grieving people find great comfort and healing in the use of personal symbols. Some frequently used symbols are hearts, roses, or food, which symbolize love; a tree, which symbolizes immortality; the moon, symbolizing the cyclical nature of life; and the sun, which is the symbolic source of life and energy.

## Sensitivity to Diverse Cultures

"The peopling of America is one of the great dramas in all of human history," wrote Thomas Sowell in his book, *Ethnic America* (in Augsburger, 1986). Over the years a stream of humanity has crossed ocean and continent to reach the United States. In this age of global interchange, interaction, and interdependency, it is imperative to develop the capacity to understand and appreciate diverse cultural values and perspectives.

Cultures have a central cluster of values, taking form in institutions, structures, and political establishments. But alongside these cultures of the powerful stand the cultures of the poor, powerless, and oppressed. Caregivers must appreciate both. The major challenge is to provide culturally sensitive care to a diverse clientele. However, even when positive efforts are made to link culture to care, unintended difficulties can occur. Becoming sensitive to the ways and symbolism of another culture, to its logic and forms of etiquette, is seldom easy or straightforward. These skills will not be developed through encyclopedic knowledge of numerous cultural traditions, but rather through a willingness to observe, listen to, and learn from families from different cultural backgrounds.

The primary skill in learning to put together this intercultural puzzle is sensitivity: being outward looking, or separating our feelings from the behavior of others. Sensitive and competent service providers are aware and respectful of the cultural "webbing" of the people they serve: their values, beliefs, traditions, and customs. These are integral parts of each person's health and wholeness.

Caregiving will continue to be an intercultural adventure in a rapidly changing and uncertain world. Because humans share a tendency to fear and reject that which they do not understand, cultural competency necessarily becomes a moral challenge and imperative as caregivers realize the tremendous influence and consequences of services which they provide.

The following are integral to effective intercultural caregiving:

1. Skilled, sensitive caregivers understand that there are as many forms and models as there are cultural contexts.

2. The work of intercultural bereavement support demands creativity, flexibility, humility, and an appreciation for the individuality of those we serve.

3. The care of patients with different cultural beliefs requires a combination of knowledge, attitudes, and skills.

In offering care to the dying and bereaved, caregivers should strive to be intercultural rather than multicultural. The intercultural person is not culture-free, but rather culturally aware. The intercultural person develops a special skill that enables him or her to enter a different culture both cognitively and affectively, to perceive and conceptualize a culture, and to respect that culture as equally valid as one's own. The intercultural person thus gains respect, understanding, and appreciation for others, which makes possible the transcendence of cultural limitations.

Cultural competency demands good communication skills including conversational style and pacing, personal space, eye contact, touch, and time orientation as well as awareness of language barriers.

Some guidelines for caregivers to assist a patient and family through a crisis include asking families how religion, beliefs, and specific cultural values and practices tend to influence health or well-being. Including family members in an evaluation of the patient can soothe fears and lend valuable insight to the care plan being designed. In assessing a patient or client, one must be aware of:

- language and communication modes,
- physical environment, apparel, and appearance,
- worldview,
- family lifestyles, including social interaction and kinship,
- religious orientation,
- educational factors, and
- food uses.

A thorough assessment must provide information not only about care recipients but also about caregivers from other cultures: doctors, nurses, and other personnel. Their beliefs and values have a major influence on care of patients in hospitals.

America is home to a variety of people with special needs. For example, when refugees experience the death of a loved one after arriving in this country, they may find it difficult to engage in their traditional religious and/or mourning practices, complicating their grieving processes. Many have lost the familiarity of their country as well as treasured belongings and loved ones. They are highly likely to become *displaced grievers* or *disenfranchised grievers*: "To disenfranchise is to deprive an individual of a right or a privilege. In the case of grief, the individual is deprived not so much of a right or privilege, but of the opportunity to perform a necessary task: grief work" (Doka, 1989, p.314-15). A disenfranchised grief response occurs when there is an absence of social support. When sustaining rituals and religious practices are inaccessible, we see psychological distress exacerbated and manifested in depression and anxiety.

Additionally, first-generation immigrants may face a particularly difficult period of grief because they do not have the traditional resources for carrying out traditional bereavement practices. They may also be uncomfortable participating in the mainstream bereavement practices of a new country. For example, group bereavement counseling may be culturally incongruent; to give voice to feelings in a group of strangers, especially if one has had little formal education and cannot speak English well, may be unacceptable.

Elderly immigrants are also at risk for disenfranchised grief. They may become distressed about acculturation and assimilation in the new country. Many elderly immigrants have lost their families and do not have the benefit of an extended support system; in some cases, their children and grandchildren have become Americanized or may have moved away. The elderly may consider it a disgrace not to have family support, and not want anybody to know they are alone.

Other factors reported to increase the psychological distress level of bereaved immigrants are environmental changes including unemployment, family and economic problems, the cultural gap between the country of origin and the country of immigration, as well as various preexisting problems.

Recognition of the individuality of each patient will result in empowering that patient during his/her healing journey. Having bilingual caregivers or translators available and written materials in different languages is one small part of that empowerment. Learning about the religious and cultural beliefs of each patient allows caregivers to be more empathic and sensitive to individual needs.

## Religious Leaders: Help or Hindrance?

Some cultures and religions recognize a *traditional healer*, a medical or spiritual leader who may enter the arena of patient care and act as a consultant to the family. Connections to life through a traditional healer may be significant and important in helping the patient successfully adapt. Cooperation with traditional healers, religious leaders, and communal spokespersons can have a very positive impact.

Traditional healers may have a wide knowledge of history, familial lineage, origin of villages, relationships, and roles in the community. The healer is prepared to exercise social power in controlling conflict. "Traditional diviners and healers have been accepted as collaborators by health treatment institutions in Zaire, Zimbabwe, Nigeria, Uganda, Tanzania, and Kenya, and in India, Pakistan, and Malaysia" (Augsburger, 1986, p.287).

Research shows positive results from the cooperation of Western-trained physicians and traditional healers. Where physicians and mental health professionals are able to work with traditional healers, the strength of friends, kin, and the community can be called on to reinforce healing.

Faith, hope, belief, relief from alienation and shame, and catharsis of anxiety and guilt are central to the therapeutic process of the folk healer and shaman, as well as to the therapeutic process of the psychologist, psychiatrist, and pastoral counselor.

The power of religious leaders such as priests, in contrast, is *authoritative*, derived from a religious organization or church. The priest is part of a succession of leaders who pass ritual, tradition, office, and authority from generation to generation. The administration of sacraments and other rituals appropriate for the care of the dying and the bereaved are highly effective in providing meaning and in conveying a vital sense of belonging (Irion, 1988). Religious faith can offer people hope, peace, and a sense of God's promise of new life. For Jews, the Exodus story, and for Christians, the paschal mystery (the death and resurrection of Jesus) are strong affirmations of faith, life, and promise.

Caregivers must always remember that the dying are also experiencing anticipatory grief for their own life. Some patients experience guilt for errors and regrets of the past, and religious faith can offer an avenue for dealing with these issues, as in the Christian practices of confession and forgiveness. Clergy sometimes remind people of present ties or ones lost in a distant past, which may help overcome feelings of isolation. Perhaps the clergy symbolize hope by bringing to mind the ways in which omissions, defeats, failures, and disappointments may be dealt with so that one's life can make sense again.

As people become concerned about completing unfinished business and bringing their personal history to its final resting place, closure can be found in each person's story, which is shaped by experiences of the family as well as ethnic, religious, and cultural communities. The use of symbolic language or rituals of the person's religious community in a time of crisis may help them maintain emotional and spiritual balance. However, not all people have strong religious or spiritual ties, and in some cases the assumption that a person needs spiritual intervention can be emotionally damaging.

Commendation of the dying, whether it follows a formal pattern or simply takes the form of a prayer, is a ritual that marks the dignified conclusion of a life and the beginning of the separation caused by death. The Roman Catholic church has moved away from the last rites, which gave the negative message that the end was near, to anointing of the sick, which gives the patient and family spiritual comfort.

Many intercultural rituals and ceremonies have been handed down for generations, and although we understand the power behind them, their overall meaning may no longer be clear. If our rituals are not repetitions of old, well established rites or ceremonies, we are free to design new ones. This may include readings, favorite quotations, prayers, and blessings.

Ritual is the vehicle by which we honor life's passages. It is common to all of our lives, and we respond with a form of ceremony on certain occasions. When we experience a loss, we need to process our feelings and the changes in our lives. Traditional ceremonies or family traditions may or may not completely meet our needs. Much of our grieving and mourning is based on personal heritage: our cultural background, our religion, our family history, perhaps even what region of the country we are from, and through rituals, new or traditional, we ceremoniously play a role that connects us with energies larger than ourselves, so that we do not feel so alone in our pain. Again, all the heritage factors play a role, particularly in the first days after a death, as the following illustration shows.

I was invited to join a friend of mine in a celebration after the death of a family member. My friend was Armenian, born in Lebanon, and came to America about 12 years ago. She told me that most of the Armenians in our community have become acculturated, but some of the original traditions are still practiced.

After the death, family and friends come to the house to offer respect and support to the grieving family members, but this is not a time to bring food. It is traditional, however, for the family to serve black coffee. Seven days after the funeral, family and friends visit again for a time of remembering the deceased and comforting the family.

On the 40th day, if the family wishes, a notice is placed in the local newspaper and a church memorial is held. The family and friends who want to participate fill out a paper listing the deceased person's name, the relationship, and the person wanting the name read. A donation is given to the church, and the priest reads every one of these requests individually during the service. At the end of the service the priest reads every name a second time and prays, "Give heaven to the dead person and give comfort to the family to grieve with hope."

At the memorial service a prayer of *Hoke-Hankist*, 'Comfort of the Soul,' is recited. After the memorial service the families gather for a meal at someone's home or a banquet hall or restaurant. Food symbolizes the prayer of *Hoke-Chash*, 'Food for the Soul.'

Many Vietnamese people also practice a formal grieving period. For seven weeks after the death of a loved one, people in mourning invite the soul of the deceased into their homes. Every seventh day they cook a special meal for the loved one and burn incense. Also customary for some people of Vietnamese descent is a visit to the grave 100 days after the death of the loved one.

In Eastern Indian culture we see the presence of many multi-generational obligations. Throughout life an individual is a member of a group, has a strong group affiliation and commitment, and is always guided by group decisions (Bhatti and Channabasavanna, 1979). Bhatti and Channabasavanna maintain that a family is united by common ancestry and property. To the property they owe protection, care, and reverent use; to the ancestors they owe dutiful obedience to tradition and the rituals of worship. In India, veneration of ancestors and prayers offered on behalf of these ancestors who are living under King Yama, the God of Death, are an obligation that unites the family and demands its procreation and continuance. The Hindu way of life demands three important steps for every individual: to marry, to have sons, and to worship the family spirits.

In some cultures in China, the most vital religious element in family life is the worship of ancestors, uniting the family present with the family past, giving departed predecessors a continuing role among the living generation. Funeral rites serve to confirm family solidarity, facilitate the comfort of the dead during the passage to the other world, notify the proper governing authority of the under-world, and protect the living from the dead (Augsburger, 1986).

In many African societies ancestors play an important part in religion, as they are vested with mystical power and retain a role in the world of the living. This link of communication and authority between the living elders and the ancestors reinforces the status of the elders. The family system in its traditional form is many layers deep in the transmission of traits through the family unconscious, and it is also reinforced by conscious loyalties and commitment to essential values.

## Multicultural Funerals as Ritual

There are a number of ways to reach out to those who are mourning, through the funeral or other grief rituals of the faith community. The funeral offers an opportunity to deal with many of the needs of the mourners, both in the immediate family and in the larger community. The funeral is a time to publicly memorialize the life that has ended, as well as to put the complex experiences of death into a framework of meaning. A supportive group gathers to express the loss, which each experiences in his or her own way, and permission is given for people to express their grief in ways that might not be considered appropriate in other settings. The funeral communicates that there are ways in which people can find comfort in believing that death is not the end, that life can begin anew.

A very sad funeral took place in our community about a year ago, and a great effort was made to address the needs of the entire community. A mentally unstable man had threatened his wife and then set fire to her apartment, killing her and her four children, ranging in age from 5 to 16. The entire community was distraught, particularly the students and teachers in the children's schools.

Mental healthcare workers spoke to students and teachers while police questioned the husband. Through the generosity of the mortuary and an incredible outpouring by the community, a beautiful service and burial were provided for the family. On a sunny, breezy afternoon, several hundred mourners gathered at the graveside and witnessed the lowering of five coffins, one quite small, into the ground; all bore traditional wreaths of flowers. Many schoolchildren and teachers attended the funeral and shared the opportunity to begin their healing journey.

Often one of the most difficult tasks after a death is the visit to the mortuary. This can be a distressing time for family members, and decisions about funeral rites can be a source of division. Here again, compassion and cultural sensitivity can offer great comfort to the bereaved, as this next example illustrates.

I accompanied a friend whose culture is very different from my own to the funeral home to make arrangements to bury her mother, with whom she had had a loving and close relationship. Since the family had known for some time that she was dying, they were able to spend time together discussing financial matters and funeral arrangements.

The funeral director demonstrated great respect and empathy for my friend. He listened closely to her needs and desires and offered many ideas to contribute to a beautiful opportunity to say good-bye to her mother. He offered music in her mother's language and cultural tradition. He helped design a memorial card that would be printed in English as well as her mother's native language and also suggested that they print a traditional prayer on the back of the folder. Arrangements would be made for family and friends to be present both evenings prior to the funeral service to partake in traditional prayers and singing.

He told us, "To share this time of acute pain with a family is a touching, sacred moment, from which I emerge a wiser, more sensitive human being."

Ritual and ceremony can fulfill the human need to be accepted by and belong with others. "Many changes in life follow the theme of death and rebirth, releasing the past to grow into the future" (Paladin, 1991, p.11). A personal ceremony (ritual) created by an individual to affirm such change serves to symbolically restore his or her spiritual and physical balance. By marking an end and a new beginning, ritual attempts to reconnect the individual to life. "When something happens to us that has no apparent purpose or meaning, it is natural to feel loss, pain, and grief. The event conflicts directly with the way we believe life should be" (Paladin, 1991, p.13). Ceremony and ritual are symbolic affirmations that a change has occurred.

The pastoral relations director at a large mortuary shared some comments about friends in the Armenian community. About 70 percent of the people in this community are connected to a church with cultural influence, so most of the funerals are presided over by a priest who delivers the eulogy as well as the chanting and singing. There is also a special time at the graveside, after the coffin is lowered, when up to 10 or 12 people shovel dirt into the grave until it is completely filled.

This ritual of lowering the casket and participating in the shoveling of dirt is a courageous act of witnessing, which validates the loss and supports those who grieve. Witnessing is integral to acknowledging the loss and encouraging people to display their emotions openly and show respect for their loved ones and their cultural traditions. On special dates such as birthdays and anniversaries family members and friends return to the cemetery to burn incense and pray for their dead. They believe the incense carries their prayers up to God.

## Conclusion

The processing of grief reminds us how essential it is to be connected to others. And grief, like history, is a living process altered by how we navigate the experience. It is also our way of letting go of life as we knew it to be and embracing life as it will grow to be. When we experience a break in our emotional, physical or spiritual connections, we naturally seek a new balance point to restore control and harmony with life. As we accept our continued existence, our grief experience helps us find new ways, and perhaps incorporate very old ways, to create our new identity in this life.

For those who choose the role of companioning the dying and the bereaved, the road can be extraordinarily demanding, though deeply rewarding. Being a caregiver is a complex emotional task that can frustrate idealism and exhaust emotional reserves. To be an effective caregiver is to remain in a state of balance; it is important to know both when to become more emotionally involved and when to pull back. And the incorporation of healing rituals can help to restore a sense of balance when one has been changed by life.

As caregivers perfect their ministry of presence, they perform an integral task of healing. Likewise, this presence strengthens the caring connection that may be one's most indispensable tool as a caregiver. Confrontations with dying and bereavement are difficult but result in a more compassionate attitude. Personal suffering is a harsh but grand teacher. As George Bernard Shaw so poignantly wrote:

This is the true joy in life, the being used
for a purpose recognized by yourself as a mighty one;
the being thoroughly worn out before you are thrown on
the scrap heap;
the being a force of Nature instead of a feverish selfish
little clod of ailments
and grievances complaining that the world will not
devote itself
to making you happy.
Life is no brief candle to me. It is a sort of splendid torch
which I have got hold of for the moment, and I want to
make it burn
as brightly as possible before handing it on to future
generations. (1903/1963, p.510-511)

Caregiving is a "splendid torch." Through our personal action we bring our visions to life. As caregivers, if we can't reach into ourselves with acceptance and love, we won't be able to reach out to others with integrity, compassion, and caring.

---

*Reverend Alice Parsons Zulli is Founder and Director of Beyond Loss, a bereavement ministry. She is a support Chaplain at Glendale Adventist Medical Center and is in private practice.*

# TWENTY-ONE

# The Wounded Healer: A Transcultural Perspective

*Douglas C. Smith*

*When we become aware that we do not have to escape our pains, but that we can mobilize them into a common search for life, those very pains are transformed from expressions of despair into signs of hope.*
— Henri Nouwen (1972)

*Healing comes not because one is whole, integrated, and all together, but from a consciousness breaking through dismemberment.*
— James Hillman (1979)

For the last ten years I have been involved in the most inspiring and invigorating work I can imagine, work that has allowed me to witness profound examples of healing. I work with the terminally ill: people in urban and rural settings, young and old, wealthy and poor, from various racial and religious backgrounds.

All of these people have been for me the ultimate examples of woundedness, facing the gradual loss of absolutely everything. They lose their possessions, their accomplishments, and their roles. They lose their talents, their abilities, and their energy. They lose their neighbors, their friends, and their family. They lose their sense of worth, their self-esteem, and their dignity. They lose their past, their present, and their future. They gradually lose everything they are.

Yet, as those of us who work with the terminally ill witness over and over again, these experts in woundedness teach us about healing. The sick and dying teach us about healthy living. Through the dying we can learn about the rightful value of possessions, accomplishments, and roles. Through the dying we can learn about the rightful use of talents, abilities, and energy. Through the dying we can learn who our true neighbors, friends, and family are. Through the dying we can learn how a sense of worth, self-esteem, and dignity can transcend our normal definitions of those words. Through the dying we can learn how to be thankful for our past, enlivened in our present, and excited about our future. Through the dying we can learn about who we were meant to be.

What we see through the terminally ill is a transcultural model of interacting with people who have emotional struggles related to loss. The model is that of the *wounded healer*, a model of how to develop counseling styles that do not attempt to cover up either our wounds or the wounds of others. We see how our wounds equip us to be good healers for others, and how the wounds of others can help us in our own healing process. Particularly through the common experiences of loss and grief, we see that woundedness allows healing for ourselves and for others that transcends cultural differences.

## The Spiritual/Religious Basis of The Wounded Healer Model

The transformation from woundedness to healing is found throughout ancient literature, most often in the spiritual and religious traditions that have existed throughout history and across cultures. In Buddhism, it was the Buddha's witnessing of suffering and death, from which he had previously been sheltered, that was the catalyst for him to begin the journey toward an enlightened life. The Jewish tradition is based on stories of woundedness and death: Adam and Eve, Cain and Abel, the destruction of the flood, the sacrifice of Isaac, Jacob's wrestling at Peniel, the captivity, the exodus; all stories in which people experienced healing through their woundedness, and in which the gift of new life came through the death of the old life. For Christians, Jesus' persecution and death reveal the purpose of his existence, leading to resurrection, permanent healing, eternal life. The Hindu teacher Ramana Maharshi (1972) spoke of this same transformation: "Your glory lies where you cease to exist." With equal succinctness, the Muslim teacher Pir Vilayat Inayat Khan (1977) said, "Die before death and resurrect now." These versions of the woundedness-to-healing message are puzzling and seem to fly in the face of rationality. Yet the fact that the message is found in all the major spiritual traditions across so many cultures leads one to believe that it must represent a profound truth.

The association of the images of wounds with healing, and dying with life, is so strong that they appear to blend together. In Jewish scripture, for example, the book of Job simultaneously portrays unimaginable suffering and unshakable faith. In fact, one might say that the suffering brings forth the faith. The Christian story of the end of Jesus' life is simultaneously a story of terrible suffering and unshakable love. Again, one might say that the suffering brings forth the love. Muslim scripture also speaks of the intertwining of suffering, faith, and love. The followers of both Hinduism and Buddhism profess that the journey towards spiritual attainment is a relinquishing of attachments and an acquiring of blessings.

A central tenet of all of these great traditions is that pain and suffering, loss and sorrow, even dying and death, carry within them the keys that unlock the secrets of healing and wholeness, the essence of spiritual advancement and an abundant life. Many traditions have a specific term to describe the process of giving up everything in order to attain so much more. The Hindus call it *moksha*; Buddhists, *nirvana*; Muslims, *fana*; and Christians refer to it as being *born again*.

The teaching that wounds lead to healing, dying to life, is contrary to much of the modern self-help psychology, which tries to persuade us that we can achieve a world without wounds, pain, and suffering. The spiritual/religious traditions tell us that wounds, pain, and suffering cannot be eliminated; the world cannot be cured of them. Yet, through wounds, pain, and suffering we can experience healing. We can grow as individuals and as a community. We can be genuine helpers to clients, family members, friends, and strangers by learning how to grow in the midst of our woundedness.

The message of these traditions is that true maturation comes in acknowledging, approaching, and using our woundedness and the woundedness of others. In life we will suffer, we will experience loss, we will err, and we will experience fear, depression, and anger. We will learn, one way or another, that any attempt to avoid suffering will only result in more problems. We must use our own woundedness for our personal growth and to facilitate the growth of others.

In the Buddhist tradition there is a story of a woman mourning the death of a child, who approached the Buddha and asked that he bring her child back to life. The Buddha told her that if she accomplished the task of acquiring a mustard seed from a household where loss and grief had not visited, she would experience healing. After calling on all the households in her community, she realized that everyone is visited by loss and grief. That realization led her to healing—not the healing she requested but healing that comes through sharing in our common woundedness and understanding that we are not alone in our suffering.

## The Role of Therapists, Counselors, and Helpers

In many ways, our goal as therapists, counselors, or helpers need not be to eliminate wounds. We can never undo the experiences of grief and loss. However, we can be models for accepting our own woundedness and loving ourselves in spite of it, paving the way for others to learn to do the same.

Although healing involves both a mental and emotional commitment, in accepting our woundedness and loving the wounded, we transcend defining and comparing and enter into a place of psychospiritual union rather than one of clinical distance. And we transcend cultural differences.

This healing process is facilitated through what Carl Rogers (1961) has labeled the *conditions for growth*, which motivate us to reach beyond our present, to transcend the psychologically and physically obvious, to become the person we really desire to be. Rogers said there are four conditions a counselor must meet for this growth and healing to occur within another, conditions that require us to transcend cultural differences: first, congruence, or authenticity—being ourselves, in all our vulnerability and woundedness; second, empathy—understanding and experiencing another's life and woundedness as if they were our own; third, unconditional positive regard—being non-judgmental, allowing the other to be authentic, allowing their woundedness without our labeling it; the fourth condition consists of the other person directly experiencing the helper's congruence, empathy, and unconditional positive regard.

## Walking the Walk as Well as Talking the Talk

How does this translate into a counseling model for a wounded healer?

1. **Being congruent.** We must receive a client with the realization that both of us (all of us) are wounded. We are all, regardless of culture, subject to loss and grief. As a counselor, I receive a client not from a position of superiority but from a position of commonality.

2. **Being empathetic.** We must transcend our cultural differences at the point of this common woundedness. Whether Hindu, Buddhist, Jewish, Christian, Muslim, or Humanist, we all experience loss and grief. In examining our own culturally based value system, we find a place where we can feel each others' suffering. As a counselor, being in touch with my own woundedness allows me to feel the woundedness of others, and likewise, being in touch with the woundedness of others allows me to feel my own woundedness.

3. **Having unconditional positive regard.** When I accept myself as having inherent value in spite of my woundedness, I can likewise accept others. When I accept the inherent value of others with all their woundedness, I can accept myself. In accepting the inherent value of humanity, I accept myself and others with unconditional positive regard, which helps all of us heal from our shared loss and grief.

4. **Being a person who conveys those three qualities.** When my clients have experienced my congruency, empathy, and unconditional positive regard, I have transcended cultural differences and provided healing for others and for myself.

## Our Common Woundedness

Unless we share in our mutual woundedness, we cannot understand, let alone minister to, those wounds which others have. We will not be able to transcend culture. Our training, degrees, and experience will be of greater value when we have learned to recognize how we, too, share in the world's woundedness. Naomi Remen (1994) has said that "at the heart of any real intimacy is a certain vulnerability. It is hard to trust someone with your vulnerability unless you can see in them a matching vulnerability and know that you will not be judged. In some basic way it is our imperfections and even our pain that draws others close to us." In being an effective therapist, counselor, or helper, our vulnerability and woundedness must be present first.

Those in our care do not want us to label and judge them, they want us to help them heal. The assurance that we will not label and judge them comes from the fact that our loss and grief are mutual and transcendent. As Nouwen (1972) has said, "Shared pain is no longer paralyzing....When we become aware that we do not have to escape our pains, but that we can mobilize them into a common search for life, those very pains are transformed from expressions of despair into signs of hope."

In respecting everyone's unique form of woundedness, we open ourselves up to share in our mutual strengths and healing. "The greatest treasure comes out of the most despised and secret places...This place of greatest vulnerability is also a holy place, a place of healing" (Kreinheder, 1991).

## A Patient Story

Sometimes the more terrible the wound, the more profound the healing.

Debbie, a hospice nurse, told with tears in her eyes about a special relationship she had with one of her hospice patients named Barbara: "I had never seen anyone so devastated by illness. It was even worse than end-stage AIDS. Barbara had cancer of the colon.

You could see her bones through her skin, as if the skin had shrunk around the bones and there was nothing else there; you could see the shape of her skull and could even fit your fist into the indentation caused by her skin sunken against her cheek bones. I once held her fragile body and just cried.... She pleaded, 'I'm ready. Why won't He just take me?'

"I have never supported assisted suicide. However, I wanted to help her; I wanted to help her end her life, but I knew I couldn't.... One day she took my hand, looked me in the eyes, and said, 'Debbie, I love you.' For some reason, I have never felt a stronger declaration of love; I have never been more moved by someone's expression of love. It was as if the very horridness of her condition lent the most profound meaning to her declaration of love. Since my divorce, I had not felt feelings of love towards anyone. I felt betrayed; I felt cold. But Barbara did something for me. She made me feel whole. Yet, she told me that I had made *her* feel whole."

## Lessons From The Dying

I have listened to many people at the end of their life's journey. From them I have learned how precious each breath can be, how wonderful it is to have people who love you, how delicious a cup of coffee can be, how blessed it is to be without pain. From the dying, I have learned much about the details of life, looking and really seeing, listening and really hearing, touching and really feeling. I have learned about not wasting time, I have learned about focusing on real needs. From the dying, I have learned about courage. I have learned about seeking meaning and purpose in my own life. I have learned how important it is for me to acknowledge that my own life will come to an end. I have learned about a deeper spiritual consciousness, realizing that our world is so much more than what we can touch, see, and measure. And yet, all of that the dying claim to receive from us when we are congruent, empathic, and show unconditional positive regard. All of this is healing in the midst of woundedness, healing in the midst of loss and grief.

## Conclusion

We learn from wounds, we teach through wounds. We grow from the wounds of others, we grow through our own wounds. Within that woundedness, we experience healing. The primitive shamans knew it. Krishna knew it. Buddha knew it. Abraham knew it. Jesus knew it. Mohammed knew it.

As therapists, counselors, and helpers, we must respect our wounds and the wounds of others, knowing that there is healing in the midst of them, not apart from them, a healing that transcends culture. As Remen (1993) said, "It's our woundedness that allows us to trust each other. I can trust another person only if I can sense that they, too, have woundedness, have pain, have fear. Out of that trust we can begin to pay attention to our own wounds and to each other's wounds—and to heal and be healed."

---

*Douglas C. Smith, MA, MS, MDiv, is Executive Director of Kanawha Hospice. He is a regular seminar leader for the American Academy of Bereavement, giving workshops for healthcare professionals around the US.*

# Conclusion

*Joyce D. Davidson*

It's enough to make one's head spin, isn't it? Race, ethnicity, religion, culture, language, gender, disability, sexual orientation, class, profession. The glorious mosaic begins to seem daunting when we consider how we are to absorb and retain all we need to know in order to assist others who must navigate the turbulent waters of death, dying, and bereavement.

Fortunately, as Barbara Koenig (1997), a medical anthropologist at Stanford, tells us, it is not necessary to be an expert in another culture. One simply needs both an understanding that cultural difference is meaningful in end-of-life care and an openness to learn from the patient and family. "Even if there is not agreement on all issues, the act of listening is crucial." This is, she says, "one of the most important tenets of a clinical practice sensitive to cultural difference" (p.10).

Author and crisis counselor Diane Ackerman (1997) agrees. "You don't have to be larger than life to help people in the darkest moments of their lives." But, she adds, it does require that "we listen athletically, with one's whole attention, and it is physically exhausting. It feels like a contact sport" (p.9).

As an African American physician, Alexandra Mazard (1997) has experienced the frustrations of both the patients and the providers participating in cross-cultural interaction in end-of-life decision-making. She has observed "a collective irritation in managing the care of a patient whose actions are discordant with the prescripts of western biomedical practices." But she also recognizes the "seemingly insurmountable barrier healthcare providers are asked to scale in such matters" (p.11). And she, too, believes that "fostering fruitful communication" begins with active listening.

She recommends using the LEARN acronym described by Fowkes and Berlin: Listening, Explaining, Acknowledging, Recommending, and Negotiating care issues in ample conversation with patients and families. But the process always begins with active listening.

We will inevitably make mistakes. But as Doka notes earlier in this volume, it is more important to reach out and make a mistake than not to reach out at all. Shukria Raad's poignant story of her sense of abandonment in an American hospital during her husband's terminal illness is a powerful reminder. The pastoral care and counseling staff were no doubt compassionate, caring people, but did not feel empowered to reach out to a family from an unfamiliar culture. We must risk making mistakes or being rebuffed in order to comfort a dying or grieving person.

A recurring theme of this volume is that healthcare professionals should familiarize themselves with the literature on cross-cultural issues and how those issues complicate or facilitate end-of-life decision-making and the grieving process. This book and the resources listed in it are a good beginning.

But perhaps it is an even more resounding imperative to use that knowledge base not as a means of possessing the answers but as the means for formulating thoughtful questions. It is the patients and their families who are the real experts on cultural knowledge and who teach us what we need to know. We must elicit the personal preferences of patients and their families, rather than assuming those preferences based on what we think we know of their cultural background. Our job is to explore, recognize, honor, and reinforce their strengths. In the end, our job is to listen.

Koenig (1995) believes that:

> The ideal of respecting diverse cultural perspectives is based on deeply held American beliefs in the value of tolerance. This does mean, however, that patients may demand unlimited treatment based on their beliefs or cultural identity. The challenge for clinical practice is to allow ethical pluralism—a true engagement with and respect for diverse perspectives—without falling into the trap of absolute ethical relativism. (p.10)

Accordingly, David Price (1997) contrasts tolerance with moral relativism, in which morality is equated with mere preference. "Tolerance," he says, "is a much more robust and demanding virtue.... It respects persons, especially as they attempt to make principled decisions. True tolerance succeeds not by devaluing the issues or traditions that divide us, but by respecting those who differ in good faith" (p.56). The rewards, for patients and for ourselves, are not just commensurate with the effort but immeasurably greater.

Navigating the healthcare system during terminal illness is a frightening and foreign experience for anyone. How much more so for people from other cultures, especially those who don't communicate primarily in English. I learned a powerful lesson from two Indian women—a patient's wife and her mother—who spoke no English. The patient was dying of heart failure and wanted to be removed from all mechanical support. He spoke some English, but his wife and her mother spoke none. When an interpreter explained her husband's conversation with the doctors, the wife was frantic. With palms together, she begged him not to give up. Unable to make herself understood to the staff, her frustration grew into keening desperation. Over the next few days, as her husband grew weaker and weaker, she and her mother kept vigil, able to communicate only with each other. There were no other visitors. I sat beside her frequently with my hand on hers. We shared only touch and facial expressions. As she wept quietly in her chair, I put my arm around her and stroked her hair. I held her mother's hand.

I felt so inadequate. But soon, every time they saw me as I stepped off the elevator and into the unit, they spread their arms out wide in welcome. Our tentative, cautious touch gave way to big bearhugs. And sad smiles touched their faces. The man died in the middle of the night while I was not there, and I never saw his wife or her mother again. But I have never connected more meaningfully with words than I did with those two women with whom I shared no words.

A number of authors here have expressed the imperative that we cultivate not only a head for cross-cultural understanding, but a heart for it as well, which is reflective of the Buddhist concept of the balance between wisdom and compassion. We come to understand our differences with our heads, but we find our common humanity with our hearts. Zulli's apt reference to George Bernard Shaw touches the core: Caregiving is indeed a "splendid torch." And as Albert Camus said, "To look in the face of humanity and not turn away is the most spiritual thing one human being can do for another."

---

*Joyce D. Davidson, MA, is the Bereavement Coordinator for Children's Hospital of New Jersey. She leads grief and bereavement groups throughout the community, and has lectured in China on death, dying, and bereavement.*

# Resource Organizations

## AIDS Caregivers Support Network

2536 Alki Avenue, SW, Suite 138, Seattle, WA 98116
(206) 937-3368
http://www.wolfenet.com/~acsn
e-mail: acsn@wolfenet.com

AIDS Caregivers Support Network is a non-profit, volunteer driven organization which provides support, referral, and education for AIDS caregivers. They publish a quarterly newsletter and offer community education about caregiving to churches and civic groups in the Seattle area. The Network's book, *Circle of Care*, has been used by caregivers and people living with HIV/AIDS throughout the country for the creation and maintenance of successful careteams.

## AIDS Information Network

1211 Chestnut Street, 7th Floor, Philadelphia, PA 19107
(215) 575-1110, Library extension 131
e-mail: aidsinfo@critpath.org

AIDS Information Network has projects related to education and prevention of HIV/AIDS and maintains a comprehensive multi-media, multi-lingual collection of over 100,000 items related to HIV/AIDS. Information requests are answered by professional staff on site, or via telephone, fax, mail or e-mail.

## Alzheimer's Association

919 N. Michigan Avenue, Suite 1000, Chicago, IL 60611-1676
(800) 272-3900

The Alzheimer's Association is the only national voluntary organization dedicated to conquering Alzheimer's disease through research, and through providing education and support to people with Alzheimer's disease, their families, and caregivers. The association sends out general information about the disease and caregiving responsibilities and refers callers to their local chapter where they can get support group information and find out about resources in their area.

## AMERICAN ASSOCIATION ON MENTAL RETARDATION
444 North Capitol Street, NW, Suite 846, Washington, DC 20001
(800) 424-3688 or (202) 387-1968
http://www.aamr.org
e-mail: aamr@access.digex.net

The AAMR is a professional organization that advances the knowledge
and skills of individuals in the field of mental retardation and related
developmental disabilities through the exchange of information and ideas.
The Association strives to enhance the life opportunities of people with
mental retardation and their families and promote public policies, research
and services.

## AMERICAN ASSOCIATION OF PASTORAL COUNSELORS
9504A Lee Highway, Fairfax, VA 22031-2303
(703) 385-6967
e-mail: info@aapc.org

The American Association of Pastoral Counselors (AAPC) was organized
in 1963 to promote and support the ministry of pastoral counseling within
religious communities and the field of mental health in the United States
and Canada.

## AMERICAN ASSOCIATION OF RETIRED PERSONS
601 E Street, NW, Washington, DC 20049
(202) 434-2277
http://www.aarp.org

AARP is the nation's leading organization for people 50 and older.
AARP serves their needs through information and education, advocacy,
and community services provided by a network of local chapters and
experienced volunteers throughout the country. The organization also
offers members a wide range of special benefits and services, including
*Modern Maturity* magazine and the monthly *AARP Bulletin*.

## AMERICANS FOR BETTER CARE OF THE DYING
2175 K Street, NW, Suite 820, Washington, DC 20037
(202) 530-9864
http://www.abcd-caring.com
e-mail: caring@erols.com

Americans for Better Care of the Dying (ABCD) is a non-profit charity
dedicated to social, professional, and policy reform and education aimed

at improving services for patients with serious illness and their families. ABCD aims to: enhance the experience of the last phase of life for all Americans; advocate for the interests of patients and families; improve communication between providers and patients; involve society in end-of-life care; control pain and other symptoms; demand continuity in service systems for the seriously ill; and limit the emotional and financial toll on families.

## AMERICAN CANCER SOCIETY

1599 Clifton Road, NE, Atlanta, GA 30329-4251
(800) ACS-2345
http://www.cancer.org

The American Cancer Society is the nationwide, community-based voluntary health organization dedicated to eliminating cancer as a major health problem by preventing cancer, saving lives, and diminishing suffering from cancer through research, education, advocacy, and service.

## AMERICAN HEART ASSOCIATION

7272 Greenville Avenue, Dallas, TX 75231
(214) 373-6300 or (800)AHA-USA1 to be connected to closest affiliate in area.
http://www.americanheart.org

The American Heart Association is one of the world's premier health organizations committed to reducing disability and death from cardiovascular diseases and stroke.

## AMERICAN PARKINSON DISEASE ASSOCIATION

1250 Hylan Boulevard, Suite 4B, Staten Island, NY 10305-1946
(800)223-2732 or (718) 981-8001
http://www.apdaparkinson.com
e-mail: apda@admin.con2.com

APDA is a not-for-profit voluntary health agency committed to serving the Parkinson community through a comprehensive program of research, education, and support, offering educational booklets and supplements, symposiums, and referrals to support groups, local chapters, and physicians specializing in Parkinson's disease throughout the United States.

## ASSOCIATION OF ASIAN PACIFIC COMMUNITY HEALTH ORGANIZATIONS

1440 Broadway, Suite 510, Oakland, CA 94612
(510) 272-9536
http://www.aapcho.org
e-mail: info@aapcho.org

AAPCHO is a national association representing community health organizations dedicated to improving the health status of Asians and Pacific Islanders (APIs) in the United States and its territories, especially the medically underserved. AAPCHO advocates for policies and programs that will improve the provision of healthcare services that are community driven, financially affordable, linguistically accessible, and culturally appropriate. AAPCHO offers technical assistance and training for medically underserved API communities.

## ASSOCIATION FOR CLINICAL PASTORAL EDUCATION

1549 Clairmont Road, Suite 103, Decatur, GA 30033
(404) 320-1472
http://www.acpe-edu.org
e-mail: acpe@acpe-edu.org

The ACPE mission is to foster experienced-based theological education which combines the practice of pastoral care with qualified supervision and peer group reflection and which is grounded in a person-centered approach to religious ministry.

## ASSOCIATION FOR DEATH EDUCATION AND COUNSELING

638 Prospect Avenue, Hartford, CT 06105
(860) 586-7503
http://www.adec.org

ADEC is dedicated to improving the quality of death education and death-related counseling and caregiving; to promoting the development and interchange of related theory and research; and to providing support, stimulation, and encouragement to its members and those studying and working in death-related fields.

## CANDLELIGHTERS CHILDHOOD CANCER FOUNDATION

7910 Woodmont Avenue, Suite 460, Bethesda, MD 20814-3015
(800) 366-2223 or (301) 657-8401
http://www.candlelighters.org

CCCF provides support, information, and advocacy to families of
children with cancer (at any stage of the illness or who are bereaved),
to professionals in the field, and to adult survivors, through local
groups, newsletters, and other services.

## THE CENTER TO IMPROVE CARE OF THE DYING

2175 K Street, NW, Suite 820, Washington, DC 20037
(202) 467-2222
http://www.gwu.edu/~cicd
e-mail: cicd@gwis2.circ.gwu.edu

The Center to Improve Care of the Dying is a unique, interdisciplinary
organization committed to research, education, and advocacy to improve
care of dying patients and those suffering with severely disabling diseases.
Its broad perspective is achieved by incorporation of insights and
experience from the social sciences, humanities, law, epidemiology,
health services research, and ethics.

## CHILDREN'S HOSPICE INTERNATIONAL

2202 Mt. Vernon Avenue, Suite 3C, Alexandria, VA 22301
(703) 684-0330
http://www.chionline.org
e-mail: chiorg@aol.com

Children's Hospice International creates a world of hospice support
for children, providing medical and technical assistance, research, and
education for these special children, their families and healthcare
professionals. CHI works with hospices, children's hospitals, homecare
agencies and other individuals and organizations to assist them in better
caring for children with life-threatening conditions.

## THE COMPASSIONATE FRIENDS

P.O. Box 3696, Oak Brook, IL 60522-3696
(630) 990-0010
http://www.compassionatefriends.org

The Compassionate Friends is a self-help organization whose purpose
is to offer friendship and understanding to parents and siblings following
the death of a child. They have 580 chapters nationwide which provide
monthly meetings, phone contacts, lending libraries and a local newsletter.
The national organization provides newsletters, distributes grief-related
materials, and answers requests for referrals and information.

## THE DOUGY CENTER

P.O. Box 86582, Portland, OR 97286
(503) 775-5683
http://www.dougy.org
e-mail: help@dougy.org

The Dougy Center provides support groups for grieving children that
are age specific (3-5, 6-12, teens) and loss specific (parent death, sibling
death, survivors of homicide/violent death, survivors of suicide). They
have additional services that include national trainings, consultations
to schools and organizations, crisis-line information, and referrals.

## HOSPICE FOUNDATION OF AMERICA

2001 S Street, NW, Suite 300, Washington, DC 20009
(202) 638-5419
777 17th Street, Suite 401, Miami Beach, FL 33139
(800) 854-3402
http://www.hospicefoundation.org
e-mail: hfa@hospicefoundation.org

The Hospice Foundation of America provides leadership in the
development and application of hospice and its philosophy of care for
terminally-ill people, conducting programs of education and providing
grants. HFA sponsors an annual *Living With Grief* teleconference series, a
monthly bereavement newsletter, *Journeys*, and other publications. HFA
has also produced an audiotape series, *Clergy to Clergy*, which helps clergy
members minister to those confronting illness, death, and grief.

## In Loving Memory

1416 Green Run Lane, Reston, VA
(703) 435-0608

Mutual support, friendship, and help for parents who have lost their only child or all of their children.

## Institute for the Study of Health and Illness

P.O. Box 316, Bolinas, CA 94924
(415) 868-2642
http://www.commonwealhealth.org
e-mail: 74512.2635@compuserve.com

The mission of The Institute for the Study of Health and Illness (ISHI) is to create a new approach to health delivery, a step beyond disease-centered care and patient-centered care called "relationship-centered care." ISHI has developed programs that focus on physician training and workshop development, as well as an active consulting and speakers program.

## Intercultural Cancer Council

1720 Dryden, Suite C, Houston, TX 77030
(713) 798-4617
http://icc.bcm.tmc.edu
e-mail: icc@bcm.tmc.edu

The mission of the Intercultural Cancer Council is to develop and promote policies and programs to assist minorities, culturally diverse, and medically underserved individuals who have higher incidence and lower survival rates from cancer.

## Last Acts Campaign

c/o Barksdale Ballard, 8027 Leesburg Pike, #200, Vienna, VA 22182
(703) 827-8771
http://www.lastacts.rwjf.org
e-mail: ballard2@aol.com

The goal of Last Acts is to achieve the following: greater awareness of problems in the care of critically ill and dying Americans; greater recognition—by various organizations and groups—of their responsibility to participate in developing and implementing solutions; and increased collaborative activities, information-sharing, and continued engagement in discussion of end-of-life issues.

## THE MAUTNER PROJECT FOR LESBIANS WITH CANCER

1707 L Street, NW, Suite 500, Washington, DC 20036
(202) 332-5536
http://www.sirius.com/~edisol/mautner/index.html
e-mail: mautner@aol.com

The Mautner Project for Lesbians with Cancer is dedicated to providing direct services and support groups for lesbians, their partners, and caregivers. The project also provides education and information about cancer to the lesbian community, education to healthcare providers about the special concerns of lesbians with cancer, and advocacy on lesbian health issues in national and local arenas.

## NATIONAL ASSOCIATION OF THE DEAF

814 Thayer Avenue, Silver Spring, MD 20910
(301) 587-1788 or TTY number (301) 587-1789
http://www.nad.org
e-mail: NADHQ@juno.com

The mission of NAD is to assure that a comprehensive, coordinated system of services is accessible to Americans who are deaf and hard of hearing. Numerous programs and activities are available enabling them to achieve their maximum potential through increased independence, productivity, and integration.

## NATIONAL ASSOCIATION OF PEOPLE WITH AIDS

1413 K Street, NW, Washington, DC 20036
(202)898-0414
http://www.thecure.org

NAPWA is a national AIDS advocacy group. They provide free publications on treatment and advocacy and have an extensive information and referral department that includes a fax-on-demand system; you can call (202)789-2222 from your fax machine to request information on HIV/AIDS. They also have a health and treatment department that provides up-to-date treatment information and a free bi-monthly publication, *Medical Alert* (available in English and Spanish.)

## NATIONAL BLACK WOMEN'S HEALTH PROJECT

1211 Connecticut Avenue, NW, Suite 310, Washington, DC 20036
(202) 835-0117

The mission of the NBWHP is to improve the health of Black women through wellness education and services, Self-Help Group development, and health information and advocacy. NBWHP works with individuals and groups at the primary prevention level; NBWHP is also active on the national and international level. There are 16 national chapters and 150 local Self-Help Groups.

## NATIONAL COALITION OF HISPANIC HEALTH AND HUMAN SERVICES ORGANIZATIONS

1501 16th Street, NW, Washington, DC 20036
(202) 387-5000
http://www.cossmho.org
e-mail: info@cossmho.org

COSSMHO is the sole organization focusing on the health, mental health, and human services needs of the diverse Hispanic communities. COSSMHO's membership consists of thousands of front-line health and human services providers and organizations serving Hispanic communities. COSSMHO's services include: consumer education and outreach; training programs; technical assistance; and model community-based programs.

## NATIONAL COUNCIL ON DISABILITY

1331 F St. NW, Suite 1050
Washington, DC 20004
(202) 272-2004
TTY: (202) 272-2074
http://www.ncd.gov

The National Council is the only federal agency charged with addressing, analyzing, and making recommendations on issues of public policy that affect people with disabilities regardless of age, disability type, perceived employment potential, economic need, specific functional ability, status as a veteran, or other individual circumstance.

## NATIONAL FEDERATION OF INTERFAITH VOLUNTEER CAREGIVERS

368 Broadway, Suite 103, Kingston, NY 12401
(914) 331-1358
http://www.nfivc.org
e-mail: nfivc@aol.com

The purpose of the National Federation of Interfaith Volunteer Caregivers, Inc. is to promote, in all congregations throughout the United States, the ministry of caregiving to disabled persons and their families without reference to age, gender, race, or religious affiliation. NFIVC provides support and training to start and operate Interfaith Volunteer Caregiving Projects (IVCPs). Through IVCPs, Volunteer Caregivers provide compassionate, one-on-one care to those in need.

## NATIONAL HOSPICE ORGANIZATION

1901 N. Moore Street, Suite 901, Arlington, VA 22209
(703) 243-5900
http://www.nho.org
e-mail: drsnho@cais.com

The National Hospice Organization (NHO) is the oldest and largest
public benefit organization in the US devoted exclusively to hospice
care. NHO operates the Hospice Helpline (1-800-658-8898) to provide
the general public and healthcare professionals with information about
hospice care, reimbursement sources, as well as referrals to local hospice
programs throughout the US. NHO publishes a variety of brochures on
hospice care, grief in the workplace, and bereavement.

## NATIONAL INFORMATION CENTER FOR CHILDREN
## AND YOUTH WITH DISABILITIES

P.O. Box 1492, Washington, DC 20013
(800) 695-0285, voice & TTY or (202) 884-8200, voice & TTY

The National Information Center for Children and Youth with Disabilities
is an information and referral center that focuses on young people with
disabilities from birth to the age of 22. Publications, referrals, and
information concerning other resources are available.

## OFFICE OF MINORITY HEALTH RESOURCE CENTER

P.O. Box 37337, Washington, DC 20013-7337
(800) 444-6472
TTY: (301) 589-0951
http://www.os.dhhs.gov/progorg/ophs/omh/omhrc.htm

The Office of Minority Health Resource Center (OMH-RC) was established
to facilitate the exchange of information and strategies to improve the
health status of racial and ethnic minorities. The center's mission is to
collect and distribute information on the health of Blacks, Hispanics,
Asians and Pacific Islanders, American Indians and Alaska Natives. The
Resource Persons Network of OMH-RC consists of minority health experts
available to provide technical assistance, offer advice, and speak at
workshops. OMH-RC publishes a bimonthly newsletter called *Closing the
Gap*. Services are provided at no cost.

## REGISTRY OF INTERPRETERS FOR THE DEAF

8630 Fenton Street, Suite 324, Silver Spring, MD 20910
(301) 608-0050

## St. Francis Center

4880-A MacArthur Boulevard, NW, Washington, DC 20007
(202) 333-4880
http://www.moore.net/~sfcgrief
e-mail: sfcgrief@erols.com

St. Francis Center (non-sectarian) specializes in support to people affected by all types of illness, loss, and grief. Services include counseling for adults and children; grief awareness programs for schools, work places, and religious institutions; education/training for mental health and health professionals in clinical applications of loss; and a volunteer program offering emotional and practical support for those living with illness, loss, or grief.

## Self Help for Hard of Hearing People

7910 Woodmont Avenue, Suite 1200, Bethesda, MD 20814
(301) 657-2248
TTY: (301) 657-2249
http://www.shhh.org
e-mail: national@shhh.org

SHHH is a volunteer, international organization of hard of hearing people, their relatives, and friends. It is a nonprofit, non-sectarian educational organization devoted to the welfare and interests of those who cannot hear well. Publishes bimonthly journal, *Hearing Loss*, as well as publications on all aspects of hearing loss. There are 250 self-help support groups throughout the US.

## Tragedy Assistance Program for Survivors

2001 S Street, NW, Suite 300, Washington, DC 20009
(800) 959-TAPS
http://www.taps.org
e-mail: TAPSHQ@aol.com

TAPS is a national non-profit organization made up of, and providing services at no cost to, all those who have suffered the loss of a loved one in the Armed Forces. The heart of TAPS is its national military survivor peer support network called SurvivorLINK, which links together the families, friends, and coworkers of those who are grieving. TAPS also offers bereavement counseling referral, provides case worker assistance that carries the work of the casualty assistance officers into the future, hosts the nation's only annual National Military Survivor Seminar and Kids Camp, publishes a quarterly journal mailed at no charge to survivors and caregivers, maintains a comprehensive web site, and offers a toll-free crisis and information line available 24 hours a day.

## The International **THEOS** Foundation
(They Help Each Other Spiritually)
322 Blvd. of the Allies, Suite 105, Pittsburgh, PA 15222
(412) 471-7779

THEOS helps persons whose spouses have died, providing educational materials and emotional support for the newly widowed. Chapters offer ongoing self-help support groups. THEOS also publishes a magazine series and hosts an annual national conference, open to both professionals and those who are recently widowed.

## Widowed Persons Service
4270 Chicago Drive, SW, Grandville, MI 49418
(616) 538-0101

WPS is a self-help support group for men and women who have experienced the loss of a spouse through death. They offer daytime and evening support group meetings, seminars, social activities and public education of the widowed experience. They have a directory of the 270 programs across the country and can refer you to one in your area. They have two excellent videos on the widowed experience that many hospices have purchased.

# World Wide Web Resource:

## Growth House
http://www.growthhouse.org
e-mail: info@growthhouse.org

The mission of Growth House, Inc., is to improve the quality of compassionate care for people who are dying through public education about hospice and home care, palliative care, pain management, death with dignity, bereavement, and related issues. This award-winning web site offers the net's most extensive directory of reviewed resources for life-threatening illness and end-of-life care. Growth House offers a free monthly e-mail newsletter covering new and noteworthy net resources for terrminal care, life-threatening illness, and bereavement.

# References

## INTRODUCTION: DOKA

Coles, R. (1990). *The spiritual life of children*. Boston: Houghton-Mifflin.

Crenshaw, D. (1991). *Bereavement: Counseling the grieving throughout the life cycle*. New York: Continuum.

Klass, D., Silverman, P.R., & Nickman, S.L. (Eds.). (1996). *Continuing bonds: New understandings of grief*. Washington, DC: Taylor & Francis.

Kübler-Ross, E. (1969). *On death and dying*. New York: MacMillan.

Martin, T.L. & Doka, K. J. (1996). Masculine grief. In K. J. Doka (Ed.), *Living with grief: After sudden loss*. Washington, DC: Hospice Foundation of America/Taylor & Francis.

Miner, H. (1956). Body ritual among the Nacirema. *American Anthropologist, 58* (3).

Neimeyer, R.A. (1997). Meaning reconstruction and the experience of chronic loss. In K. J. Doka & J. Davidson (Eds.), *Living with grief: When illness is prolonged* (pp. 159-176).Washington, DC: Hospice Foundation of America/Taylor & Francis.

Parkes, C.M. (1972). *Bereavement: Studies of grief in adult life*. New York: International Universities Press.

Prend, A. (1997). *Transcending loss: Understanding the lifelong impact of grief and how to make it meaningful*. New York: Berkeley.

Rando, T.A. (1984). *Grief, dying and death: Clinical implications for the caregiver*. Champaign, IL: Research Press.

Rando, T.A. (1993). *The treatment of complicated mourning*. Champaign, IL: Research Press.

Sanders, C.M. (1989). *Grief: The mourning after*. New York: Wiley.

Sanders, C.M. (1992). *Surviving grief and learning to live again*. New York: Wiley.

Sanders, C.M. (1993). Risk factors in bereavement outcome. In M. Stroebe, W. Stroebe, & R. Hansson (Eds.), *The handbook of bereavement: Theory, research, intervention* (pp. 255-267). Cambridge: Cambridge University Press.

Stroebe, M. & Stroebe, W. (1993). Determinants of adjustment to bereavement in younger widows and widowers. In  M. Stroebe, W. Stroebe, & R. Hansson (Eds.), *The handbook of bereavement: Theory, research, intervention*. Cambridge: Cambridge University Press.

Stroebe, M. & Schut, H. (1995, June). *The dual process model of coping with loss*. Paper presented at the meeting of the International Work Group on Death, Dying and Bereavement, Oxford, England.

Sue, D.W. & Sue, D. (1990). *Counseling the culturally different: Theory and practice* (2nd ed.). New York: J. Wiley & Sons.

Worden, J. W. (1991). *Grief counseling and grief therapy*. New York: Springer.

## 1: KLASS AND GOSS

Doi, T. (1973). *The anatomy of dependence* (J. Bester, Trans.). Tokyo: Kodansha International.

Gilday, E. T. (1993). Dancing with the spirit(s): Another view of the other world in Japan. *History of Religions, 32* (3), 273-300.

Horn, G. S. (1971). *Chinese Argonauts.* San Jose: Foothill Community College District.

Klass, D., Silverman, P.R., & Nickman, S.L. (Eds.). (1996). *Continuing bonds: New understandings of grief.* Washington, DC: Taylor & Francis.

Lee, P. C. (1995). Understanding death, dying and religion: A Chinese perspective. In J. K. Parry & A. S. Ryan (Eds.), *A cross-cultural look at death, dying, and religion* (pp. 170-182). Chicago: Nelson Hall.

Levine, S. (1982). *Who dies? An investigation of conscious living and conscious dying.* New York: Anchor Books.

Plath, D.W. (1964). Where the family of god is the family: The role of the dead in Japanese households. *American Anthropologist, 66* (2), 300-317.

Smith, R.J. (1974). *Ancestor worship in contemporary Japan.* Stanford, CA: Stanford University Press.

Volkan, V. (1981). *Linking objects and linking phenomena: A study of the forms, symptoms, metapsychology, and therapy of complicated mourning.* New York: International Universities Press.

Winnicott, D. W. (1953). Transitional objects and transitional phenomena. *International Journal of Psychoanalysis, 34,* 89-97.

Yamamoto, J., Okonogi, K., Iwasaki, T., & Yoshimura, S. (1969). Mourning in Japan. *American Journal of Psychiatry, 125,* 1661-1665.

## 2: GROLLMAN

Dershowitz, A.M. (1997). *The vanishing Jew.* Boston: Little, Brown.

Goldberg, C. (1991). *Mourning in Halacha.* New York: Mesorah.

Grollman, E.A. (1974). *Concerning death: A practical guide for the living.* Boston: Beacon Press.

Isaacs, R.H. (1992). *Rites of passage: A Jewish guide to the Jewish cycle.* Hoboken, NJ: KTAV.

*Jewish mourner's book.* (1994). New York: Behrman House.

Kolatch, A.J. (1993). *The Jewish mourner's book of why.* New York: Jonathan David.

Lamm, M. (1969). *The Jewish way in death and mourning.* New York: Jonathan David.

Moore, G.F. (1946). *Judaism.* Cambridge: Harvard University Press.

Riemer, J. (1974). *Jewish reflections on death.* New York: Schocken.

Sonsino, R. & Syme, D.B. (1990). *What happens after I die?* New York: Union of American Hebrew Congregations.

Weiss, A. (1991). *Death and bereavement: A Halakhic guide.* Hoboken, NJ: KTAV.

## 3: McConnell

LaGrand, L. E. (1997, September/October). Are we missing opportunities to help the bereaved? *The Forum 23* (5).

Lewis, C. S. (1961). *A Grief Observed.* London: Faber.

## 4: Raad

*The Holy Quran* (A.Y. Ali, Trans.). Brentwood, MD: Amana Corp.

Smith, J. I. (1991). Islam. In C.J. Johnson & M.G. McGee (Eds.), *How different religions view death and afterlife* (pp. 185-284). Philadelphia: The Charles Press.

# Part II. Ethnicity and Culture

Barrett, R. K. (1995). Contemporary African-American funeral rites and traditions. In L. A. DeSpelder & A. L. Strickland (Eds.), *The path ahead: Readings in death and dying* (pp. 80-92). Mountain View, CA: Mayfield.

Doka, K.J. (1997, July/August). Grief in the Arctic Circle. *The Forum, 23* (4), 7-9.

Glazer, N. & Moynihan, D. (1963). *Beyond the melting pot: The negroes, Puerto Ricans, Jews, Iranians and Irish of New York City.* Cambridge, MA: MIT Press.

Irish, D.P., Lundquist, K.F. & Nelsen, V.J. (1993). *Ethnic variations in dying, death, and grief: Diversity in universality.* Washington, DC: Taylor & Francis.

Kalish, R. A. & Reynolds, D. K. (1981). *Death and ethnicity: A psychocultural study.* Amityville, NY: Baywood.

Parkes, C. M., Laungani, P. & Young, B. (1997). *Death and bereavement across cultures.* New York: Routledge.

Sue, D.W. & Sue, D. (1990). *Counseling the culturally different: Theory and practice* (2nd ed.). New York : J. Wiley & Sons.

Walsh, F. & McGoldrick, M. (1991). *Living beyond loss: Death in the family.* New York: W.W. Norton.

## 5: Cable

Aries, P. (1974). *Western attitudes toward death: From the middle ages to the present.* Baltimore: Johns Hopkins University Press.

Bliatout, B. T. (1993). Hmong death customs: Traditional and accultured. In D. P. Irish, K. F. Lundquist, & V. J. Nelsen (Eds.), *Ethnic variations in dying, death, and grief* (pp.79-100). Washington, DC: Taylor & Francis.

Corr, C. A., Nabe, C. M. & Corr, D. M. (1997). *Death and dying, living and life* (2nd ed.). Pacific Grove, CA: Brooks/Cole Publishing Company.

Irish, D. P., Lundquist, K. F., & Nelsen, V. J. (1993). *Ethnic variations in dying, death, and grief.* Washington, DC: Taylor & Francis.

Kastenbaum, R. J. (1998). *Death, society, and human experience* (6th ed.). Needham Heights, MA: Allyn and Bacon.

Rando, T.A. (1988). *Grieving: How to go on living when someone you love dies.* Lexington, MA: Lexington Books.

Rando, T.A. (1993). *The treatment of complicated mourning*. Champaign, IL: Research Press.

Raphael, B. (1983). *The anatomy of bereavement*. New York: Basic Books.

Scheff, T. J. (1975). Labeling, emotion, and individual change. In T. J. Scheff, (Ed.). *Labeling madness*. Englewood Cliffs, NJ: Prentice-Hall.

Tanner, J. G. (1995). Death, dying, and grief in the Chinese-American culture. In J. K. Parry & A. S. Ryan (Eds.), *A cross-cultural look at death, dying, and religion* (pp. 183-192). Chicago: Nelson Hall.

Worden, J. W. (1991). *Grief counseling and grief therapy* (2nd ed.). New York: Springer.

## 6: SHOWALTER

Carter, F. (1976). *The education of Little Tree*. New York: Delacorte Press/E. Friede.

Deloria, V. (1994). *God is red: A native view of religion*. Golden, CO: Fulcrum Publishing.

Doka, K.J. (Ed.). (1989). *Disenfranchised grief: Recognizing hidden sorrow*. Lexington, MA: Lexington Press.

Garrett, J.T. & Garrett, M. (1996). *Medicine of the Cherokee: The way of right relationship*. New York: Bear & Company.

Good Tracks, J.G. (1973). Native American noninterference. *Social Casework, 18* (6), 30-34.

Kubler-Ross, E. (1969). *On death and dying*. New York: Macmillan.

Laski, V. (1959). *Seeking life*. Austin, TX: University of Texas Press.

Lindemann, E. (1944). Symptomatology and management of acute grief. *American Journal of Psychiatry, 101*, 141-148.

Locust, C. (1985). *American Indian beliefs concerning health and unwellness*. [Monograph]. Native American Research and Training Center, University of Arizona.

Mankiller, W. (1993). *Mankiller: A Chief and her people*. New York: St. Martens Press.

Mooney, J. (1982). *Myths of the Cherokee and sacred formulas*. Nashville, TN: Elder Booksellers.

Showalter, S.E. (1997, March/April). Walking with grief: The trail of tears in a world of AIDS. *Healing Ministry 4* (2), 29-39.

Tafoya, T. (1989). *Circles and cedar: Native Americans and family therapy*. New York: Hawthorne Press.

## 7: BARRETT

Barrett, R. K. (1986). Cultural mistrust as a contributor to mental health and psycho-pathology. *ERIC/CADS Resources in Education*, 261-296.

Barrett, R. K. (1993). Psycho-cultural influences on African-American attitudes towards death, dying, and funeral rites. In J. Morgan (Ed.), *Personal care in an impersonal world* (pp. 213-230). Amityville, NY: Baywood.

Barrett, R. K. (1994). Reclaiming and reaffirming African-American funeral rites. *The Director*, 36-40.

Barrett, R. K. (1995). Contemporary African-American funeral rites and traditions. In L A. DeSpelder & A. L. Strickland (Eds.), *The path ahead: Readings in death and dying* (pp. 80-92). Mountain View, CA.: Mayfield.

Barrett, R. K. (1997a). Bereaved Black children. In J. Morgan (Ed.), *Readings in thanatology* (pp. 403-419). Amityville, NY: Baywood.

Barrett, R. K. (1997b, May). *Blacks, death, dying and funeral rites: Everything you've wondered about but thought it politically incorrect to ask*. Presentation at the 15th King's College Annual International Conference on Death, Dying, and Bereavement, London, Ontario.

Dixon, B. (1994). *Good health for African Americans*. New York: Crown.

Holsendolph, E. (1997, October). Insurance companies race for the market. *Emerge: Black American News Magazine*.

Irish, D.P., Lundquist, K.F. & Nelsen, V. J. (1993). *Ethnic variations in dying, death, and grief: Diversity in universality*. Washington, DC: Taylor & Francis.

Kalish, R. & Reynolds, D. (1981). *Death and ethnicity: A psychocultural study*. Amityville, NY: Baywood.

Nichols, E. (1989). *The last mile of the way: African American homegoing traditions 1890 - present*. Columbia, SC: Dependable.

Parry, J.K. & Ryan, A.S. (1995). *A cross-cultural look at death, dying, and religion*. Chicago: Nelson Hall.

Perry, H. (1993). Mourning and funeral customs of African Americans. In D.P. Irish, K.F. Lundquist & V. J. Nelsen (Eds.), *Ethnic variation in dying, death and grief: Diversity in universality* (pp. 51-63). Washington, DC: Taylor & Francis.

Sue, D.W. & Sue, D. (1990). *Counseling the culturally different: Theory and practice*. New York: J. Wiley & Sons.

Sullivan, M. (1995). May the circle be unbroken: The African-American experience of death, dying and spirituality. In J.K. Parry & A.S. Ryan (Eds.), *A cross-cultural look at death, dying, and religion*. Chicago: Nelson Hall.

Terrell, F. & Barrett, R. K. (1979). Interpersonal trust among college students as a function of race, sex, and socioeconomic class. *Perceptual and Motor Skills, 48*.

Terrell, F. & Terrell, S. (1983). The relationship between race of examiner, cultural mistrust, and the intelligence test performance of Black children. *Psychology in the Schools 20*, 367 - 369.

Washington, H. (1997, October). Fear of medical care can become deadly. *Emerge: Black American News Magazine*.

## 8: DeSpelder

Barrett, R.K. (1995). Contemporary African-American funeral rites and traditions. In L.A. DeSpelder & A.L. Strickland (Eds.), *The path ahead: Readings in death and dying* (pp. 80-92). Mountain View, CA: Mayfield.

DeSpelder, L.A. & Strickland, A.L. (1996). *The last dance: Encountering death and dying* (4th ed.). Mountain View, CA: Mayfield.

Galanti, G.A. (1997). *Caring for patients from different cultures: Case studies from American hospitals* (2nd ed.). Philadelphia: University of Pennsylvania Press.

Lipson, J.G., Dibble, S.L., & Minarik, P.A. (1996). *Culture and nursing care: A pocket guide*. San Francisco: UCSF Nursing Press.

# Part III. Varied Experience: Gender, Development, Class, and Cultural Influences on Grief

Coles, R. (1977). *Privileged ones: Children of crisis*. Boston: Little and Brown.

Doka, K. J. (Ed.). (1989). *Disenfranchised grief: Recognizing hidden sorrow*. Lexington, MA: Lexington Press.

Garreau, J. (1981). *The nine nations of North America*. Boston: Houghton-Mifflin.

Gordon, M. (1975). *Human nature, class and ethnicity*. New York: Oxford University Press.

Hollingshead, A. (1949). *Elmstown's Youth*. New York: Wiley.

Warner, W.L. (1959). *The living and the dead: A study of symbolic life of Americans*. New Haven: Yale University Press.

## 10: SANDERS

Ball, J.F. (1977). Widows' grief: The impact of age and mode of death. *Omega, 7*, 307-333.

Helsing, K.J., Szklo, M., & Comstock, C.W. (1981). Factors associated with mortality after widowhood. *American Journal of Public Health, 71*, 802-809.

Lund, D.A., Caserta, M.S. & Dimond, M.F. (1993). The course of spousal bereavement in later life. In M. Stroebe, W. Stroebe, & R. Hansson (Eds.), *Handbook of bereavement*. New York: Cambridge University Press.

Martin, T.L. & Doka, K.J. (1996). Masculine grief. In K.J. Doka (Ed.), *Living with grief: After sudden loss*. Washington, DC: Hospice Foundation of America/Taylor & Francis.

Parkes, C.M. & Brown, R.J. (1972). Health after bereavement: A controlled study of young Boston widows and widowers. *Psychosomatic Medicine, 34* (5), 449-461.

Raphael, B. (1984). *The anatomy of bereavement*. London: Hutchinson Publishing.

Sanders, C. M. (1989). *Grief: The mourning after*. New York: John Wiley & Sons, Inc.

Sanders, C.M. (1995). The grief of children and parents. In K.J. Doka (Ed.), *Children mourning, mourning children*. Washington, DC: Hospice Foundation of America/Taylor & Francis.

Stroebe, W. & Stroebe, M. (1993). The impact of spousal bereavement on older widows and widowers. In M. Stroebe, W. Stroebe, & R. Hansson (Eds.), *Handbook of bereavement*. New York: Cambridge University Press.

## 11: MARTIN AND DOKA

Doka, K. J. (1990). The therapeutic bookshelf. *Omega, 21*, 321-327.

Martin, T. L. & Doka, K. J. (in press). Masculine responses to loss: Implications for counselors. *Journal of Counseling and Development*.

Rando, T.A. (1993). *The treatment of complicated mourning*. Champaign, IL: Research Press.

Rogers, C. R. (1951). *Client-centered therapy*. Boston: Houghton-Mifflin.

Shuchter, S. R. & Zisook, S. (1993). The course of normal grief. In M. Stroebe, W. Stroebe & R.Hansson (Eds.), *Handbook of bereavement*. New York: Cambridge University Press.

Silverman, P.R. (1986). *Widow to widow*. New York: Springer.

Worden, W. (1991). *Grief counseling and grief therapy: A handbook for the mental health practitioner* (2nd ed.). New York: Springer.

Wortman, C. B. & Silver, R. C. (1989). The myths of coping with loss. *Journal of Counseling and Clinical Psychology, 57*, 349-357.

## 12: CORR

Blos, P. (1979). *The adolescent passage: Developmental issues*. New York: International Universities Press.

Bowlby, J.A. (1961). Processes of mourning. *International Journal of Psychoanalysis, 42*, 317-340.

Bowlby, J. A. (1973-1982). *Attachment and loss* (3 vols.). New York: Basic Books.

Corr, C.A., & Balk, D.E. (Eds.). (1996). Handbook of adolescent death and bereavement. New York: Springer.

Corr, C.A., & Corr, D.M. (Eds.). (1996). *Handbook of childhood death and bereavement*. New York: Springer.

Corr, C.A., Nabe, C.M., & Corr, D.M. (1997). *Death and dying, life and living* 2nd ed.). Pacific Grove, CA: Brooks/Cole.

Erikson, E. (1963). *Childhood and society* (2nd ed.). New York: Norton.

Erikson, E. (1968). *Identity: Youth and crisis*. London: Faber & Faber.

Levinson, D. J. (1978). *The seasons of a man's life*. New York: Knopf.

Levinson, D. J. (1996). *The seasons of a woman's life*. New York: Knopf.

Parkes, C.M. (1970). "Seeking" and "finding" a lost object: Evidence from recent studies of reaction to bereavement. *Social Science and Medicine, 4*, 1887.

Parkes, C.M. (1987). *Bereavement: Studies of grief in adult life* (2nd ed.). Madison, CT: International Universities Press.

Rando, T.A. (1993). *The treatment of complicated mourning*. Champaign, IL: Research Press.

Stroebe, M., & Schut, H. (1995, June). *The dual process model of coping with loss*. Paper presented at the meeting of the International Work Group on Death, Dying and Bereavement, Oxford, England.

## 13: LAVIN

Adlin, M. (1993). Health care issues. In E. Sutton, A. R. Factor, B. A Hawkins, T. Heller, & G. Seltzer (Eds.), *Older adults with developmental disabilities* (pp. 49-60). Baltimore, MD: Paul Brookes Publishing.

Berman, A. L. (1992). Treating suicidal behavior in the mentally retarded: The case of Kim. *Suicide and Life-threatening Behavior, 22*, 504-513.

Biklen, B. (1989). Redefining schools. In D. Biklen, D. Ferguson, & A. Ford (Eds.), *Schooling and disability: Eighty-eighth yearbook of the National Society for the Study of Education: Part II* (pp. 1-24).Chicago, IL: NSSE.

Deutsch, H. (1985). Grief counseling with the mentally retarded clients. *Psychiatric Aspects of Mental Retardation* Reviews, *4*, 17-20.

Doka, K. J. (Ed.). (1989). *Disenfranchised grief: Recognizing hidden sorrow*. Lexington, MA: Lexington Press.

Edgerton, R.B., & Gaston, M. A. (1991). *I've seen it all: Lives of older persons with mental retardation in the community*. Baltimore, MD: Brooks Publishing Co.

Edgerton, R.B., Gaston, M.A., Kelly, H., & Ward, T.W. (1994). Health care for aging people with mental retardation. *Mental Retardation, 32*, 146-150.

Gambert, S. R., Liebskind, S. & Cameron, D. (1987). Lifelong preventative health care for elderly persons with disabilities. *Journal for the Association of Persons with Severe Handicaps, 12*, 292-296.

Ghaziuddin, M., Alessi, N., & Greden, J. F. (1995). Life events and depression in children with pervasive development disorder. *Journal of Autism and Developmental Disorders, 25*, 495-502.

Harper, D.C. & Wadsworth, J.S. (1993). Grief in adults with mental retardation: Preliminary findings. *Research in Developmental Disabilities, 14*, 313-330.

Kanner, L. (1943). Autistic disturbances of affective contact. *Nervous Child, 2*, 217-250.

Kauffman, J. (1994). Mourning and mental retardation. *Death Studies, 18*, 257-271.

Kirk, S. A. (1989). *Educating Exceptional Children* (6th ed.). Boston: Houghton Mifflin.

Lavin, C. (1989). Death and the developmentally disabled. In K.J. Doka (Ed.), *Disenfranchised grief: Recognizing hidden sorrow* (pp. 229-237). Lexington, MA: Lexington Press.

Lipe-Goodson, P.S. & Goebel, B.L. (1983). Perception of age and death in mentally retarded adults. *Mental Retardation, 21*, 68-77.

Luckasson, R., Coulter, D., Polloway, E., Reiss, S., Schalock, R., Snell, M., Spitalnik, D., & Stark, J. (1992). *Mental retardation: Definitions, classifications, and systems of support*. Washington, DC : American Association of Mental Retardation.

Overeynder, J., Turk, M., Dalton, A. & Janicki, M. P. (1992). *I'm worried about the future: The aging of adults with cerebral palsy*. Albany, NY: New York State Disabilities Planning Council.

Rothenberg, E.D. (1994). Bereavement intervention with vulnerable populations: A case report on group work with the developmentally disabled. *Social Work with Groups, 17*, 61-74.

Schopler, E., & Sloan, J. (1989). Autism. In C. Reynolds & L. Mann (Eds.), *Encyclopedia of special education* (Vol. 1, pp. 163-165). New York: John Wiley.

Seltzer, M.M., & Seltzer, G.B. (1991). Classification and social status. In J.L. Matson & J.A. Mulik (Eds.), *Handbook of mental retardation* (2nd ed., pp. 166-180). New York: Pergamon Press.

Steppe-Jones, C. (1987). Cerebral Palsy. In C. Reynolds & L. Mann (Eds.), *Encyclopedia of special education* (Vol. 1, pp. 293-296). New York: John Wiley.

Turner, M. (1990). *Practical guidelines for understanding and assisting clients with concerns about death and dying*. New York: Young Adult Institute.

Wadsworth, J., & Harper, D.C. (1991). A strategy to train health care professionals to communicate with persons with mental retardation. *Academic Medicine, 66*, 495-496.

Walz, T., Harper, D., & Wilson, J. (1986). The aging developmentally disabled person: A review. *The Gerontologist, 26*, 622-629.

## 14: Zieziula

Dolnick, E. (1993, September). Deafness as culture. *Atlantic Monthly,* 37-53.

Gannon, J. R. (1989). *The week the world heard Gallaudet.* Washington, DC: Gallaudet University Press.

Greenberg, J. (1970). *In this sign.* New York: Holt, Rinehart and Winston.

Hairston, E. & Smith, L. (1983). *Black and deaf in America: Are we that different?* Silver Spring, MD: T. J. Publishers.

*Neither silent nor alone* [video]. (1997). Heritage Hospice, Inc.: Danville, KY.

Kübler-Ross, E. (1969). *On death and dying.* New York: Macmillan Publishing Co.

Lane, H. (1984). *When the mind hears: A history of the deaf.* New York: Random House.

Lane, H. (1988). Is there a "psychology of the deaf?" *Exceptional Children, 55,* 7-19.

Lane, H., Hoffmeister, R. & Bahan, B. (1996). *A journey into the deaf-world.* San Diego, CA: DawnSign Press.

Levine, E. (1956). *Youth in a soundless world.* New York: New York University Press.

Lou, M. & Charlson, E. (1991). A program to enhance the social cognition of deaf adolescents. In D. Martin (Ed.), *Advances in cognition, education, and deafness* (pp.329-334). Washington, DC: Gallaudet University Press.

Meadow, K.P. (1972). Sociolinguistic, sign language, and the deaf subculture. In T.J. O'Rourke (Ed.), *Psycholinguistics and total communications: The state of the art* (p. 19-33). Washington, DC: American Annals of the Deaf.

Meadow, K.P. (1980). *Deafness and child development.* Berkeley, CA: University of California Press.

Meadow-Orlans, K. (1990). Research on developmental aspects of deafness. In D. Moores & K. Meadow-Orlans (Eds.), *Educational and developmental aspects of deafness* (pp. 283-298). Washington, DC: Gallaudet University Press.

Moore, M.S. & Panara, R.F. (1996). *Great deaf Americans: The second edition.* Rochester, NY: MSM Productions, Ltd.

Moses, K. (1991). *Notes on shattered dreams & growth: Loss and the art of grief counseling.* Evanston, IL: Resource Networks, Inc.

Myklebust, H. (1964). *The psychology of deafness* (2nd ed.). New York: Grune & Stratton.

Pintner, R. (1933). Emotional stability of the hard of hearing. *Journal of Genetic Psychology, 43,* 293-309.

Schildroth, A. & Hotto, S.A. (1996). Changes in student and program characteristics, 1984-85 and 1994-1995. *American Annals of the Deaf, 141* (2), 68-71.

Schein, J.D. (1989). *At home among strangers.* Washington, DC: Gallaudet University Press.

Schlesinger, H.S. (1978). The effects of deafness on childhood development: An Eriksonian perspective. In L.S. Liben (Ed.), *Deaf children: Developmental perspectives* (pp.69-84). New York: Academic Press.

Zieziula, F.R. & Meadows, K. (1991). The experience of loss and grief among late deafened people: A report of research and theory. In S.J. Larew, K.M Saura, & D. Watson (Eds.), *Facing deafness* (pp. 58-63). DeKalb, IL: Northern Illinois University.

## 15: WILDER

Feinstein, H. (1979). *Torch song trilogy*. New York: The Gay Presses of New York.

Garnets, L.D., et al. (1991). Issues in psychotherapy with Lesbians and Gay Men. *American Psychologist, 46* (9), 964-972.

Garnets, L.D. & Kimmel, D.C. (1993). *Psychological perspectives on Lesbian & Gay male experiences*. New York: Columbia University Press.

Rando, T.A. (1995). Grief and mourning: Accommodating to loss. In H. Wass and R.A. Neimeyer (Eds.), *Dying: Facing the facts* (3rd ed., pp. 218-219). Washington, DC: Taylor & Francis.

# Part IV. Making Sense Out of Loss

Gennep, A. (1950). *The rites of passage*. Chicago: University of Chicago Press.

Mumford, L. (1951). *The city in history: Its origins, its transformations and its prospects*. New York: Harcourt, Brace and World.

Sue, D.W. and Sue, D. (1990). *Counseling the culturally different: Theory and practice* (2nd ed.). New York: J. Wiley & Sons.

## 17: NEIMEYER AND KEESEE

Anderson, H., & Goolishian, H. (1992). The client is the expert. In S. McNamee & K. J. Gergen (Eds.), *Therapy as social construction*. Newbury Park, CA: Sage.

Attig, T. (1991). The importance of conceiving of grief as an active process. *Death Studies, 15*, 385-393.

Attig, T. (1996). *How we grieve: Relearning the world*. New York: Oxford University Press.

Becker, E. (1973). *The denial of death*. New York: Macmillan.

Braun, K. L., & Nichols, R. (1997). Death and dying in four Asian American cultures. *Death Studies, 21*, 327-359.

Braun, M. L., & Berg, D. H. (1994). Meaning reconstruction in the experience of bereavement. *Death Studies, 18*, 105-129.

Corr, C. A. (1993). Coping with dying: Lessons we should and should not learn from the work of Elisabeth Kübler-Ross. *Death Studies, 17*, 69-83.

Dula, A. (1997). The story of Miss Mildred. In K.J. Doka & J. Davidson (Eds.), *Living with grief: When illness is prolonged* (pp. 83-95). Washington, DC: Hospice Foundation of America/Taylor & Francis.

Gilbert, K. R. (1996). "We've had the same loss, why don't we have the same grief?" Loss and differential grief in families. *Death Studies, 20*, 269-284.

Goss, R. E., and Klass, D. (1997). Tibetan Buddhism and the resolution of grief. *Death Studies, 21*, 377-396.

Hagemeister, A. K., and Rosenblatt, P. C. (1997). Grief and the sexual relationship of couples who have experienced a child's death. *Death Studies, 21*, 231-251.

Haussaman, B. (1998). Death and syntax. *Death Studies, 22*.

Horowitz, M. J. (1986). *Stress response syndromes*. Northvale, NJ: Jason Aronson.

Janoff-Bulman, R. (1989). Assumptive worlds and the stress of traumatic events. *Social Cognition, 7*, 113-116.

Kelly, G. A. (1955). *The psychology of personal constructs*. New York: Norton.

Klass, D., Silverman, P.R., & Nickman, S.L. (Eds.). (1996). *Continuing bonds: New understandings of grief*. Washington, DC: Taylor & Francis.

Martin, T.L., & Doka, K. J. (1996). Masculine grief. In K.J. Doka (Ed.), *Living with grief: After sudden loss* (pp. 161-172). Washington, DC: Hospice Foundation of America/Taylor & Francis.

Milo, E. M. (1997). Maternal responses to the life and death of a child with developmental disability. *Death Studies, 21*, 443-476.

Nadeau, J. W. (1997). *Families making sense of death*. Newbury Park, CA: Sage.

Neimeyer, R.A. (Ed.). (1994). *Death anxiety handbook: Research, instrumentation, and application*. New York: Taylor & Francis.

Neimeyer, R.A. (1997a). Death anxiety research: The state of the art. *Omega*.

Neimeyer, R.A. (1997b). Meaning reconstruction and the experience of chronic loss. In K. J. Doka & J. Davidson (Eds.), *Living with grief: When illness is prolonged* (pp. 159-176). Washington, DC: Hospice Foundation of America/Taylor & Francis.

Neimeyer, R.A. (1998). Can there be a psychology of loss? In J. H. Harvey (Ed.), *Perspectives on loss: A sourcebook*. Philadelphia: Taylor & Francis.

Neimeyer, R.A., Keesee, N. J., & Fortner, B. V. (1997). Loss and meaning reconstruction: Propositions and procedures. In S. Rubin, R. Malkinson, & E. Wiztum (Eds.), *Traumatic and non-traumatic loss and bereavement*. Madison, CT: Psychosocial Press.

Neimeyer, R.A., & Mahoney, M. J. (1995). *Constructivism in psychotherapy*. Washington, DC: American Psychological Association.

Neimeyer, R.A., & Stewart, A. E. (1996). Trauma, healing, and the narrative emplotment of loss. *Families in Society, 77*, 360-375.

Nord, D. (1997). *Multiple AIDS-related loss*. Philadelphia: Taylor & Francis.

Rando, T. A. (1995). Grief and mourning: Accommodating to loss. In H. Wass and R. A. Neimeyer (Eds.), *Dying: Facing the facts* (pp. 211-241). Washington, DC: Taylor & Francis.

Richards, T. A., & Folkman, S. (1997). Spiritual aspects of loss at the time of a partner's death from AIDS. *Death Studies, 21*, 515-540.

Stroebe, M., Schut, H., & Stroebe, W. (1998). Trauma and grief: A comparative analysis. In J.H. Harvey (Ed.), *Perspectives on loss: A sourcebook*. Philadelphia: Taylor & Francis.

Tedeschi, R., Park, C., & Calhoun, L. (Eds.). (1998). *Post-traumatic growth: Positive changes in the aftermath of crisis*. Mahwah, NJ: Lawrence Erlbaum.

Viney, L. L. (1991). The personal construct theory of death and loss. *Death Studies, 15,* 139-155.

Wolowelsky, J. B. (1996). Communal and individual mourning dynamics within traditional Jewish law. *Death Studies, 20,* 469-480.

## 19: ELLIS

Barra, D. M., Carlson, E. S., Maize, M., Murphy, W. I., O'Neal, B. W., Sarver, R. E., & Zinner, E. S. (1993). The dark night of the spirit: Grief following a loss in religious identity. In K. J. Doka & J. D. Morgan (Eds.), *Death and spirituality* (pp.291-308). Amityville, NY: Baywood.

Bliatout, B. T. (1990). Hmong death customs: Traditional and acculturated. In D. P. Irish, K. L. Lundquist, & V. J. Nelsen (Eds.), *Ethnic variations in dying, death, and grief* (pp.79-100). Washington, DC: Taylor & Francis.

Choney, S. K., Berryhill-Paake, E., & Robbins, R. R. (1995). The acculturation of American Indians. In J. G. Ponterotto, J. M. Cassa, L. A. Suzuki, & C. M. Alexander (Eds.), *Handbook of multicultural counseling* (pp.73-92). Thousand Oaks, CA: Sage.

Corr, C. A., Nabe, C. M., & Corr, D. M. (1997). *Death and dying, life and living* (2nd ed.). Pacific Grove, CA: Brooks/Cole.

D'Andrea, M., & Daniels, J. (1995). Promoting multiculturalism and organizational change in the counseling profession: A case study. In J. G. Ponterotto, J. M. Cassa, L. A. Suzuki, & C. M. Alexander (Eds.), *Handbook of multicultural counseling* (pp.17-33). Thousand Oaks, CA: Sage.

DeSpelder, L. A. & Strickland, A. L. (Eds.). (1996). *The last dance: Encountering death and dying* (4th ed.). Mountain View, CA: Mayfield.

Grieger, I. & Ponterotto, J. G. (1995). A framework for assessment in multicultural counseling. In J. G. Ponterotto, J. M. Cassa, L. A. Suzuki, & C. M. Alexander (Eds.), *Handbook of multicultural counseling* (pp.357-374). Thousand Oaks, CA: Sage.

Hayes, C. L. & Kalish, R. A. (1995). Death-related experiences and funerary practices of the Hmong refugee in the United States. In L. A. DeSpelder & A. L. Strickland (Eds.), *The path ahead: Readings in death and dying* (pp.75-79). Mountain View, CA: Mayfield.

Kerwin, C. & Ponterotto, J. G. (1995). Biracial identity development: Theory and research. In J. G. Ponterotto, J. M. Cassa, L. A. Suzuki, & C. M. Alexander (Eds.), *Handbook of multicultural counseling* (pp.199-217). Thousand Oaks, CA: Sage.

Lee, C. C. & Armstrong, K. L. (1995). Indigenous models of mental health intervention. In J. G. Ponterotto, J. M. Cassa, L. A. Suzuki, & C. M. Alexander (Eds.), *Handbook of multicultural counseling* (pp.441-456). Thousand Oaks, CA: Sage.

Lee, C. C., Oh, M. Y. & Mountcastle, A. R. (1992). Indigenous models of helping in nonwestern countries: Implications for multicultural counseling. *Journal of Multicultural Counseling & Development, 20,* 3-10.

Morrison, T., Conaway, W. A., & Borden, G. A. (1994). *Kiss, bow, or shake hands: How to do business in sixty countries.* Holbrook, MA: Bob Adams, Inc.

Murray, J. (1997). *Alaska.* Oakland, CA: Compass American Guides (Fodor).

Parkes, C. M., Laugani, P., & Young, B. (1997). *Death and bereavement across cultures.* New York: Routledge.

*Random House Dictionary of the English Language* (2nd ed., unabridged). (1987). New York: Random House.

Root, M. P. P. (1992). Within, between, and beyond race. In M. P. P. Root (Ed.), *Racially mixed people in America* (pp.3-11). Newburg Park, CA: Sage.

Rosenthal, P. C. (1997). Grief in small-scale societies. In C. M. Parkes, P. Laugani, & B. Young (Eds.), *Death and bereavement across cultures* (pp. 27-51). New York: Routledge.

Scheper-Hughes, N. (1995). Death without weeping: The violence of everyday life in Brazil. In L. A. DeSpelder & A. L. Strickland (Eds.), *The path ahead: Readings in death and dying* (pp.41-58). Mountain View, CA: Mayfield.

Sue, D. W. & Sue, D. (1990). *Counseling the culturally different: Theory and practice* (2nd ed.). New York: J. Wiley & Sons.

U.S. Bureau of the Census. (1991). *1990 census count of American-Indians, Eskimos, or Aleuts and American Indian and Alaska Native Areas*. Washington, DC: Bureau of the Census, Racial Statistics Branch, Population Division.

Vontress, C. E. (1991). Traditional healing in Africa: Implications for cross-cultural counseling. *Journal of Counseling and Development, 70*, 242-249.

## 20: ZULLI

Augsburger, D.W. (1986). *Pastoral counseling across cultures*. Philadelphia: Westminster Press.

Bhatti, R. & Channabasavanna, S. M. (1979). Social system approach to understanding marital disharmony. *Indian Journal of Social Work, 40* (1), 79-88.

Dobson, S. M. (1991). *Transcultural nursing*. London: Scutari Press.

Doka, K.J. (Ed.). (1989). *Disenfranchised grief: Recognizing hidden sorrow*. Lexington, MA: Lexington Books.

Efan, J. S. & Spangler, T. J. (1979). Why grown-ups cry. *Motivation and Emotion 12* (3), 63-72.

Hiebert, P. (1976). *Cultural anthropology*. Philadelphia: J.B. Lippincott Co.

Irion, P.E. (1988). *Hospice and ministry*. Nashville: Abingdon Press.

Klass, D., Silverman, P.R., & Nickman, S.L. (Eds.). (1996). *Continuing bonds: New understandings of grief*. Washington, DC: Taylor & Francis.

Kottler, J.A. (1996). *The language of tears*. San Francisco, CA: Jossey-Bass Publishers.

Larson, D. (1993). *The helper's journey: Working with people facing grief, loss, and life-threatening illness*. Champaign, IL: Research Press.

Leininger, M.M. (1991). *Culture care diversity and universality: A theory of nursing*. New York: National League for Nursing Press.

Levy, R. I. (1984). Emotion, knowing, and culture. In R. A. Shweder & R. A. LeVine (Eds.), *Culture theory: Essays on mind, self, and emotion*. Cambridge, MA: Cambridge University Press.

Mariechild, D. (1995). *Open mind: Women's daily inspiration for becoming mindful*. New York: HarperCollins.

McNees, P. (1996). *Dying: A book of comfort*. Garden City, NY: GuildAmerica Books.

Miller, J.E. (1997). *One you love is dying*. Fort Wayne, IN: Willowgreen Publishing.

Olson, M. (1997). *Healing the dying*. New York: Delmar Publishers.

Paladin, L. S. (1991). *Ceremonies for change*. Walpole, NH: Stillpoint Publishing.

Schneider, J. (1994). *Finding my way*. Colfax, WI: Seasons Press.

Shaw, G.B. (1963). *Complete plays with prefaces* (Vol. 3). New York: Dodd Mead. (Original work published 1903).

Sowell, T. (1986). In D.W. Augsburger, *Pastoral counseling across cultures*. Philadelphia: Westminster Press.

Williams, D.R. & Sturzl, J.A. (1990). *Grief ministry*. San Jose, CA: Resource Publications.

## 21: SMITH

Hillman, J. (1979). Puer's wound and Ulysses' scar. In *Puer papers* (pp. 100-128). Dallas: Spring Publications.

Khan, P.V.I. (1977). *Samadhi with open eyes*. New Lebanon, NY: Messenger Press.

Kreinheder, A. (1991). *Body and soul: The other side of illness*. Toronto: Inner City Books.

Maharshi, R. (1972). *The spiritual teaching of Ramana Maharshi*. Boulder, CO: Shambhala.

Nouwen, H. J. M. (1972). *The wounded healer*. New York: Doubleday.

Remen, R. N. (1993). Wholeness. In B. Moyers, *Healing and the mind*. New York: Doubleday.

Remen, R. N. (1994). *Kitchen table wisdom*. New York: Riverhead Books.

Rogers, C. R. (1961). *On becoming a person*. Boston: Houghton Mifflin.

## CONCLUSION: DAVIDSON

Ackerman, D. (1997). *A slender thread*. New York: Random House.

Koenig, B. (1997, August). A medical anthropologist examines the case example and cautions against a simplistic view. In *Last Acts: Care and caring at the end of life* 3, 7-10. The Robert Wood Johnson Foundation Quarterly.

Koenig, B. and Gates-Williams, J. (1995) Understanding cultural difference in caring for dying patients. *The Western Journal of Medicine, 163* (3), 244-249.

Mazard, A. (1997, August). Patient diversity creates major challenges. In *Last Acts: Care and caring at the end of life* 3, 1-11. The Robert Wood Johnson Foundation Quarterly.

Price, D. (1997). Hard decisions in hard times: Making ethical choices during prolonged illness. In K.J. Doka & J. Davidson (Eds.), *Living with grief: When illness is prolonged* (pp. 51-66).Washington, DC: Hospice Foundation of America/Taylor & Francis.